Modern American Cities

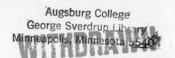

Modern American Cities

Edited with an Introduction by
Ray Ginger

✺ a New York Times Book

Quadrangle Books
CHICAGO

Preface

VICTORIA GRANLEY GINGER has done so much of the work for this book that she should be listed as co-editor. I have also been especially privileged over the years by opportunities to discuss the history of cities in the United States with four friends: A. Theodore Brown of the University of Wisconsin, Milwaukee; Corinne Gilb and Sidney Glazer of Wayne State University; and Richard C. Wade of the University of Chicago.

A special kind of debt is also owed to Rafael Tufiño. Although I had greatly respected his posters and paintings and linoleum blocks and murals, I had never met him personally. At our first encounter in a lovely patio in Old San Juan, he reminded me that the road to productivity is from "the inside out, not from the outside in."

My dedication is for friends in Puerto Rico: Dr. and Mrs. Antonio J. Colorado, Lt. Col. and Mrs. William D. Hunter, and the late B. G. Stern.

R.G.

Barrio Morcelo
Caimito Alto
Puerto Rico
February 1969

Contents

2. Some Characteristics of Cities

3. Toward the Future of Cities

Modern American Cities

Introduction:
What Is a City?

MANY PLACES flaunt their distinctive emblems. Tourists in the
countryside of New England quickly see that the dominant images
in the landscape are the white steeples of the churches; the eye
picks them out, soaring above the green foliage, before it distinguishes other objects. If religious spires are the visual symbol
of Cape Cod, secular ones serve the same function in Wyoming—
grain elevators. A passerby will see few people, but every few
miles he will encounter a cluster of four or five giant silos.

Similarly with the contemporary American city. Towering above
the skyline of Chicago or New York or Houston is the tool that
is incessantly reshaping that skyline: the crane. More than sixty
years have passed since the novelist Henry James watched the
construction of the apartment buildings along Riverside Drive in
Manhattan, and summed up his reaction by remarking that each
structure, even as it was going up, seemed to be merely holding
the spot for whatever was to replace it. Since that time, the bull-
dozer and the crane have become deities. They run the show. If
the moving van is a fitting token of the mobility of the typical
American, construction equipment represents his penchant for
replacing anything that exists. A giant metal ball swings out of the
sky and—crunch—smacks into a roof, so that within a few days

an architectural landmark (the Larkin Building in Buffalo, for instance, designed by Frank Lloyd Wright) ceases to exist, often to be replaced by an inferior building or, worse yet, a parking lot. This is not to deny that much recent construction has been magnificent; almost at random I think of Hartford with its stunning Phoenix Mutual Life Building and its St. Joseph's Cathedral. But the creation of such masterpieces is hit-or-miss, while the total environment of the city is left simply to sprawl. In some metropolitan areas (I think of Detroit) even isolated buildings worthy of praise are virtually nonexistent.

As with sight, so with the other sensory organs. The taproot of a good life is a stream of stimulating sense-perceptions. Moreover, the chief perceptions of the various senses tend to fit together into a tone, a mood. Let me contrast a typical city in the United States today with another mode of existence. I have been living this winter on a rather isolated mountaintop in Puerto Rico, about ten miles south of San Juan. The view from the terrace is northward toward the Atlantic. Starting at your feet are several abrupt mountain ranges. Then the city—white buildings by day, a white and yellow dazzle after dark. Then the white dance of the breakers, and beyond them the blue-green of the ocean. The scene is not static, for the sky and the light on the land change moment by moment. But if the landscape begins to bore you, watch the lizards, little creatures that invade your house, make no noise, leave no mess, eat up ants and gnats, and are more entertaining than any domestic pet I have ever seen. For sound, you have a steady rhythmic harmony from about four o'clock every afternoon until eight in the morning from tree toads, with their "co-qui, co-qui" (supplemented by chickens before dawn, cows intermittently, and the packs of disowned defrocked dogs that yawk half the night and turn over trash cans in search of food). The dominant smell is of flowers: African tulip trees, in the spring the flamboyant, bougainvillea, hibiscus, honeysuckle. The chief touch is the wind, howling in January, soothing most of the year, but nearly always present. The dominant taste is food and drink: little cornsticks, a concoction called *asapao* which is chiefly rice with chicken or shellfish, rum with water.

Now look at a contemporary American city. The sound by day is air hammers being used in demolition or construction; by day and by night it is the static of traffic. A fitting partner is the sense of touch—the unwelcome smash of strange bodies on the subway or bus. On the street you can choose summer with an atmosphere so heavy you must carry it on your shoulders, or winter when the wind slashes through you as if you were gossamer. The senses of smell and of taste combine to register industrial wastes: the gas works, automobile-exhaust fumes, oil refineries, chemical plants, steel mills. If you think you cannot "taste" air, you have probably never lived in Pasadena, or Dearborn, or Bayonne, or Gary, or any of dozens of coal towns in West Virginia or smelter camps in the Far West (or Covington, Kentucky, where, the last time I visited, you could get drunk by simply standing on a street corner and breathing).

Obviously, either of these environments, town or country, New York or Puerto Rico, is stunted. If persisted in, either could be stultifying. Man is a sociable animal, and an outlander finds little companionship on a semi-tropical mountain. The literature of the United States is aflood with tales of the miserable loneliness and monotony sustained by farmers and even more by their wives, whether in the Dakotas (Ole Rölvaag's *Giants in the Earth*) or in New England (Edith Wharton's *Ethan Frome*) or in Virginia (Ellen Glasgow's *Barren Ground*) or in Nebraska (Willa Cather's "A Wagner Matinee"). There is no need to idealize rural isolation, not even on an island where you can swim in a benign ocean in February. As a lifelong pattern, it stupefies you. A cliché about New York says: "It's a great place to visit, but I wouldn't want to live there." The same thought applies to the countryside. At least, it applies unless you can run off to the city quite often.

II

But when you get to the city, where are you? What is a city? What are the unique functions of cities? Here is testimony about Asia Minor more than sixteen hundred years ago, about the city of Antioch which had some sixteen miles of colonnaded streets:

"Well, it seems to me that the pleasantest, yes, the most profitable side of city life is society and human intercourse, and that, by Zeus, is truly a city where they are most found. . . . People in other cities who have no colonnades before their houses are kept apart by bad weather; nominally, they live in the same town, but in fact they are as remote from each other as if they lived in different towns." Please replace the phrase "bad weather" in the preceding sentence by "traffic and parking" and you have a neat description of a major modern frustration. Two close friends may say when in California that they both live in New York City. But if one lives in Princeton, New Jersey, and the other in Chappaqua, New York—a hundred miles apart—they won't see each other from one year to the next. In fact, they might see each other more often if one of them moved to Gloucester, Massachusetts.

What is a city? To quote a profound student of the history of cities, Lewis Mumford: ". . . it is a place designed to offer the widest facilities for significant conversation." Conversation differs from noise; it is not raucous automobile horns and shouted profanities. When two persons discuss a problem together, the process is not tumultuous. When people enjoy each other's company, the outcome is not 47th Street off Broadway. Merely to list certain realities is to reveal how the contemporary city in the United States has not only sold out its present but also betrayed both the past and the future of cities.

What can you do in a city that you can't do equally well elsewhere? Well, you can have specific kinds of fun that the hillsides don't offer. Some scholars would say that you can "think." That, it seems to me, is wrong. Most of us can think better in bare and silent rooms. What the city does offer is a concentration of the materials upon which thought must operate. Without cities, no libraries. No art museums, no planetariums, no zoos, no botanical gardens. No concerts. And especially and forever and ever, not much diversity in the human condition. Hill folk, by necessity, are generally the same. A man does not have to strain to understand his neighbor; he is almost a replica of his neighbor. Just read a description of an agricultural region near Lynchburg, Virginia, a century ago: ". . . I could not help thinking that people living in such a country were excusable, amid their dearth of amusements and mental excitants of any kind, if they busied themselves with sectarian differences in theology and speculative questions in politics." (Karl Marx was not being merely petulant when he referred to "the idiocy of rural life.")

A city differs. It rubs one culture against others. It produces marginal men who are no longer sure that their own traditions are the only possible ones. These collisions make everybody uneasy. To some men, they are threatening. The result is mass distrust and even mass hatred—an Italian Catholic parish versus an Irish Catholic parish, ethnic voting on election day, black against white, race riots, a boom in the sale of guns to private citizens. But to a few persons—unhappily, still, only to a small fraction of the population—contact with alien ways is invigorating. They don't cower and they don't shoot; they think. They create. They put together formerly disparate elements into a new whole. By producing, over and over, clashes between men who embody variant civilizations, a city speeds up innovations. Unlike Moses and the Ten Commandments, the great inventions do not come down from the mountain. It is the cities that spawn new methods, new materials, new products, and new ideas.

History can tell us a good deal about the conditions of creation. Movable type and the art of printing came about only after Europeans began to look around in China. The great murals of modern Mexico came after painters carrying with them their indigenous Indian traditions went to Paris and felt the impact of modern impressionism. Productive work in low-energy physics has ensued from the collaboration of the theoretical mathematics of the Soviet Union with engineering in the United States. Dixieland jazz and its myriad descendants followed when Southern rural blacks with their own musical heritage moved to New Orleans and encountered the instruments and the melodic notions of Europe. Could this achievement have occurred anywhere other than New Orleans, which was in 1900 the second largest port city in the United States?

The abrasion between cultures that is facilitated by cities is not limited to a clash between, say, the modes of a Vermont Yankee in 1969 and the modes of an immigrant from Puerto Rico in 1969. It reaches back through time. Many of the city's institutions are meant to make the past available to the present. We can, of course, still choose to ignore the problems and accomplishments of former times; André Malraux once observed that no man can inherit his culture, that he must conquer it. But cities do offer the objects of conquest.

That is, real and true cities do. But a giant agglomeration of people is not necessarily a real and true city. One of the great libraries in the world, the Boston Public, has seen its budget for buying new books virtually disappear and its visiting hours pared to the bone. Or consider Newark. You may think the reputation of Newark was bad enough before its race riot in 1967, but at least it had good libraries and a good museum. Now the city fathers have voted to close down both institutions for economy's sake. The program was implemented on April Fool's Day, 1969.

III

How large must a city be? The Census Bureau of the United States simply counts heads; for instance, an urban resident is anybody living in a town with more than 2,500 inhabitants, and so on. This quantitative approach has its uses as well as its defects. We are told that some eminent cities in ancient Greece had fewer than four thousand residents. Quite a few American clusters (clots, I want to call them) number more than a million, but are they cities? The area of Rome in the late Empire was only about five square miles, whereas the metropolitan area of New York today is five hundred times as large. But do such figures tell us much about the social role played by various cities? What is the ideal size of a city? The ancient Romans thought each cosmopolis should be limited. The original two score cities of Rome had, by the age of Augustus, planted more than four hundred others in what is now Italy. Apparently the idea was that each of them would be confined to about fifty thousand people. Earlier, Aristotle had written of the city that in "size and extent it should be such as may enable the inhabitants to live at once temperately and liberally in the enjoyment of leisure." Later, an Italian general struck a similar note when he was surrendering his troops amid the Sahara sands. The British, he said, were more than welcome to the wretched place; he would go back to his beloved Florence and enjoy *la dolce vita.*

That is the kind of life Benjamin Franklin had in his adopted city. Although Philadelphia in the eighteenth century was second in population to London in the entire British Empire, it had only fifty thousand inhabitants. But in the most important ways it was more deserving of the accolade "city" two centuries ago than it is today. Size is relevant but not sufficient to define the genus. Nor is physical layout sufficient. The description of colonial Williamsburg by Albert Jay Nock in his *Thomas Jefferson* reads much like the setting for "An Arkansaw Difficulty" in *The Adventures of Huckleberry Finn.* But the Jefferson who read law with George Wythe and attended sessions of the House of Burgesses was a cosmopolite in a puddle that, however small, was urban, while what Mark Twain portrayed in the Old Southwest almost a hundred years later was nothing but a hamlet, with citizens whose minds and manners were as filthy as their main street.

What was true of Virginia in 1760 was true of Massachusetts. John Adams' *Diaries* show us a young lawyer who lived in Quincy, a country town about twenty miles from the State Capitol in Boston. Quincy was still so open that Adams bought a farm in the town. But his daily life included many urban amenities. Night after night he dined at a tavern with friends, lingering afterward to empty wine bottles, discuss civic affairs, plot the defense of "the ancient rights of Englishmen" (Was it revolution?), and swap off-color jokes.

Mention of Virginia and Massachusetts prompts us to ask why certain locations spawned towns, and why some of those towns became cities. To revert momentarily to the primitive standard of size, the birth and growth of American towns up to 1830 is fairly easy to understand. All of the largest were on deep water. Sailing southwestward down the Atlantic you could find Boston, New York, Philadelphia, Baltimore, Charleston. But north from Boston you could find another large town: Salem. What happened to Salem? After the Revolution, in one year seven-eighths of all pepper to enter the United States came through the customs house in Salem. Samuel McIntyre worked there, designing the most gracious street of houses in the land. A local merchant, Elias Hasket Derby, was called "King." But the town declined rapidly as the tonnage of ships increased: its harbor could not receive vessels of deep draft, and the international trade of New England migrated to Boston. So the aspiring lads went traipsing off to Boston—and within a very few years thereafter, aspiring lads in the Hub were traipsing off to New York.

The origin and growth of towns after 1830 is more complicated. Navigable water was still a factor; Lexington had once been the main town in Kentucky, but the inability of the new steamboat to swim on land caused Lexington to atrophy just as Salem was doing at the same time. But other factors began to weigh heavily. Perhaps the most important was governmental insight and competence. Considering the natural assets that God had embedded at Manhattan on the one side and at Boston on the other, the former was almost certain to prevail. But many of us have blown a sure thing. New York used its head start when the state undertook to build the Erie Canal from Albany to Buffalo. Completed in 1825, it was more than 350 miles long, forty feet wide, and four feet deep. The traffic was so heavy that it was enlarged almost at once. As a toll canal it not only paid for itself but helped to finance other activities.

While Boston was being overwhelmed by Manhattan, Philadelphia tried to compete for the trade of the Old Northwest. The consequence was disaster. What had been genius in New York was folly in Pennsylvania. The Erie Canal traversed virtually flat land, but as anybody knows who has driven the Pennsylvania Turnpike, the best route from Philadelphia to Pittsburgh must deal with some substantial mountains. Thus New York's lead, gained gratuitously by virtue of native endowments, was consolidated by the prescience of politicians who built the perfect canal. Wall Street became the financial center of the country, and entrepreneurs in Manhattan used their control of money to build railroads westward, until by 1880 five trunk lines connected New York to booming Chicago. In the struggle to win traffic, those five railroads fought each other viciously. Their charges to customers fell and fell. In terms of freight charges per ton-mile, the merchants and manufacturers of New York had the best deal in the world.

But they had, to a degree, earned it; they had not just fallen into a mud puddle and come up with their pockets loaded with gold. They had a good deal going for them from the start, but they knew how to improve their opportunities. Commercial rivalries between cities are as old as the United States, and the outcome has often depended on the presence in one city of a small handful of shrewd men. It has depended on the quality of the local leadership. Philadelphia fought bitterly with Baltimore for the trade of the Susquehanna Valley, and, if she was vanquished by New York, she was generally victorious over her enemies on Chesapeake Bay. The men who mattered in St. Louis, founded seven decades before Chicago, thought for many years that they could outstrip their competitor, but look what happened. Turning to a ridiculous case, Independence, Missouri, once believed it could conquer Kansas City in the battle for business, but a handful of K.C. boosters grouped around a newspaper editor named Van Horn gave Independence its come-uppance. Of course, the fact that Independence had Confederate sympathies during the Civil War was also a drag on the town when the battles were over and the peace was signed. (If Independence had known that a century later it would own a former President, would the foresight have boosted the imagination and zeal of its citizens from 1850 to 1870? Probably not: once a dullard, always a dullard.)

These instances suggest generalizations. The job of being a town promoter, a boomer, has been a career since before the first Englishman landed in North America. Pamphlets distributed in London early in the seventeenth century to lure settlers and investors told many of the same lies you can find in match booklets trying to sell you a home site in Florida or New Mexico. Second, it wasn't what you knew, it was whom you knew. Avenues to political or financial strength could be crucial for a town. Some of the most vicious and hilarious combats in American history involved whether Roaring Gap or Hambone would become the county seat. Even more of those frays involved the routing of a new railroad and the location of its station. Easy and cheap cartage has always been essential: a port for ocean-going ships, a canal, a railroad, to-day those divided streamers of asphalt or concrete. Businessmen in Grand Island, Nebraska, must weep because Interstate Highway 80 bypasses them so far away, and some motel owners in Omaha must rejoice that it ends abruptly in their immediate neighborhood.

A promising place can become obsolescent because of transportation. Surprisingly, transportation can be too good as well as not good enough. Many prosperous farmers no longer live on the land they cultivate; they don't even live near it. They may live fifty miles away where they can get at the slot machines and the dice tables. Wives don't buy at the general store in the crossroads town; they prefer to drive a hundred miles to a big suburban shopping center. After the census of 1960, a map was printed to show how the population of the country had redistributed itself since 1950. The counties that had declined were colored in red: a light pink for those that had lost fewer than 10 per cent of their people, a darker pink for 10 to 20 per cent, and so on. The counties that had gained population were shaded in various blues, using the same scheme. Rural counties had atrophied. Save for a few urban counties, the whole interior of the United States was painted red, and it sported a solidly blue border around the seacoasts.

The steamboat ruined the chances of some once promising towns, the railroad of others, the automobile of more. Or the economic base of an entire region and of all the towns in it might be undermined, as happened to the anthracite district in Pennsylvania. Or an epidemic might drive people away: Memphis shriveled in the late nineteenth century after it suffered a siege of yellow fever. Boston has gone through eras of absolute decline for two distinct sorts of reasons. Its first regression came just before the American Revolution, and the main cause evidently was a shortage of firewood. Any reader of *The Scarlet Letter* will recall the omnipresent forests; for a long time the presence of cheap timber was probably the chief base on which Boston rested. But in 150 years the area had been lumbered out, and wood had to be imported from as far away as Nova Scotia. The price soared. People fled rather than freeze. (Not until the large-scale mining of anthracite coal after 1820 was it possible to jam thousands of people together and keep most of them warm in winter.) The second phase of a Boston fade is the immediate past. The state census of 1965 revealed that the city had lost about 15 per cent of its residents in ten years. Reasons are many. It was natural that in prosperous times as incomes rose, many families would want to buy or rent more space to live in, and, since additional space could not be had in Boston, they retreated to Framingham or another new development. But compounding the natural causes of the flight from Boston has been the stupidity, or the cupidity, or both, of the men who run the show. Perhaps they are simultaneously dumb and greedy. Whatever the character of those responsible for it, urban renewal in Boston is a device for converting the city into a slum for the benefit of the suburbs. On that topic, more later.

IV

The melding together of people—up to a point—has brought immense benefits to mankind. Not least among them has been the federal government of the United States. When the First Continental Congress met in 1764 to discuss matters, the men did not convene in a cornfield near Pittsburgh, or even in a cornfield near Pittsfield; they met in the center of Philadelphia. Except for George Washington, all of the men in the Constitutional Convention of 1787 who really mattered were urban types. Some of the others who certainly mattered, for instance James Madison, may seem to be exceptions because they were plantation owners and such, but it seems to me that Madison and his wife were about as urbane as a couple can be. The point is simple: in 1787, when the total of urban residents probably was not more than 5 per cent of the country, they dominated government. It was a sharp break from their English heritage, for there the country lords had held the whiphand. But from Governor John Winthrop to the present, the ideas and the propulsion in American politics have spiraled out of high densities of population.

Lord Bryce long ago observed that in politics as in war, organization counts for everything. Voters are easier to organize when they are packed side by side along a street. Or are they?

Maybe not. The common charge that cities have been unique seed-beds for "machine politics" is almost surely mistaken. England at the beginning of the seventeenth century, or at the end of the eighteenth, had no political parties, but it did have machine politics, at once corrupt and coercive, a politics of deference. Most voters did what the powerful landholders bade them do. This type of republicanism came over on the Mayflower (and few would venture to call the Plymouth of William Bradford a "city").

It had come even earlier to Virginia. Look at the civic beginnings of the man who became the Father of His Country. The sole elections in the province were those which named two members from each county to the House of Burgesses. The technique was open; on election day a citizen could go to his polling place, stand up in front of all others, and state his preferences. The first time George Washington stood for office, he lost. By the second time he had learned the game. On this occasion the polls were opened by a vote for Mr. Washington from Lord Thomas Fairfax, the richest landlord in the area. Next came a succession of well-to-do landowners and distinguished ministers. All were for Washington. By the time tenants and parishioners could raise their voices, they had heard the voices of their betters and the message had registered. Washington won. That is a sample of how the suffrage worked in the countryside. The notion that rural America was pure and proper until tainted by the advent of cities is just not sound. We might say that farming districts in America made one major contribution to government in this country: they preserved the corrupt and coercive traditions of their English forebears.

In economics as in politics, innovations have come from cities. A peasant is a conservative. He plants what his father planted, and he grows it using the same tools and identical techniques. I can stand on my terrace in Puerto Rico and look in every direction, and the only cash crop visible is plantain. It may appear that the American farmer is another breed, and, with the rise of scientific agriculture in the last century, many of them are. All the successful ones are. But this was not always so. The typical man who moved from central Illinois to western Kansas after the Civil War actually believed that he could go on growing the same crops using the same methods. Sometimes he discovered differently in time to rectify his mistakes; or perhaps his sons went off to the state agricultural college and encountered the sciences that had burgeoned in cities. Often, however, he would just flounder and go under.

A city, for the alert few, is a hothouse. The fortunes it fertilizes can be the soil where imaginations flourish. Boston in 1775 contained only fifty merchants engaged in international trade, with roughly the same number of hangers-on of the bar and the cloth. But these few men were the movers and shakers for the colony. Confronted by a shortage of money in New England, they established reliable commercial banks. They seized on new technologies and set up the Boston Manufacturing Company a few miles away to make cotton textiles. When their needs outran the available water power on the Charles River in Waltham, they founded new towns with larger factories: Lowell, Lawrence, Nashua. A model protagonist came along later: John Murray Forbes. His first fortune came out of China, from goods that had a proven market in Boston. As the promise of the Far Eastern trade paled, he put money into the booming field of textile manufacturing. That began to fade after 1850, so he went heavily into Midwestern railroads. Tea from China, cheap sheetings from Massachusetts, cartage in Iowa—he didn't care, just so the market was profitable. Few rural folk are so flexible. Of course, few urban folk are that flexible, but the odds are much better.

It is nearly two centuries since Adam Smith wrote one of the most incisive remarks ever composed: "The division of labor depends upon the size of the market." The zone within which a producer can sell his output depends basically on (1) low costs of transportation, (2) the absence of governmental restraints such as import and export duties, and (3) the concentration of people. Because the British colonies in North America were thin strips along the Atlantic and a few rivers, they had the first advantage from their origins. The Constitution with its interstate commerce clause brought the second. The third, as has been suggested already, ensued for several reasons, but when it came, it reinforced the first. Masses of men turned out to be masses of buyers, and they made specialization possible. In Boston, before it had existed fifty years, coopers (barrel-makers) were distinct from carpenters as well as from shipwrights. As a result, each worker did his job more efficiently. So they, and of course their employers, earned more. Recognizing that Charles Goodnight and other ranchers could build impressive spreads, it is accurate to note that the main chance for success in American business has been the concentration of humanity. Go to the city, young man, to the city. Better yet, be born there, to affluent parents, and go to the best schools. Inherit your father's business. If your father does not have a going concern, get attached to a father-in-law who does. Eon by eon, the formula for success stays pretty much the same.

Today in the "developed" world a city must justify itself chiefly in the social sphere. It must be a good place to live. It should be sane and civilized. It should also be exciting because it is dramatic, and dramatic because it is variegated. A city can muster more hardware for this rivalry than can the countryside. Patrons of high culture will not rub their heads at all while trying to decide between the two modes of life—but neither will patrons of low culture. For them, no choice is involved. A man who does not read books can hardly be expected to vote a tax raise to support libraries. If you despise the graphic arts, an art museum is meaningless. An astonishing number of people don't like music at all. Many music-lovers are content with pop or folk-rock on the radio. If they want Bach, they can tune in on FM or buy a stereo and a tape recorder and a few dozen records. This particular pleasure can be purchased anywhere in the United States. If you don't want a rare book, or paintings, or to watch musicians doing their thing, what does a city have for you?

Maybe quite a bit. Food, for instance. Some love eating; some do not. But in rural areas it is unspeakably dull, a chore to be surmounted. Five years ago I lived for several days with a family in the tobacco region of Puerto Rico. The barrio did not have one road. Transportation was by foot, by mule, by horse. Food, like anything else, was toted in laboriously or not at all. Salt, sugar, a little coffee—those were the supplies from outside. Nobody could buy more anyway; the typical family did not touch more than a hundred dollars cash in the course of a year. Everything eaten was home-grown. It was plentiful, nourishing, and some of it was tasty. But it was the same day after day. Plantain and coconuts, breadfruit and mangos. Maybe a chicken on Sunday, maybe not. It got tedious in less than a week. In contrast, townfolk who shopped at the supermarket ten miles away had innumerable options. In the United States the offerings at any first-rate store are staggering. A greengrocer, any time of year, will sell you five or six kinds of salad greens. In winter you can pick among russet or Comice pears, various melons, and citrus fruits. If you are willing to allow frozen foods, you can serve virtually any meat or fish that you ever heard of. As for the occasional stewed chicken on the Sabbath in the barrio, a good American family screams when asked to eat roast chicken one evening and then chicken salad for lunch the next day.

If business takes you away from home or if you just feel like dining out, some cities offer great gratifications. The most fortunate cane-cutters around Mayaguez may have to content themselves with salted mackerel and rice and red beans, but a well-heeled tourist can go to Bolo's and have his red snapper with Spanish sauce or broiled in butter. After a five-minute walk in Boston you could choose among three magnificent Italian restaurants: Joe Tecce's with its incredible antipasto, Felicia's for veal margherita, Stella's for shrimp marinara. The Henning Hotel in Casper, Wyoming, will give you as good a steak dinner as you can get outside of private homes. Try the bouillabaisse at Del Pezzo in Manhattan, or the almond boneless chicken at Chung's in Detroit. If you have a yen for quiche lorraine or for snails, go to L'Orangerie in San Francisco. For a trencherman, exquisite cuisine is found in cities, and you are not likely to discover it in the provinces where I was born and reared.

Thus does a city provide for men who like to eat. It gives them chances to make money, and it offers them worthwhile things to spend their money for. How does it provide for their mates? A few years ago the historian David M. Potter noted that the existence of immense tracts of unoccupied land had contributed mightily to the liberation of American males, because it had freed them from dependence on landowners. He added that the single influence that had done most to promote the equality of women had been the growth of cities. Whether you choose to talk about the movement of blacks into cities in the United States or about the migration of *jibaros* in Puerto Rico, you find that often more jobs are open to women than to men. With economic opportunity, women have gained other kinds of freedom. Some of the results are not delightful: psychological breakdowns, broken families, soaring divorce rates. But that cities have brought profound changes in the relations between men and women—changes that had to be made —can hardly be doubted. Is it accidental that the decade after 1840, which produced a greater relative rise in urban population than any other ten years in American history, also witnessed the first national convention for the emancipation of women?

Until very recently, a city child had much more to look forward to than his country cousin. True, a country boy can hunt and fish, and he may believe in the tranquility and excitement of the big two-hearted river. He can learn to scale fish and skin rabbits. But he will probably lack companionship. Without the friction of foreign minds and foreign consciences, his life becomes a stutter.

Unfortunately, today our cities seem intent on matching the confining ways of the countryside. They often stifle the potential of their young. If your family is wealthy you might go duck-shooting or casting for trout. But you might never experience the exuberant anger that comes from trying a hundred times to dam a creek, only to realize in the end that the attempt was foolish to start with. Usually the best an American city offers today is the chance to learn other kinds of lessons: how to play the violin, how to dance "Swan Lake." Indeed, in these respects the city can bewilder nearly anybody. A few years ago I knew a seven-year-old boy. With parents who were both attached to a university, he encountered many of the normal "advantages" of an upper-middle-class, cultured milieu. He had tennis lessons; he had swimming lessons; he had this kind of music lesson and that kind of music lesson; I think he even took lessons privately in some foreign language. One evening the boy unexpectedly asked his father:

"Dad, are we Jewish?"

Pause. "Well, yes, we're Jews, but we're not practicing Jews."

Pause. "Dad, thank God. If I had to practice one more thing I'd go out of my mind."

V

With its virtues, a modern city in the United States has the power to squelch, to destroy, to stamp out. Many of its defects are rooted in "massive forces working obscurely in the background." To be precise, there are three forces. First, cities have been increasingly regarded by Americans not as places to live in but as places to make money. Go to the Board of Trade, grab whatever you can, then go home to the little woman and the kids in Kenilworth. An Italian does not think that way about Florence, nor does a Frenchman think that way about Paris. Nor did a member of the governing class a couple of generations ago think of Boston in that fashion: unless the weather was atrocious, he walked to his office on State Street, perhaps took lunch in the Men's Grill at the Parker House where he could get tripe or scrod, ate dinner at his club if his family was away in Manchester, admired the beauties of the Common and the Public Gardens as he strolled back to his home on Beacon Hill, and in his spare time he served as a director of a half-dozen institutions aimed at civic improvement.

The other two corrosive elements relate to the first. Recently I listened to specialists in the history of modern France compare it with their native United States. An American citizen, they contended, has no sense of public property. When a taxpayer goes to the county courthouse he unconsciously feels that it belongs to "them." To illustrate, in 1961 I went to the capitol in a Midwestern state to look at some well-known murals. The floor of the lobby was littered with pigeon droppings, and I felt sure it had not been mopped for some time. In contrast, so I was told, the typical Parisian in a municipal building will view it with pride because he regards it as "partly mine."

Third, the mobility of Americans is not conducive to the health of any area. In the United States, people migrate frequently; an appropriate symbol for the nation is the moving van. According to Peter H. Rossi: "About three-quarters of our urban citizens were living in 1950 in places in which they did not reside in 1940." Why bother about the long-term future of your neighborhood? In a few years you are going to sell out and move elsewhere anyway, so your only worries are short-run. You will resent a black family who might be fine companions for the next thirty years if they seem to threaten the immediate resale value of your property.

A traveler who merely crosses the border into Canada will soon see that these generalizations about the United States do not hold universally. In September 1968 I visited friends in Toronto. Their apartment is a five-minute drive from downtown, but when you look out the windows the view is of green, grassy ravines, hills, and trees; you can watch black squirrels a few feet away. Looking out the window of my century-old house a comparable distance from downtown Detroit, I could see nothing green except weeds overgrowing the sidewalk; parking lots surrounded me on three sides, and on the fourth was a street where lunatics drove 40 or 50 miles an hour with their horns raving. My Toronto friends early on a Saturday afternoon deposited me in front of their new City Hall. It is breathtaking, an object of beauty, a credit to its city and to its builders. Facing on a large and lovely park, its lawns bear a couple of discreet signs: "Please walk on our grass." An outdoor stage in front of the building was featuring a show of women's fashions with attractive models. At least a thousand people were lounging about, watching the exhibit, apparently self-contained and relaxed. An hour or so later the models vanished and a respectable band began to play. The public comfort-station in the park turned out to be immaculate. So were the lawns, partly because public employees were steadily picking up any scrap of refuse they could find, perhaps largely because residents of Toronto have learned not to litter their own property. I got thirsty and went in search of a bubbler; the water was deliciously cold, and no one had tossed his used chewing gum into the fountain. In contrast, the City-County Building (also new) in Detroit is inhumane and mechanically ghastly. Not a bench to sit on, not a blade of grass, not a tree to be seen. It looks like what the Martians would build if they conquered Earth.

The exterior of the City-County Building projects what happens inside it. If your credentials are perfectly in order, it may take five hours to get a driver's license in Detroit, or five weeks to get a marriage license. The bureaucrats don't care, because they live in Dearborn or St. Clair Shores. Recently the police in Detroit argued that it was a deprivation of their civil rights to require them to live inside the city limits; when told that abolition of the rule would cause them to be seen by blacks as an army of occupation, they seemed unable to comprehend the argument. So tax rates rise to pay more police who want to live elsewhere. So taxpayers move outside the city. More and more of the men who run Boston live in Weston or Newton. They want to get back and forth to the city fast. Land comes off the Boston tax rolls to provide space for the Massachusetts Turnpike extension. More land is removed to build colleges and religious institutions and other tax-exempt ventures. City libraries and art museums close for lack of money. The city becomes a dying carcass, its flesh serving parasites from the suburbs.

VI

Are remedies at hand? Can we keep the good and reduce the bad? Yes, but only if we are willing to cut down these "massive forces working obscurely in the background." An American city today is a captive, held in the tentacles of absentee owners. Let's look at the matter from two angles—which actually turn out to be one. The tangible object that has done the most to destroy cities in the United States is the automobile. With so many cars you can't move. And you can't stop moving because you can't park your car. As a further debit to the account put air pollution, with sooty buildings and catarrh. On the other hand, a rural area for most of us today is too sparse, too meager. It offers tranquility but it does not encourage one to create. Meanwhile a city affords not stimulation but noise. It confuses. Psychologists have shown experimentally that a dearth of sensory stimuli will drive anybody mad. Almost certainly the cacophonies of New York City have driven many persons mad; otherwise it is hard to account for the usual rudeness of bus drivers and shop clerks. Our problem, then, is to create an environment that will fluctuate from the nodding petals of "Tintern Abbey" to the jagged spurs of a metropolis.

You are about to read a plan directed toward this end. But first it seems wise to fend off an objection that many will want to make: It sounds great, they will say, but it is foolish because it can't be carried out. The quibble will not stand up. Most citizens of the United States now live in homes or apartments that have been built since World War II. Likewise, most of them work in offices or factories that are less than twenty-five years old. We have, in physical terms, restructured the country. While doing so we have improved it little if at all. The aim itself was cancerous. Any sound scheme should aim at an ambience in which both boys and girls can grow up (meaning mature), work at useful and sometimes exciting jobs, and find a lot of peace and a fair amount of glee when they are off duty.

The federal government alone could have done much to promote such a society, because it has had a large say in where those factories and offices and homes were placed. The metropolitan area in southeastern Virginia that centers on Norfolk holds 750,000 and survives on federal moneys. So with Waltham, Massachusetts, and its electronics plants. So with the entire state of Mississippi, where more than 25 per cent of all personal incomes issue from federal agencies. If defense contracts had been awarded on condition that new installations would be built in specific locations, we could have rationally revised whole regions as places meant to offer possibilities for a better life.

Now to the model. Imagine a circle a hundred miles in diameter. Place on the circle a half-dozen dwelling clusters, fifty or sixty miles apart. Let each of them hold from fifty thousand residents to five or six or seven times that number. (In some cities with 350,-000 residents, traffic and parking are no problem. On the other hand, a town of fewer than 50,000 will not be able to provide services that must be available.) With so much open space between the dwelling clusters, a family in any one of them can have more space inside its home, and more space between it and surrounding homes. Scatter through and around each of these clusters a number of shopping centers where a customer can not only buy groceries and liquor and clothing but can also have a good meal with a friend or just sit down and watch the birds. Each of these dwelling clusters will have a public library, but it will be essentially a small-city library, not meant for scholarly research. The art museum in each, the concert hall in each, will function and function well, but they will depend heavily on visiting collections, visiting orchestras. Botanical and zoological parks can be located in the dwelling clusters and in almost empty zones between them. Next, connect each cluster to the two nearest it by an expressway. From anywhere on the circle you can reach any other spot on the circle in two hours or less—and it won't be downtown driving, or in low gear. You can easily visit friends who live "far away."

The six dwelling clusters on the circumference will contain at least a half-million inhabitants. Together they have purchasing power, and a person from any one of the clusters can reach the center of the circle in an hour. So there will go the big library, which will lend books to the peripheral libraries for use by specialists. There we can build a college, and it can be large enough to be good because we have sufficient patronage. A sports coliseum and a gymnasium will not be blighted by the parking difficulties that afflict the facilities of so many city teams. Which brings us, I think, to one of the main advantages of the plan. People oppressed daily by the fumes of generating plants, by the poisonous-looking rings around the lavatories after the plugs are pulled, by the blemishes on their faces that disappear so miraculously after their faces have spent a week in the country—sometimes like to escape. When urbanites want to watch Shakespeare's plays they will go to Stratford, Connecticut, or to Stratford, Ontario. They love a concert at Ravinia, north of Chicago, at Castle Hill, north of Boston, at Meadowbrook, north of Detroit. They love to lie on the grass and hear a good quartet play Mozart. They want to be rural, and they want to be urban. Today the combination need not be silly.

Part 1

BOOMTOWNS AND PLACID PLACES

A CITY IS a place that offers great variety. Bringing diverse types of people into contact with each other, it makes life more dramatic. Although a city's size is relevant, neither total population nor density is definitive. But each of these factors establishes a limit for a given time and place, depending on the fortuities of technology and on the eternals of man's make-up. In terms of aggregates, a minimum of 50,000 and a maximum of 500,000 would seem today to be the boundaries. That gives us Casper, Wyoming, as a possibility, and Indianapolis, Indiana, as another. Even the Boston area is still in the recuperation ward, but it will not last long if those in charge continue to run affairs. New York is a lost cause, and Los Angeles was a lost cause from the beginning. The solid economic base of Chicago has disintegrated until it now compares with the area's geological base, while the cultural base acquired by zeal and ingenuity has also turned to mud. Philadelphia, once a magnificent city, has become a plaything for snotty children who now, having aged, are called stuffed shirts.

The articles in this section point up two curbstones. First, size can be too great or too small. Second, growth can be too fast or too slow. Either factor, left to itself, is likely to get out of hand. Juneau, to cite one piece below, is not a city, and never will be. It simply cannot suck into itself enough ingredients from the surrounding region to become a city. A steady influx of goods, of people, of ideas makes a city. Manhattan outstripped Philadelphia in the nineteenth century because it could service the hinterland at lower cost. Its market ran up the Hudson, then into the interior for thousands of miles, and ultimately to China.

If Juneau never had a potential of growth, the potential of San Francisco and Los Angeles is spent by now. Beverly Hills was once the capital of low culture for the nation and for much of the world, but now the glamour and the profits have leaked away. What remains is a sanctuary for elderly widows: on good days they warm the marrow of their bones, on all days they support local hostels, and on election days they vote Neanderthals into high office. San Francisco is another story. Whereas so much land was open around Los Angeles that the settlement sprawled, so little was open around San Francisco that it jammed. Living space is stinted; highways are clogged. San Francisco has become known as a great city for a simple reason: the standards of comparison are abysmal. If you live west of the Mississippi and want "a weekend in the city," where else can you go? To Tulsa, or Kansas City, or Dallas, or Los Angeles? Of them all, I'd pick Casper.

The towns that are not too big and not too small still seem promising. To think of only two states, Michigan and Indiana, I can mention Flint and Grand Rapids and Muskegon, South Bend and Fort Wayne. Each of these towns has already sacrificed a great deal, but the losses can be regained. Flint, discussed below, had a huge debit because it was a protuberance of absentee ownership, a company town. But I have friends who live there and like living there. It will never have a great orchestra, but it could have a fine trio or quartet playing chamber music. With the emerging electronic systems in libraries, any student in Flint could quickly get any book from Detroit. Flint can be civilized. Russell Porter's account describes what Flint was formerly like.

Houston? Decide for yourself about Houston.

Speed, Speed, and Still More Speed! —That Is Flint

by Russell B. Porter

FLINT, MICH.

THE ESSENCE of Flint is speed. The tempo of the production line, where the speed-up was one of the grievances of the sit-down strikers who tied up the mammoth General Motors automobile plant throughout the country, has spread to the entire life of the city.

Company executives fly here in airplanes to save precious minutes. Others roar over the wide Dixie Highway, sixty-five miles from Detroit, past Father Coughlin's Shrine of the Little Flower, at breakneck speed in fast automobiles. Huge factories covering hundreds of acres turn out thousands of high-powered cars capable of a hundred miles an hour, for distribution all over our speed-mad country.

Taxicabs and private cars wheel through the streets and spin around corners at rates which make a New Yorker dizzy. People dash in and out of hotels, offices, stores and restaurants in this fast-moving town. The workers speed to the factory in their own cars, spend eight hours at high pressure keeping up with the speed of the conveyor line and assembly line, speed home from work, speed to the movies at night, and speed to work again the next morning to begin another round.

Charlie Chaplin's "Modern Times," with its burlesque of the speed-up, is the town's favorite film. It was shown with great success to the sit-down strikers in their seized factories.

Speed, speed, speed—that is Flint morning, noon and night. If every city has its own distinctive voice, as O. Henry wrote, it needs little imagination to hear the voice of Flint as it unceasingly cries: "Hurry up—hurry up—hurry up."

Speed presided even at the birth and growth of this fabulous, incredible town as a modern city. Most cities grow to large size slowly and gradually, as a result of a natural development of geographical, economic and social factors. Flint was different. It grew from a tiny market town of 10,000 or 15,000 people to its present population of 165,000 by an artificial, forced method.

In the past quarter-century the city has undergone an amazing transformation from a village typical of the horse-and-buggy age, in which it produced some of the best known carriages and wagons in the country, to the city typical of the great American automotive industry. It is to the automobile what Pittsburgh is to steel, what Akron is to rubber.

But it is more. It is not only a one-industry town; it is also practically a one-company town. Eighty per cent of the families are directly dependent upon General Motors, and the rest are indirectly dependent upon it. The few other factories in the city sell mostly to the big company, and of course all the banks, business concerns, stores and restaurants do their business almost entirely with the corporation and its employes.

As General Motors is responsible for 45 per cent of the automobile production of the United States and as Flint, with its Buicks and Chevrolets, contains the largest grouping of G. M. production units in the country, with about one-third of the company's automobile workers, there could be no better place to use as a laboratory for a study of the social and economic results of the great technological progress which has brought the American automobile industry to its present position and has spelled out American civilization to the rest of the world.

As a piece of God's green earth, upon which trees and grass might grow, Flint has always sacrificed the natural beauties of life to the urge for money.

In early days it must have been a lovely spot, situated in the river valley at a ford known as "Grand Traverse of the Flint River." The Seneca Indian name of Genesee County, of which Flint is the seat, meant "beautiful valley." The Indian name from which "Flint" is derived meant flint or flint stones. There is a certain efficient hardness to life in the city today which makes the name appropriate.

But the lumber barons were ruthless in denuding the countryside of its superb pine forests, and the profits were taken away by absentee owners even as they were in the later years of the automobile industry. The natural beauty of the river valley has never been restored, trees and grass will not grow under the pall of heavy smoke from the multitudinous factory chimneys.

For some years after the destruction of the forests Flint remained a quiet market town. Not long after the Civil War, the carriage industry began to expand, and in the Gay Nineties Flint was regarded as one of the leading towns of the country in the carriage and wagon trade.

In one way it was a natural transition from carriage making to automobile production, but in another way it was purely accidental that Flint became the most typical city in the automotive industry, for this community has no geographical advantages over many other places in central and southern Michigan.

James H. Writing, president of the Flint Wagon Works, whose product was one of the leaders in making this town known as "the vehicle city" before the birth of the automobile, invited David D. Buick to move his new and struggling automobile concern from Detroit. Thus in 1904 the Buick Motor Company was founded and housed in a small one-story building which proved to be the foundation for the vast General Motors Corporation.

Buick, who was no business man, later sold out and died in

poverty. The man who created General Motors and did more than any one else to make Flint what it is today was William C. Durant, an Easterner who came here as a boy, whose grandfather had one of the largest lumber mills in Flint, and who had become a millionaire in the Durant-Dort Carriage Company. "Billy" Durant, as Flint calls him, is an old man now, but in his heyday he was the embodiment of the American speculative entrepreneur.

He organized General Motors. He lost control of it to the bankers. He regained his power, then he lost it to the bankers again in a series of spectacular financial manipulations which kept the country in a frenzy for years. For good or evil, it was "Billy" Durant who set the feverish pace for the Flint speed-up. He made all his associates and subordinates keep up with his own killing rate of speed, working day and night. It was not until years afterward that they discovered he used to sleep all around the clock occasionally, sometimes twice around in order to restore what seemed to be his superhuman energy.

When Mr. Durant was forced out of control by the bankers, after a period of overexpansion, two other outstanding figures in the automotive industry impressed their personalities upon the history of Flint, Buick and General Motors. They were Charles W. Nash and Walter P. Chrysler, both of whom left later to head their own concerns.

But instead of following further the history of the automotive industry, let us come at once to the present troubled hour. Let us see what sort of city and what sort of life have evolved here out of the grandiose dreams and schemes of Mr. Durant and his associates. Today Flint is a city absolutely dependent for its economic and social health upon the employment situation at the Buick and Chevrolet plants, at the two Fisher Body plants which feed them with car bodies and at the A. C. Spark-Plug plant, named after Albert Champion, the French inventor. All of them are part of General Motors.

When a comparative "handful" of men, not more than 2,000 at most and probably fewer, sat down and folded arms at their places in key points of the two Fisher plants late in December, they closed the bottleneck of the whole G.M. machine in Flint.

Because no bodies could be obtained, one department after another in both Buick and Chevrolet had to close down until eventually not a wheel was turning in either of the huge plants.

This threw 38,000 General Motors employes out of work, not to speak of clerks in retail stores laid off subsequently. It left only 6,100 factory workers at their jobs—5,300 in the A. C. plant and 800 in small independent establishments. This was only about one-third the number of Flint factory workers still employed at the depth of the depression. It meant the loss of about $266,000 a day in wages, or six-sevenths of the town's factory payroll just before the strike.

This brought about a creeping economic paralysis in which retail trade collapsed, workers' families buying nothing but groceries and other absolute necessities; the nearly complete stoppage of normal credit, and a rapid increase in the relief rolls. Moreover, it divided workers against one another—union men against non-union, father against son, brother against brother, wife against husband—in a way unpleasantly suggestive of civil warfare.

Life in Flint has its peculiarities. Flint is a labor town, but not a union town. The atmosphere is entirely different from that in intensely democratic Seattle, another "labor" town, but also a union one. In Seattle a teamster or longshoreman thinks the best is none too good for him, and has not the slightest hesitation in walking into the best hotel in town for dinner or a drink. And no one thinks of lifting an eyebrow so long as he is properly dressed and behaves respectably. Not so in Flint.

The class distinctions here might be compared to those of an army post. There is what might be called an officers' club, with an exclusive circle of society composed chiefly of General Motors top executives and their wives and some members of old families in the pre-motor age. Among the five other clubs where drinks and food may be consumed—there are State liquor stores, but nothing except beer is served in public places in this factory town —one might be described as a non-coms' club, although the brass hats drop in once in a while. The rest of the town belongs to the privates in the ranks.

There are no visible signs of widespread poverty, hunger or misery in town—quite the contrary. The automobile industry, especially in Flint, has always paid good wages. Workers, their wives and children seen on the street appear well-fed and well-clothed, the men in heavy woolen mackinaws or leather coats, overalls, great cloth caps with peaked visors, and long boots and heavy socks.

Housing conditions on the whole are good, although there are complaints of rising prices, natural in the boom period the automobile industry was enjoying up to the time of the strike. According to a local housing expert, perhaps some 30,000 persons, or nearly one-fifth of the population, live in homes he does not consider proper under the American standard of living.

As far as this writer could see in trips about the city, only a few hundred seemed to be living in disgraceful conditions.

Nearly everybody has an automobile and a radio. Many people have electric refrigerators and other modern devices, even if some be second-hand and ramshackle. In front of the most disreputable habitation one may sometimes see the latest model Buick, all shiny and streamlined, a car probably worth more than the home and its furnishings.

Here we have the logical development of the American machine age, with all its marvelous scientific, mechanical, engineering and business efficiency. On the top economic level many millionaires have been made by Flint. The middle class enjoys the luxuries and pleasures which Kings and Emperors of bygone days could not command. The average workers earn enough when times are good to buy all or most of the material comforts of life.

At the same time that Flint illustrates the physical advantages of the machine age, it emphasizes the shortcomings of that age from the esthetic, cultural and intellectual points of view. The millionaires do not stay in Flint any longer than they have to. They move to New York, Detroit or Chicago. The middle class is always rushing off to Detroit for parties, the theatre or music. The workers, although many recreational facilities are provided for them, perhaps in some cases are unable to enjoy either these or material comforts because of the mental and physical fatigue induced by the speed-up.

Flint is a city of speed, a city of efficiency, but it is not a city of beauty. Perhaps it points the way to the ultimate realization of the American dream. Can beauty be added to efficiency to produce a new American way of life? The answer is for the coming generation.

L'Enfant's Capital
—*and* Boomtown, Too

by James Reston

WARTIME WASHINGTON is finally fulfilling the dreams of its found-
ers. The small town on the banks of the Potomac is growing up.
The "Federal City" of Major Pierre Charles L'Enfant's imagination is here at last. The capital is no longer, as Charles Dickens
described it, "a monument raised to a deceased project . . .
whose spacious avenues begin in nothing and lead nowhere." Its
avenues are reaching out now to the ends of a melancholy universe; it is the wartime capital of the Western World, an eager,
scurrying overcrowded metropolis, the hope of Athens and Amsterdam, and even of Dickens's own London.

Look down on it in the early morning from the pinnacle of
the Washington Monument. The geometric pattern of its streets
stretches out in the early sun to a rim of blue water and green
hills. From this peephole in the sky it looks like an architect's
dream, a World's Fair model city turned on by an electric switch,
a study in shine and shade and movement, a fabulous and incon-
gruous mixture of long, straight modern boulevards and classical
pillared buildings out of Greece and Rome.

Promptly at 7 o'clock every morning the government machine

From the *New York Times Magazine,* June 1, 1941, copyright © 1941,
1969 by The New York Times Company.

begins to turn. The government workers start converging on the city. Thousands of cars, miniature from this height, roll down from the Virginia Hills, sweep across the bridges of the Potomac, swing around the Capitol on Jenkins Hill, and finally settle down like so many mechanical black beetles along the gutters of every street downtown. This is the new Army of the Potomac starting its daily invasion—an army which has changed the whole atmosphere and tempo of life in the nation's capital.

When Lord Bryce, writing of post–Civil War America, said that the United States was "the only great country in the world which has no capital," Washington was just a small green city with a population of 147,293. By the turn of the century this had increased to 278,718, and by the end of the World War to 437,571. When President Roosevelt took office the population was about 488,000. Now, with the centralization of government and the defense boom, it is more than 700,000, and Greater Washington will soon be pushing the million mark.

This sharp change is due almost entirely to the arrival of new Federal employes with their families. In June, 1933, there were 65,437 government workers in the capital; now there are more than 170,000 or 52,000 more than at the peak of our World War production. In the past year alone some 40,000 persons have been added to the payroll, and the total population of the city in this same period has jumped by some 75,000.

Washington, in consequence, has growing pains. The boom has touched every section of the community; it has affected the cost of living; produced, like every boom, a dozen new social problems; changed the working hours and conditions of most people in the District, cut into the social and night life of the capital, and opened up again the whole question of Washington's future.

Consider first the social changes, starting with housing, which, except for the war and Mr. Roosevelt, seems to be the main topic of conversation. About 80 per cent of the 40,000 persons hired by the government to work here in the past year were paid less than $38 dollars a week, which means that they were looking for houses in the $40-a-month bracket. The demand for these houses was so great that the supply had been exhausted by January last, when, according to a Congressional committee report, 1,972 families were looking for houses of this class and only 605 houses were available.

The apartment shortage is just as serious. Last August, a month after the real boom started, 7.94 per cent of the apartments in town were vacant. On Sept. 1 the percentage of vacancy had dropped to 5.99, and on March 1 to 1.51. By Easter virtually every apartment in the city was filled.

This housing problem in turn has produced several other social problems. Rents have naturally gone up with the demand, and as they have gone up hundreds of people living in the modest but respectable $30-a-month houses have gradually been forced into more or less slum quarters. Many families have been doubling up. In the very lowest wage brackets as many as eight families have been found living in an eight-room house, with twenty-four persons using a single bathroom. These conditions have produced problems for the District Department of Health which are now being investigated by a Congressional committee.

Coincidentally, district officials are concerned about the problem of housing the thousands of young women who have been crowding into the capital from all over the country for the past year. More than 12,000 stenographers and typists have been hired by the government since the first of the year. The supply of single rooms in private houses has long since vanished; young women are now living two or three to a room in unsupervised quarters, and the Civil Service Commission is about to issue a new nationwide call for thousands of additional workers of this class.

The problem of fitting these newcomers into the educational and transportation systems of the capital has already caused several fundamental adjustments in the whole organization of the city's life. In the vicinity of the navy yard and in the Anacostia section the influx of youngsters in the schools has been overwhelming, and for a while the traffic problem threatened to tie up the entire capital.

Old-timers like to point out how mechanization and centralization have complicated life here in the past few months. A year ago the Federal employes, who dominate the activities of

Washington, went to work at 9 in the morning. Getting to the center of the city during the rush hours in Washington was never a very easy task, because L'Enfant laid out the capital in a series of tree-lined circles, which, while picturesque and useful in the event of an enemy invasion, provided a ring of traffic bottlenecks all around the city.

Nevertheless, with a little ingenuity and a great deal of noise, Washington got to work on time—until the defense workers arrived. Then the traffic problem became urgent. Every morning at 9 o'clock and every evening at 5 some 81,000 workers tried to get in and out of the Federal Triangle, which looked during these hours like the environs of the Yankee Stadium after the Army-Notre Dame game. Appeals were made to the employes to leave their cars at home and, when these appeals failed, the entire Federal working schedule was changed to bring the employes to work gradually, starting at 7:30 in the morning. Some of the departments even introduced a night shift.

Increased demands for all commodities and services, and the breaking of the normal routine of the city's life have naturally boosted the cost of living. On Sept. 15, last, it was 100, or normal, according to the Department of Labor's statistics. On March 15 it had increased to 100.9 in the low-salary brackets and soared in the middle brackets. Eating at noon in downtown Washington, for example, is nothing more than an expensive scrimmage. Prices have gone up from 10 to 25 per cent in the past six months, and indigestion, like sinus trouble, is becoming a popular complaint.

To commercial and industrial Washington, however, the boom has been a boon. A year ago, the Federal Government's Washington payroll was $22,582,980 a month; since then it has increased by $5,000,000 a month. As a result, when the stenographers leave the office in the afternoon, downtown Washington looks like Fifth Avenue during the Christmas rush. All the stores have had to increase their staffs; by last January department-store sales in the capital were already 21 per cent higher than in January of 1940. The architects and contractors are profiting too. Even before the war, of course, the Washington of the New Deal was bursting its borders. In 1938, for example, 4,275 new family units were built in the District. When the defense workers were beginning to arrive, however, 6,151 family units were knocked together in the last six months of 1940 and that pace has been maintained ever since. The government itself is building or planning six slum-clearance projects for Negroes, putting up 4,275 new family units around the fringe of the District, and working on a new dormitory to house 1,000 women workers.

The social and night life of the city has been affected in minor ways. High society in Washington has always radiated from the White House and the embassies. The principal characters in these quarters, however, are now preoccupied with the war. It is not good taste to be festive, and, besides, as the war spreads, sending invitations to the diplomatic corps becomes more and more complicated.

But while entertaining is reduced around the White House and the embassies, it has increased elsewhere. The arrival of new executives—and they arrive daily—is the sign for a round of parties; similarly, the departure of officers from the War and Navy Departments for new posts in the field is also an excellent and popular excuse. Normally at this time of year when the heat begins to descend on this valley, the more important social section of the population begins to leave for the country. There is too much work for that this year.

The sheer weight of the new arrivals, too, has increased social activity. Everybody with a clean shirt here seems to be in society, and as a result the roofs and dining and ball rooms of the hotels are in a constant state of confusion. That noisiest and most unsatisfactory of all modern institutions, the cocktail party, has staggered up to new heights of popularity.

Washington has never been able to support a night club comparable to any of the main clubs in the Fifties in New York, but the few night clubs that are operating are doing a land-office business. Similarly, the movies are jammed to the roof almost every night, and the drive-in movie lots around the city are flourishing. This much being said, however, it must be added that social life still centers around the dinner tables of Georgetown and Alexandria.

Where, then, is this boom going? Will these war workers return to their homes when the war is over, or will they remain here to run a government that is increasing its control over the whole nation every month?

One's first guess is that this vast influx of people will be permanent. The move toward centralization in government is not restricted to the United States. In London, the government has steadily grown and has now spilled over from Whitehall into Berkeley Square and Bloomsbury. In Berlin, similarly, one sees a gigantic centralized machine providing new Ministries and spreading well beyond the confines of Unter den Linden.

Washington seems determined to take advantage of this world trend. The emergency building program, one notes, is much more permanent than the ramshackle gray stucco dreadfuls thrown up in the last war. The attitude of the people who own things here, too, is different now from that in 1919, when they expected and got a serious drop in the population. Now there is a tendency to talk and plan on a large scale.

When Lord Bryce said Washington was no capital back there in the Eighties, he meant that it had not, like the great capitals of Europe, gathered together the great minds of the nation and made itself the cultural and commercial as well as the political center of the nation. That criticism was undoubtedly valid then and is valid today. In the past decade, Washington has undoubtedly exerted a greater political influence on the whole nation than ever before and, through its supervision of business, it has gone far toward becoming the financial and commercial capital of the nation, but it is still far from taking the lead in the fields of culture.

Though one bows to Carl Sandburg, Archibald MacLeish and many noted and able university professors along The Mall, though indeed the New Deal has contributed a great deal toward that ideal cultural community, it cannot yet be said that Washington has inspired any great drift of her thinkers toward the Potomac. It does hold in its great galleries and libraries many of the great treasures of the world of art and literature, but here again the community's record is disappointing, for these great libraries and museums are used mainly by the people from other communities who come here to use them.

Above all things, Washington is still a city of violent contrasts: of the hurry of the North and the leisure of the South; of whites and Negroes and rich and poor, living door to door; of dreamers, patriots and statesmen, and cynics, liars and cheats; of good causes and bad causes and lost causes. In some curious way it combines the country and the city.

In building this capital we have copied shamelessly from that Europe we are now trying to save. Here on Capitol Hill are the Congressional office buildings looking for all the world like the buildings fronting the Place de la Concorde in Paris; here around the corner the Supreme Court Building looking like a Roman temple; here the great Lincoln Memorial with its Doric columns. Unlike the White House, the first and still the most beautiful building in the capital, all these seem strangely foreign.

And yet for just that reason, for just that contrast between the Old World and the New, Washington seems just right for its present role. By the statement of the present Administration, the United States is the champion of all that is meant by Western civilization. And for that momentous role, this strangely beautiful city provides the perfect setting.

Juneau, Fifty Years After the Gold Rush

by Richard L. Neuberger

JUNEAU CAN talk to New York now. It costs $7.50 for the first
three minutes and a Signal Corps sergeant rather than a girl switch-
board operator places the call, for Alaska is still enough of a
military zone to have the Army handling all communications. But
it is a genuine thrill to establish contact by land line between
North America's last frontier and the continent's greatest city, and
many Juneau families have pinched slightly at mealtimes so that
they could make use of the new wilderness telephone system strung
from cedar pole to cedar pole along the 1,519-mile Alaska
Highway.

Not that Juneau's people think of their compact little community of 7,000 as the last frontier—far from it. In this autumn
of 1948, half a century after the first rush of Americans into the
distant north, they feel that Juneau has become quite a metropolis.
And when reminded that Juneau, which is the capital of Alaska,
has fewer inhabitants than one or two big apartment houses in
New York or Boston, they answer that these urban giants were
not so stupendous, either, after only fifty years in business.

For Alaskan history, in the opinion of Juneau's population,

From the *New York Times Magazine,* October 10, 1948, copyright © 1948
by The New York Times Company.

stems not from the Pleistocene Age when the prodigious 20,000-foot mountains were thrust skyward, nor from the exploring voyage of Capt. George Vancouver in H.M.S. Discovery in 1794, nor even from the purchase of Alaska from Czar Alexander II of Russia by the United States in 1867.

Alaska's year of origin, if you ask man, woman or child on the narrow streets of Juneau, was 1898. That was the year prospectors found naked, gleaming nuggets in the sands of Bonanza Creek in the Klondike. It brought a frantic, searching rush of people from Seattle and San Francisco to the mysterious land their government had bought. It was the first time Americans in any numbers had migrated to Alaska, so the Territory this fall will celebrate what Governor Ernest Gruening has called "the half-century anniversary of the discovery of Alaska by the American people."

At 50, Juneau is still different things to different people; it still illustrates the truth of a casual remark by one of the most celebrated of the men who made that desperate trek in 1898. "It all depends," said Jack London, "on whether you are coming or going."

Voyagers stepping ashore from the luxury steamers from the states see Juneau's docks of crumbling timbers, the one gravel road which ends twenty-eight miles from town, the price tags in grocery and drug stores 30 per cent above Seattle's already high costs, the antiquated room over the fire station which serves as a public library, the liquor stores and bars that nearly outnumber the groceries and restaurants.

But the men down from the lonely "bush" see a different Juneau. Their eyes are taken by the new $250,000 hotel with its chicken and roast beef dinners, by the thirty-six-seat buses which absorb the bumps on the rutted Glacier Highway, by the pretty girls wearing the latest styles who pour down the marble steps of the Territorial Capitol at 5 o'clock, by the grocery and drug store prices a full 30 per cent below those at the log trading posts along the surging Yukon.

Juneau itself was a mere outpost when the *cheechakos* (tenderfeet) sailed northward in 1898. Yet Jack London, who saw it from the decks of the old cargo vessel Umatilla, probably would be more stirred today by Juneau's awakening social conscience than by its seven-story hotel and its modern bus system. If any mood characterizes the most northerly capital under the American flag, it is a mood traditionally American—rebellion against colonialism.

"I'm tired of trudging to the top of a hill every time I want to get my mail or post a letter," protested a white-haired grandmother selling Eskimo handiwork in walrus ivory behind a jewelry store counter, "If we were a state with a couple of Senators in Washington, they wouldn't dare treat us this way."

Juneau's 1,961 postoffice boxes actually outnumber those in Philadelphia. This is because everyone in Juneau must call for his mail at the Federal Building, which is on a high hill. Nor do citizens forget that the postal windows are on the second floor. "Must have been designed by one of those fellows down in Washington" is a frequent comment.

Alaska's capital has no letter carriers and no pick-up mail boxes. More than one wayfarer has missed his boat roaming Juneau in quest of the familiar green receptacle. Juneau families complain about the $6 a year they must pay for postoffice boxes, and they also chafe at having to carry home every Christmas package and delivery from a mail-order firm. Alaska's universal Eighth Zone parcel-post rate is an even more constant cause of grumbling. It costs a Juneau housewife as much to send a package the ninety miles to the neighboring Alaskan town of Skagway as to New York City, 4,000 miles distant.

These quirks, regarded in Juneau as outrageous impositions, have stirred within the community a demand for statehood which the town's most cautious burghers have not been able to quell. When the executive committee of the local Chamber of Commerce adopted a wait-and-see attitude on statehood, the full membership revolted and came out for immediate inclusion in the Union. And when the *Juneau Daily Empire* refused to print Governor Gruening's name because of his leadership of the statehood movement, public indignation compelled the newspaper to abandon this act of censorship.

Prices are another symbol to the people of Juneau of their Territorial serfdom. They blame prices on the highest ocean freight rates under the American flag, and they know the United States Supreme Court has ruled that Alaska as a state could no longer be denied access to competing cargo service by Canadian ships. Today a series of legal restrictions force all Alaskan freight to originate in Seattle, and Juneau housewives attribute to this a cost of living which eclipses that anywhere in the United States.

These are a few comparisons made by the Alaskan Department of Labor showing the gap several months ago between Juneau food prices and those in New York City:

	N.Y.	Juneau
Round steak	79c	$1.02
Pork chops	69c	98c
Milk	21c	30c
Bread	15c	22c
Peas, can	16c	28c
Tomatoes, can	16c	27c
Sugar	10c	13c
Coffee	49c	58c
Eggs	81c	94c
Carrots, bunch	16c	13c

Juneau shoppers jocularly tell themselves that only the carrots were produced in Juneau, and did not have to be freighted 1,000 miles northward from Seattle.

Although a score of waterfalls plunge down the mountains near Juneau in Corinthian columns of spray and foam, local power rates are high and there is no regulation by a public utilities commissioner. A governmental official, moving north from Portland, says that he pays $15 to the Alaska Electric Light and Power Company for the same quantity of kilowatt-hours that cost him $4.50 off the lines of Portland General Electric. And, adds the Federal employe, a 25 per cent increase in his salary for Alaskan service does not begin to atone for the difference in living costs between Juneau and his former home in Oregon.

Heavily though they are nicked by the utilities company and at the grocery store, Juneau's people are let off lightly by the tax collector. They pay all Federal levies, but Territorial taxes are practically nonexistent. The sole levy by the Territory is a $5 annual school tax, and it applies only to wage-earners—and to none of them over the age of 60. The solitary tax to support the city is a 20-mill levy on real and personal property.

Juneau's economic welfare is delicately reliant on two sets of payrolls—those of the government and of the salmon fisheries. The salmon runs have declined, because traps and nets have made heavy inroads on the Pinks and Kings surging upstream to spawn. Yet in 1947 Juneau fishermen received $2,250,000 for the salmon and halibut they brought into harbor.

No one, not even the census taker, ever has known exactly how many commercial fishermen there are in Juneau. This is because the taxi driver, the hotel clerk and the pretty wife of the new store-keeper all become fishermen at the time of the salmon runs.

And government in Alaska, like government everywhere else, is burgeoning. Federal and Territorial offices have overflowed into many buildings "downtown." Among the largest public employers are the United States Forest Service, Fish and Wildlife Service, Alaska Native Service and Territorial Department of Health. As in that other and distant capital, Washington, D.C., girls who hit typewriters far outnumber the professional and staff workers. Approximately 1,000 people in Juneau owe their pay checks to either the Territorial or United States Government.

The connection between these two dominant industries and Juneau's economic well-being is direct and easily discernible. Businessmen protested vehemently when a threat was made to move part of the Indian Service to Anchorage. A poor fishing season so curtailed employment of waitresses and cooks in Juneau that Julius Heinemann, German-born secretary of Local 871, AFL Culinary Workers, had to announce a withdrawal of the union's delegate to the Territorial Federation of Labor convention at Mount McKinley Park. The $500 expense money could not be raised.

Juneau's other economic activities are diverse and widely scattered. A few hardy souls raise mink and silver fox on the tiny timbered islets near Juneau. A small group of longshoremen service the Alaska Line and Canadian Pacific boats which put into the harbor. With the world outside pleading for lumber, the Juneau Spruce Mill has had a monthly payroll of $120,000, but this plant has been frequently shut down by strikes, leading even governmental New Dealers in Juneau to concede that local sentiment was probably favorable to the Taft-Hartley Act.

It is a symptom of a new era in Alaskan economics that the industry which first brought a prospector named Joe Juneau to the blue waters of Gastineau Channel is now closed down. Only a colossal heap of tailings tells of the millions in gold taken from the Alaska-Juneau Mine. The lure responsible for the frenzied boom of 1898 is virtually gone by 1948. In its place the capital of Alaska looks forward to a vast pulp plant which may produce 500 tons of newsprint a day.

Juneau is surrounded by immense forests of hemlock and spruce. These forests may be of more value—and, of greater importance, more enduring—than the bright flecks that colored the sands of Gold Creek, which still foams through Juneau. Yet this wilderness treasure-trove that may make Juneau rich tends to dwarf it in the eyes of newcomers. From a steamer in the channel the capital of Alaska, clinging to the rocky apron of 3,700-foot Mount Roberts, stockaded by measureless evergreen solitudes, seems a mere cluster of toy buildings.

Only on closer inspection does Juneau assume metropolitan stature. Indeed, it is infinitely more metropolitan than its sister cities of similar population in "the states." From a place of 7,000 anywhere in the United States it is generally only a short drive to Newark or Omaha or Los Angeles, where sister can have her tonsils extracted and mother can do her fall shopping.

But Juneau must be self-contained. It is 1,000 miles by sea or air to Seattle. Edmonton is 1,519 miles away over the Alaska Highway, and a brief voyage by car ferry is required to reach a feeder road of the highway on salt water. In fact, it is even 300 miles to the closest Alaskan town of equal size: Ketchikan.

So Juneau is big for its population. Charley Goldstein's store might grace a community of 50,000 in "the states." Charley was in Juneau in 1898, a status in Alaska comparable to having one's ancestors come over on the Mayflower in New England. And Dick Harris, son of the man who was Joe Juneau's partner, is in the sign business in the town his father helped to found.

Juneau is also picturesque. Like many other Alaskan communities, it is compressed snugly between salt water and mountain wall. The tilted apron of the mountain begins almost at the timbered wharves, which rest on spruce and cedar pilings.

Flats and cottages cling precariously to the steep hillsides, and are reached by a series of paths and ladders reminiscent of Navajo cliff dwellings. Zoning is unknown. Residences intrude on the business district, mine residue creeps out into the harbor, Gold Creek foams through lawns and back yards. From the harbor the massive masonry piles of the Territorial Capitol, Goldstein Building and Baranof Hotel tower indiscriminately above rooming houses, bungalows and Indian shacks.

The wilderness does not stop at the Juneau city limits. Many houses—some multi-windowed and modernistic, others dating nearly from the gold rush—are stockaded by evergreen trees. More than one frightened Juneau mother has thought she heard a big brown bear growling in the underbrush.

Small as Juneau is in the great galaxy of American cities, it is not too small to participate in the rush to suburbanism. The particular lure at the moment is the Glacier Highway, which winds through the Tongass National Forest. Juneau businessmen and clerks are taking up five-acre plots of the Public Domain as homesites. The Glacier Bus Lines operates a commuters' service, although these titans of the road must pick their way carefully through the narrow streets of Juneau—streets laid out before the internal-combustion engine was shipped north.

Although the last nugget has been panned in Gold Creek, Juneau is close to its pioneer beginnings. Seated in the Baranof's lavish "Bubble Room," most famous and Sybaritic bar in the North, two girls from an office of the Territorial Government had a bearded young man in checkered cruiser come up and introduce himself by name. He sat down without invitation, ordered Bourbon and soda for three, and explained that they were the first white women he had seen in fourteen months.

After half an hour of painful silence, broken only by the girls' feeble attempts to initiate conversation, the whiskered young man departed as abruptly as he had arrived.

To some extent, Juneau dramatizes the universality of American customs and behavior. It is 1,000 miles from America's continental soil; it is on the fringe of the last great frontier under our flag. Yet it is not so profoundly different from its sister Pacific Coast capitals of Olympia, Salem and Sacramento—or those of any others of the forty-eight states.

Juneau has a Lions Club, American Legion, Elks, Veterans of Foreign Wars, Knights of Columbus, Scottish Rite, CIO and AFL. The local Chamber of Commerce favors the Taft-Hartley Law; the Fishermen's Union opposes it. The wives of Federal and Territorial officials fret when they are not included in the teas and luncheons held at the Governor's Mansion with its stately white pillars and Haida totem poles. The League of Women Voters and the Juneau Women's Club tiff over who shall honor the handsome young college professor just stopping over between boats.

A few years ago the descendants of Alaska's original owners often were considered "lesser breeds without the law" in Juneau. They frequently were barred from taxis, hotels and beauty parlors. An occasional restaurant put up a sign: WE DO NOT CATER TO NATIVE TRADE.

But as tolerance and understanding spread in the United States, they also advanced northward. The Alaskan Legislature, like the Legislatures of four of the United States, passed a law forbidding discrimination based on race, creed or color. The signs came down. And now the Juneau division has sent three Indians to sit in the seats of the lawmakers—Senator Roy Peratrovich and Representatives Andrew Hope and Frank Johnson.

On the other hand, Juneau has no golf course, no organized professional sports, no football games. Movies are frequently from one to five years behind current releases. Because of only 28 miles of roads, there are comparatively few automobiles.

This has diverted Juneau money into other channels. Clothing has been one of the beneficiaries. Juneau is well up on the "new look," and the people of Alaska's capital wear their best clothes on all possible occasions.

Juneau was also perceptibly less affected by the end of the war than was the continental United States. Much of the tension and mood of wartime still endure here. The boy at the front door in Juneau with a telegram is not a Western Union messenger but an Army corporal. The U.S.S. Wachusett, a Coast Guard cutter with a crew of more than 220 men, is based in Juneau. Not far offshore is the great Navy yard on barren Kodiak Island.

Alaskans realize that their land is the American soil nearest the Soviet Union. They are aware that the Eskimos of the Arctic coast may soon again be mobilized for guerrilla warfare, as they were when the Japanese squatted on Attu. The average Juneau merchant or professional man will tell you he is reconciled to Alaska becoming the first battleground, should Russia and the United States ever clash.

"I don't need to pick up our little paper to find out how things are going in Berlin," a local steamship agent confided. "I can tell by the number of calls I get asking if I have any cabins left on an outgoing boat. Whenever the news looks as though there might be serious trouble between the East and the West, the people here want reservations on the next boat—to get their families out."

In one respect the residents of Juneau—and of most of Alaska for that matter—seem even more American than are their relatives and friends and ancestors farther South on the continent. Their most ardent desire is the right to vote for a President of the United States. They participate avidly in straw polls. They debate Territorial politics in terms of national issues.

On street corners in front of the old Greek Orthodox churches left over from the Russian settlement, Juneau citizens argue whether Truman or Dewey might deal more effectively with the Soviet colossus just 55 miles from Alaskan soil across the Bering Strait.

In the hillside bungalows that look down on Seward Street much as Telegraph Hill apartments look down on San Francisco, the people of Juneau translate local political contests into terms of the Presidential race itself. They hope that by 1952 they will not have to resort to this play-acting.

The Two States
of California

by R. L. Duffus

WHILE THE population of the United States increased about 20 per cent during the last decade, the population of California went up about 50 per cent. This is one of the outstanding facts of our time. It is astonishing and almost unbelievable. However, it has happened and is continuing to happen.

A symbol of this phenomenon is perhaps that the Golden State, with what almost seems like a single stride, has assumed a majestic political importance. The Republicans have recognized this notable truth by selecting San Francisco as the scene of their 1956 nominating convention. Moreover, California, like Virginia in the old days and Ohio and New York in more recent times, is making an effort to be the mother of Presidents—or at least of Presidential candidates.

Senator William F. Knowland has admitted that under certain circumstances he will declare himself in January. Vice President Richard M. Nixon has made no such declaration, but he is a potential candidate, at least for Vice President, and some of his friends have still higher ambitions for him. A third and even more distinguished Californian, Chief Justice Earl G. Warren, has

From the *New York Times Magazine,* December 18, 1955, copyright © 1955 by The New York Times Company.

been mentioned, although his stated position is that he is not and will not become a candidate.

Such is the situation. This is California a little over a century after the Gold Rush. California is no longer a place. It is an event. One can well be aware of this truth as he stands on the top of one of the rugged hills of San Francisco. He can be even more aware of it—in fact, he can hear it shouting in his ears— if he goes over the Tehachapi Pass and down into the valley of southern California.

This is California. Two cities dominate it. What isn't in some way hooked up with San Francisco is hooked up in some way with Los Angeles. But there has been a change not only in the size of its population but in the weight of its distribution. A generation or so ago, whenever anybody in California spoke of going to "The City," his hearers knew approximately where to address him. Now they don't. Now, unless they are inherently prejudiced in favor of north or south, they ask, "Which city?"

The old balance between north and south has changed. The forty-four counties of California which are generally considered as northern have this year a population of about 5,170,000, or 40.7 per cent of the whole state. The remaining fourteen, which include Los Angeles City and County, have the other 59.3 per cent—7,000,000 and up, always up.

The relative populations of the political cities are misleading because San Francisco is confined to a small county and cannot cross county lines, whereas Los Angeles has a big county to play around in. Thus, San Francisco has about 800,000 persons on a little over ninety-one square miles, of which only about forty-five square miles are dry land. Los Angeles, on the other hand, has 453 square miles, most of them dry, on which to house its 2,150,000 (and more) inhabitants.

The metropolitan areas, as defined by the Bureau of the Census, tell a more accurate story. For Los Angeles the Bureau allocates Los Angeles and Orange Counties and gets a total of 5,221,000 and up. For San Francisco the bureau allows six counties and achieves a total of about 2,500,000. If there were complete justice, and California cities did not have to stop at county lines, Los

Angeles would still be about twice as populous as San Francisco.

The drift is south. Why, a San Franciscan doesn't know. A Los Angeleno knows but is too busy to find the words.

Los Angeles is California's runaway child. The old philosophers who used to sit around the parks, maybe playing a few games of horseshoes once in a while, the worshipers of the sun, the cultists: these have not disappeared from Los Angeles—not by any means —but they aren't news any more, or at most they are what journalists call feature material. The news is the intrusion into sunny southern California of the spirit of Chicago and Detroit.

With this change has come, within California, a conflict of places and cultures. Californians stand as one in agreement that all sane persons would, if they could choose, live in California. But which California? That is the question.

It is impossible to be unbiased in this argument. All the observer can do is to state the facts with respect for the truth as he sees it.

The first fact is that a judgment between San Francisco and Los Angeles must derive from temperament. Nobody can be deliriously happy about both these cities. All the judicious can do—all that even an impartial visitor from Florida, the French Riviera, Little America or Mars can do—is to mention certain qualities and leave the rest to the judgment of posterity.

Los Angeles is warmer than San Francisco, but not so much warmer as most of us think—an annual mean temperature of 63, as compared with San Francisco's 56.5. It is less humid—there is an annual rainfall of 15.23, as compared with San Francisco's 22.18.

Los Angeles is not so dramatically hilly as San Francisco. Some who have examined it carelessly would say it is flat. This is not true—one point in the city is over 5,000 feet above the sea. You can see a lot of Los Angeles from Beverly Hills, which is inside it but not a part of it, or from a highly respectable ridge called The Strip, which is also inside but is believed to belong to the county. There are mountains to the north, east and south. You cross or go around one range of hills to get to a part of the city—

the San Fernando Valley. There are hills in downtown Los Angeles that you can skid down on your two feet, just as you do on Mason and a few other streets in San Francisco.

But generally, in Los Angeles you think of valleys and plains. In San Francisco you think of hills and water. That is the topographical difference, and in spite of the inequalities in the Los Angeles terrain it is a big one. It is a psychological difference, too, and it is a tremendous one. The Los Angeles area is a basin. The San Francisco area, except for that part of it occupied by water, is a bulge.

Let us look more closely at each of these cities. San Francisco, which came into prominence at the time of the Gold Rush more than a century ago, was known around the world before anybody outside of the immediate neighborhood ever heard of Los Angeles. San Francisco crowns one of the lordliest sites on earth; a great harbor with a narrow approach; hills in the city itself and real mountains to the north, southwest and east; canyons that could be, and were, broadened and tamed.

Under the stimulus of gold, then of silver, then of the railway and the opening markets of the Pacific, it grew with tremendous vigor. It grew impulsively, without much planning. When the important part of it burned after the earthquake of 1906—and though it was fire that did the vast damage there really was an earthquake—it rebuilt gaily on its old foundations.

In recent years it has spread—across the bay on a mighty bridge, across the Golden Gate on another, down the peninsula. It continues to grow, inside and outside its political limits. It remains charged with vigor. It takes life joyfully, but not easily.

But, as a friendly critic said, it is a completed city; it is a city built on the older pattern; it is a city that will not, within its political boundaries, much alter its character in the years to come. A recent visitor tested this observation; he saw vast developments all along the land periphery, but in ten years the inner nature of the city had not greatly changed. Why should it? It was already good.

San Francisco is the kind of city that will boast officially of all the material evidences of wealth and progress. They are there. Trade increases. Industries multiply and grow. Each dawn brings into the north new settlers from the East, to work and to buy.

But this is not so much a city as it is a way of life. What other metropolis would cherish the outmoded cable cars as San Francisco does? San Francisco loves them. San Francisco rides up and down Powell and California Streets in a kind of frantic delight, the city falling away and rising, as though it were alive.

San Francisco is daily work. To be sure, San Francisco is getting ahead in the world. Certainly—though not in the desperate way the redshirted miners from the Mother Lode and the silk-hatted adventurers from the Comstock strove to get ahead.

But San Francisco is the ships coming and going in the mighty bay; it is the lights at night from Nob, Telegraph and Russian Hills; it is Golden Gate Park, a lovely monument forever to a man named McLaren, who nursed it for a long lifetime; it is the beach below the Cliff House; it is the restaurants where whole families go night after night; it is Fisherman's Wharf, Lone Mountain and the Twin Peaks; it is the hills down which you must not walk without rubber heels, if you value your bones; it is the sunset gleam on long rows of stucco-covered houses that used to be bleak, unpainted wood but have been beautified in later decades; it is joy and sin and colds in the head and fog stinging the throat like wine; it is the neighborhood pride that makes the Potrero distinguish itself from the near-by Mission District, and North Beach look down on both, and all of them, including the relatively new Marina, feel sorry for commuters and villagers.

This is San Francisco, and if you don't look out, if you listen to the returned exile, if you converse a little with the outwardly cynical native-born and permanent inhabitants, you will be captured and never get away.

But is it a good thing to live in a city that is completed and perfect? Is such a city right and proper in this changing world? Should any city be dedicated to a slightly mystical way of life, a strayed romanticism, a golden, however beautiful, illusion?

Let us not distort the picture. San Francisco is one of the world's great ports. In value of cargo, its harbor surpasses Los

Angeles. In any other part of the world the fact that it has quadrupled its manufacturing output since 1919 would be regarded as impressive. It is less so only because industrial Los Angeles has gone ahead so much faster that it has outrun San Francisco and the San Francisco area three to one.

San Francisco works, no doubt about that. But it isn't the work one thinks of in and around San Francisco, it is the play the work buys.

But in Los Angeles one cannot help thinking it is the work that is the fun; it is the work that is the big game. The working and the playing cannot always be pulled apart.

For Los Angeles is building, some of its inhabitants believe, a new kind of city. It will be a kind of city without any recognizable center. Its important functions will be scattered. Its energy will be felt far and wide.

Whereas San Francisco, even with its immediate suburbs, is compact, Los Angeles sprawls. The old city that was made up, so the jest went, of country villages tacked together, has become an almost violently aggressive organism. It has acquired, as one young Los Angeles businessman said, an explosive quality.

Its increasingly eager quest for water is a good illustration. Half a century ago it solved all its foreseeable water problems by running an aqueduct 254 miles down from the Owens River. Almost immediately it felt the need for still more water and soon began the steps that brought part of the Colorado River into Southern California. The time is now foreseeable when even this will not be enough, and the city has its eyes on the Feather River, far to the north and east.

The Easterner may think of motion pictures and oranges when he visualizes Los Angeles and its neighborhood. Motion pictures are indeed a big element measured in prestige and in value of product. Yet early this year they were employing only about 33,000 persons. There were nearly 700,000 in various kinds of manufacturing and more than 458,000 in the service occupations.

Aircraft, petroleum and metal-working of various kinds do not appeal to some imaginations as do motion pictures and oranges, but they are the elements that keep Los Angeles going and growing. They are the elements that make one think of Detroit and Chicago. They have sent a throb of energy through the plains and hills of Los Angeles and into the neighboring counties of Orange and San Bernardino.

This is no longer an area of rest and contemplation, if ever it was. The retired farmer may still find its outflung areas relaxing but it is not the retired farmer or the retired anybody who has made Los Angeles grow and spread. The slice of population that has come into Los Angeles in the last few years is probably no older than that of the national population in general, and it may be younger. The old Plaza sleeps under its tattered palms and shabby oaks, but the Plaza belongs in another world.

In San Francisco the inhabitant who seeks recreation is likely to leave his home for a while. He may do this also in Los Angeles —and he may not. He may visit many miles of beaches without going outside the city. He has his theatres, his restaurants, his parks. He can go up to the mountains and find city-owned land up there. But this is not a city which one can grasp as a whole as he can grasp San Francisco. He can scarcely go downtown. Although there is a neighborhood called downtown, there is no center; there is no area in which people by common consent congregate in their lighter moments.

More and more, as it may seem to one who inspects some of the miles and miles and miles of new housing, big and little, sprawling over Los Angeles, the people of this city try to get away from it all within the four walls and the patios of their own homes. True, almost every reasonably expensive house has room for two or more cars in its garage or, more likely, its "car port."

But it also has a swimming pool. This luxury is not confined to the motion picture aristocracy. The bourgeoisie who engage in more prosaic occupations also have swimming pools as broad, as long and as deep as available income allows.

Whatever the statistics may show, the eye tells one that Los Angeles has taken to its heart the one-family home. These may be little and they may be big, but nowadays they all tend to be flat and they fit into the slopes on which they are built. The Mediterranean style of architecture is out of fashion. One does not live in a Florentine villa if he can afford something more modern and perhaps funnier.

If one seeks a final distinction it seems to be that the joy of life in San Francisco is external and visible, whereas in Los Angeles life tends to withdraw into groups and neighborhoods and even into the family circle. The joy of life is undoubtedly there, but it is a joy that is at once fiercer and more reserved than San Francisco's.

For the whole of Los Angeles is in a way a kind of workshop. Here the architect plays with his plans, but the bricks, the mortar, the steel of the city that is to be, are still strewn around. It takes a particular kind of person to endure this situation, much less to love it. It takes a kind of energy that used not to be associated with Los Angeles. It takes an eye and an imagination that can project lines into the future.

If California were Italy and the days of small wars were still with us, we might expect the people of California's Rome—that is to say, Los Angeles—to build their forum and their temples, but also to form hard-marching legions. We might expect those legions to proceed with a certain dourness and discipline, munching their dried olives and their wheat, northward and eastward.

We might expect a relative lack of color in this modern Rome and in the lives of its people. We might look for an intense practicality. We might look for a cultivation of the things of this world, with an occasional turning toward the sibyls and prophetesses in moments of relaxation. We would take it for granted that the dream of empire was in the making and that decadence was far away.

As for San Francisco, one would expect always the glint of burnished steel and the flash of bright colors in the flags and raiment of its defenders. The energy is there, but it is an energy of preserving and enjoying and not of expanding. Expansion will happen, to be sure, but it will happen more or less by law and nature and not out of the feverish human spirit.

The spirit of San Francisco will never again be feverish. It lost that quality when the last of the ruins of 1906—of the earthquake and fire—were cleaned up. Now the city is dedicated to the love of life, whose indulgence it does not postpone until some later time.

Los Angeles may be the last of our great cities to grow dramatically beneath our eyes, to emerge some day stark and beautiful out of the present dust and rubble of its building. Some day it may solidify into a kind of form and pattern and create a new tradition.

But San Francisco is here already. Let Rome march. San Francisco rejoices still in being beautifully and impregnably Florence.

Houston, Texas:
A "Yes, But—" Town

by Stanley Walker

THE POWERFUL Chamber of Commerce of Houston, employing the accepted gadgets of the honest statistician, figures that on July 3 the so-called metropolitan area of Houston reached the 1,000,000 population mark. The event was duly observed, though with little excitement, and the city now turns its attention to gaining its second million—much easier, say the experts, than the first.

There really doesn't seem to be a foreseeable end to the growth of Houston and environs so long as the industries keep on growing and new ones keep coming in. The boosters say—and they may be right—that the 200 or so miles along the Gulf Coast which contains Houston and many other smaller but thriving spots is the richest area of its size in the world. Oil and gas, cattle and cotton, sulphur and buried beds of oyster shells, lumber and salt, sea water and rice—these are only some of the principal raw materials. On them rest the railroads, the heavy construction work, the refineries, the chemical plants, and so on.

Well, there she sits, or squats, or sprawls, or festers, or blooms, depending upon how one looks at it. The city is quite vigorous, quite messy, and full of apparent contradictions. Not even its leading residents can agree on what is good about the place and what is wrong with it. And, paraphrasing the old line about New York, many a Texan says he likes to go to Houston to transact a little business, but he wouldn't want to live there if you gave him the place.

"It's a mining camp," said an old friend of mine from New York as he was catching a plane after two busy days and nights in Houston. "It's a roaring, wild, up-to-date frontier spot, and very high-class." Another man will confide that it is nothing but an old country town that has grown up rather rapidly. Another estimates that, culturally, it is about where New York was sixty or seventy years ago. The charge has been made that the city's affairs are run by a hard-fisted, arrogant oligarchy—rich and often able men who are devoid of any genuine public spirit. It has also been declared that Houston is notable for its well-to-do, civic-minded leaders who will pitch in and give generously of their time and money for the betterment of the city. Even a chilly-souled Yankee, they say, can come to Houston, intent only on multiplying his millions, and in a short time, in these wonderful surroundings, he is transformed into a open-handed Southern gentleman and a doer of good of the first rank.

In its very early days, more than 100 years ago, in the time of the Texas Republic, Houston must have been one of the most unprepossessing of towns. Laid out by its promoters on Buffalo Bayou, some fifty miles from the Gulf of Mexico, it really seemed to have little economic excuse, and its mud, heat and mosquitos, among other things, made life there far less pleasant than in such more favored towns as Galveston, Austin and San Antonio. The dream of making the bayou a ship channel to the Gulf was nursed for decades; modern Houston really dates from the dredging of the channel, which was finally accomplished forty years ago. As a port, Houston now ranks second in gross tonnage to New York.

But there were many other considerations. For example, the Southern Pacific Railroad, long a main artery for Houston trade, is still Houston's biggest employer. The big oil companies began making their headquarters in Houston. Cotton exporting boomed.

And, finally, the big chemical companies began coming in. The economy is not only vast; it is extraordinarily diverse.

Some of the more excitable commentators have referred to Houston as a "magic" city, and the skyline, looming suddenly from the flat coastal plain, has affected some observers with a fair amount of astonishment. Such solid citizens as the editorial writers of the *Chronicle* and the *Post*, however, who yield to no one in the belaboring of the obvious, take a more common sense view. For example, the *Post* said, on the occasion of the 1,000,000-metropolitan-area arrival:

"Population growth, for the mere sake of bigness, would be of little value and might be a bad thing. The cities of China, for example, long have been bursting with people, but the standard of living of the people is so low, there is no happiness for them in being crowded among millions of their fellow men."

Well spoken! Nobody is going to sue on that. Houston has grown, it is rich, and the standard of living is relatively high. But that is not the whole story. Houston (and this, of course, could be said of many other great cities) is a yes-but town. It seems that for almost every obvious advantage there is a disadvantage—sometimes important and sometimes only an annoyance which can be removed. Examples:

The skyline, much of which is the handiwork of Jesse Holman Jones, now eighty years old, is quite clearly a solid and striking sight. But the city has grown formlessly; indeed, every attempt to put into effect a city plan, with effective zoning, has been defeated. Unkempt blocks, decayed houses and unsightly parking lots are located among the finest buildings.

There is a pathetic shortage of parks in the main part of the city. Two or three years ago, St. John Garwood, a Houston lawyer who is now a Justice of the State Supreme Court, wrote an eloquent letter to a Houston newspaper suggesting that property for a midtown park, a place of quiet and beauty and contemplation, might rather easily be acquired and developed. The Chamber of Commerce was not enthusiastic. There was no way to prove that Garwood's park would mean a thing at the turnstiles. (Houston residents, viewing what has been done in New York, sometimes say, "What we need in Houston is a Bob Moses"; maybe so, but Moses, or his double, would be hooted out of town within twenty-four hours.)

Houston has become a paradise for architects and they have done some fine stuff. The houses in the excellent residential district of River Oaks reflect their work and some of the newer developments are even more magnificent. Private swimming pools are having a great vogue. Air conditioning is widespread both in the business houses and in the better homes. The newer stores—notably Foley's and Sakowitz'—are enormously attractive. But—Houston is still one of the hottest, muggiest places in America. And its slums, sometimes situated near fancy establishments, are as shocking as the worst of New York or Chicago.

The great bulk of the ordinary citizens of Houston, and most of the well-to-do, might fairly be called "moral" people—at least as righteous as might reasonably be expected. There are many large churches. The more spectacular forms of human misbehavior are frowned upon. Gambling houses have a tough time of it. And yet Houston has been severely plagued in the last few years by gangs of young toughs. The traffic in narcotics seems to be serious. A prosecuting attorney was indicted recently on a charge of being in a sort of partnership with the keeper of a disreputable house. The call-girl business flourishes. The Mayor and members of the City Council spend so much time in mutual abuse and recrimination that Mr. Jones' *Chronicle* suggested recently that "Maybe it is time to get a new Council."

One of the striking things about Harris County, in which Houston is situated, is that it contains more cattle than any other of the 254 Texas counties. The prairies are filled with them—cattle of many shapes and colors, most of them showing the hump-backed Brahma strain from India. The Houston Stock Show is a big event every winter and many fine animals are shown. Many rich oil men have established beautiful ranches near Houston. And the people of Houston consume 64,000,000 pounds of beef a year. But, here again there is a joker: the Harris County cattle are simply not very good, as a rule, and never were. Pests and diseases bother them, and the coastal grasses are not as nutritious as some others, notably the buffalo grass of the west. If a Houston tycoon invites you to dinner at his home or club, and feeds you a good steak, you may be pretty sure that it did not come from an animal that was raised and fattened in Harris County.

The clubs of Houston—including the Houston Club, the Bayou, the Tejas, the Ramada, and the new Petroleum on top of the Rice Hotel—are in every way superior to anything that may be encountered in the Southwest. Not even Dallas, which is inclined, and with some reason, to be a bit patronizing toward Houston in all realms where the life more beautiful and abundant is concerned, can approach Houston in the sound luxury of its clubs. Even the food is good, and that is a rare circumstance in Texas, except in a few homes.

Houstonians worry about problems which are possibly of more lasting importance than good food. There is the airport, which is much too small; should it be enlarged, or should a new one be built? And who is to pay? Who, indeed, is going to pay for a lot of things that are needed? Several committees made up of both the elder and the younger statesmen of the city are trying to figure out some way of meeting the staggering side costs of rapid growth.

Rice Institute is generally acknowledged to be an excellent institution. The University of Houston, to which Hugh Roy Cullen has contributed generously, has almost as many students as the University of Texas, but it is deficient in plant and in faculty quality. The public-school system of Houston is by no means bad, though the watchful eyes of the Minute Women of America make some of the teachers nervous. The hospitals and the great medical center are improving all the time; in a few years Houston will have something to be proud of. Indeed, it already looks good.

It comforts some of Houston's leaders to reflect that most of Houston's problems have come about, not from decay, but from solid and rapid growth. Indeed, some of the more articulate citizens seem to think that most of the problems can be set down as mere petty matters that can be attended to without much trouble. They had better think again. The problem of growth, of the increasing cost of all sorts of public services, is one that bedevils every city.

It is, indeed, so serious that in some places the theory has been set forth that there is a law of diminishing returns in the growth of great cities. At the moment, the great mass of Houston's citizens —these are not millionaires, but ordinary folks who have trouble making ends meet—are not in a humor to stand higher taxes or increased bus fares.

The question is often asked outside Houston: What of all these new-rich Houstonians who like to show off? Are they as crazy as we hear? The answer is yes. Some of them are quite impossible. A few are so obnoxious that they would soon be tossed out of any reasonably decent Third Avenue saloon in New York. Others are loudmouths. Others seek publicity by giving silly and extravagant parties.

However, there is not much to be alarmed about. For one thing, the ostentatious boys are very much in the minority, and are not held in very high esteem on their home grounds. They will pass, and their pranks will be forgotten. There is nothing wrong with them except money, ignorance, and a desire to express themselves —the same thing that was wrong with Diamond Jim Brady in New York in his day.

There is a great division of opinion in Houston over the probable quality of tomorrow's civic leaders. H.R. Cullen is getting along in years. Jesse Jones, who loves property that he can see and touch (that is why he became a real-estate millionaire instead of a really big oil millionaire), will have to stop work before much longer; indeed, he is already cutting down on his activities. Harry Wiess and the other old oil men—many of them sensitive and generous and farseeing men—are mostly gone. The Brown brothers, Herman and George, the big builders, are not doddering, but they are getting along. There is one theory that the new times will always bring forth adequate leadership—that the new men coming along will be in every way as good as the old, and probably better. The theory is debatable. One thoughtful architect said last week:

"The new ones haven't got it. Don't fool yourself. Houston needs big men and they are not coming along. Pretty fair men, yes, but not big. There are many reasons. The old-timers—men like Jones and Will Clayton and a lot of others—had brains, character, drive and a strange pride in Houston. They were all individualists, which in most cases turned out to be good for Houston. The new ones are corporation men, career men, bank officials, managers of this and that property, members of big law firms and representatives of outside capital. They are push-button men, very good in their way, but they are not pioneers, they are not original thinkers at heart and sometimes it seems that at heart they don't give a damn. I hope I'm mistaken."

Another man, always looking for something to complain about, put his finger on what he said was the fundamental trouble with Houston:

"Let an ordinary man, a man of little schooling and no particular background and no real depth, make a great pile of money over the course of a very few years, and what happens? First, he fancies that it was his own genius that made the money, when it probably was owing to other factors, including luck. But, having granted that he has a touch of genius, this fellow immediately begins to throw his weight around.

"It takes many forms. He may develop a habit of shooting off wires to Senators, Presidents, and even foreign political figures. He organizes and backs groups which are bent on saving the country from something or other. He sees our very vitals threatened—without knowing in the least what these vitals are.

"He worries about the textbooks in the schools. He chips in for an automobile for Senator McCarthy. He becomes a self-made expert—maybe on the tariff, maybe on theology, on geology, or anything. He may get the idea he ought to nominate and control the next Governor, or Senator, or President. He becomes an awful nuisance, far out of proportion to his brain content."

Is it really as bad as all that? It may be questioned. The strange bird thus described is, after all, not peculiar to Houston, or to Texas. The omniscience of the new-rich has been observed over the centuries. It is not new. Like love's old sweet song, it will be with us down to the last gasp of the universe. *Viva* Houston!

Part 2

SOME
CHARACTERISTICS
OF CITIES

NEARLY A half-century ago, Robert S. and Helen M. Lynd published *Middletown,* a book that still stands as a classic of community studies. In it they set forth six common activities among all the things people do in American cities:

Getting a living.

Making a home.

Training the young.

Using leisure in various forms of play, art, and so on.

Engaging in religious practices.

Engaging in community activities.

The Lynds did not spend much time with the simple problems of protecting life and property, but today "law and order" (and its antagonist, violence) is a crucial matter. In less than a year I was burglarized twice, once from my home in Detroit, once from a parked car in San Juan. The attitude of the police is nonchalant. For me the combined losses (something over $500) were hardly sufficient to wreck me. But what of the elderly people leaving churches along Woodward Avenue in Detroit who are set upon by gangs of boys not yet in their teens, knocked down, stomped upon, and robbed of their pittances? The violence to persons is little more destructive than the wanton destruction of physical values. He who takes my goods takes my life.

In American cities a century ago, uncontrolled fire was a terror equivalent to today's violence. In a city fire can start by carelessness or by insatiable hatred. Ancient empires pioneered in the horrors of fire ("Nero fiddles . . .") as well as in the horrors and delights of professional sports. By the end of the Empire, Rome was worse than we can believe: a year held 175 days of public games, and you could watch the slaughter. Rural sports in colonial America were comparatively benign: horse racing, the hunt. Not until the rise of cities did spectator sports, with paid admissions, become an important part of life. Fortunately they did not focus on systematic murder, but they had their grim aspects. One was the trouble of getting in and out of the ball park. Another was the same as the common charge against television: the games promoted passivity. But they also promoted activity. How many of the boys who went one day a month to watch Babe Ruth or Stan Musial spent the other twenty-nine days trying to copy him? A huge plus for cities has been that in some spheres of excellence they have not only set higher standards but have publicized them.

The last two general themes in this section overlap. The easiest place to read the box score is in elections. Long ago Lincoln Steffens wrote that a city machine may rest on a few immigrant groups —or it may not. Martin Lomasny in Boston had the Irish. Fiorello LaGuardia boasted that with an Italian father and a Jewish mother, he couldn't lose in New York. Carmine DeSapio, in spite of his name, proved that *he* could lose in New York. In Memphis, Ed Crump was not sustained by Irish, or by Jews, or by Italians, but by white Anglo-Saxon Protestants. He certainly was not sustained by blacks.

The deprivations and indecencies imposed upon blacks in American cities today need all of the attention they are getting and a lot more besides. But they need more thought as well as more action. Everybody who is small-minded, threatened, fearful—and that includes nearly everybody—will try to fend off all threats. If he is in, he will try to keep "the others" out. Jews will try to keep gentiles out. In the Roman Catholic Church, descendants of Irish and Germans have done a good job of keeping Italians out of the hierarchy, and—need I add—blacks. Most people dislike anybody who is different in a way that cauterizes *my* ego, and blacks can be immediately seen as different. Why should I get to know him? I can already see that he ain't like me. For most whites, the rainbow of prejudice runs from heaven to the sandpit, and blacks stand at the bottom of the slide.

Fire in Chicago, 1871

THE RUINED CITY

TERRIBLE CONDITION OF THE CITY OF CHICAGO

FURTHER DETAILS OF THE APPALLING CONFLAGRATION

THE FLAMES PROVIDENTIALLY STAYED BY A RAIN-STORM

INCENDIARIES DETECTED AND SUMMARILY EXECUTED

EXTRAORDINARY SUFFERINGS OF THE HOMELESS CITIZENS

THE AGGREGATE LOSS ESTIMATED AT NEARLY $200,000,000

THE CHICAGO CALAMITY

A Review of the Devastation, Its Nature and Extent—What Remains of the City—Three-Fourths of the City Intact—The Best

From the *New York Times,* October 11, 1871.

Residences and Manufacturing Interests Spared—Features and Aspects of the Visitation.

SPECIAL DISPATCH TO THE NEW-YORK TIMES

(Englewood, Seven Miles South of CHICAGO, Tuesday, Oct. 10,
1871—9 A.M.)

I am able to commence my dispatch with the joyful intelligence
that the ravages of the devouring element are checked, and the
blessed rain has removed the appalling dread of total extermination
that seemed at one time certain. Accepting the boundaries of the
devastation as already defined in your advices, and to be more
certainly specified in the later dispatches of today—a few lines in
review of the devastation. From reports constantly arriving, and I
go immediately to the city to confirm them, I am sure that many
will rejoice at exemption not promised in last night's aspects. Numerous outlying blocks and many exposed edifices of the better
class in the more thinly occupied Wabash-avenue and Michigan-
avenue, below Twelfth-street, have been spared. Among these is
certainly the noble First Baptist Church, on Wabash, at Harmon-
court, and the Michigan-avenue Hotel, on the corner of Michigan-
avenue and Congress-street.

It will not do for the outside world to believe that Chicago is
"burned over." It is far from being a howling wilderness as yet,
and I am surrounded by abundant evidences in men and means
that, in spirit and force, tell of recuperation. Take any map of
Chicago and study it by section line (one mile square), and make
these your only boundaries to be taken into the question. State-
street is the first north and south section line west of the lake. Next
is Halsted, half a mile west of the river. Then come Reuben-street
and Western-avenue—three miles and a half, therefore, from the
lake to the western city limits, taking no account of the trend of
the southern lake shore.

On the south is Egan-avenue, the southern city limits. Then
come Thirty-first-street, Twenty-second-street, Twelfth-street,
Madison-street, Chicago-avenue, North-avenue and Fullerton-ave-
nue, streets representing by section lines Chicago from north to

south a distance of six miles. Here, therefore, are the dimensions of Chicago, twenty-one square miles, or six miles by three miles and a half. The fire, in its worst reported extent, and I hope to give you the boundaries and more notable exemptions, today has ravaged the tract lying one mile along the lake, on both sides of the river, and irregularly extending from Sixteenth-street to North-avenue, through the section lines of Twelfth, Madison, and Chicago-avenue to North-avenue, a distance of a little over three miles from Sixteenth-street. This, therefore, is three square miles, represented by your previous advices as very largely swept by the devouring element, leaving eighteen square miles unvisited.

Now as to the area burned, and the area that remains. It literally cuts out the heart of the city topographically, but the figure is not to be taken too literally, for, in this case, the heart was the result of the life of the city, and not the life itself. The overwhelming share of the homes of Chicago, her best and choicest residence and manufacturing sections remain, and a vast area of her best and most characteristic business, as I shall proceed to show. Nothing can be said to lighten the disaster that has fallen on the central portion of Chicago, lying east of Wells and north of Jackson streets, to the main river. It contained structures and institutions that were the pride of Chicago and the marvel of her visitors from all over the world. Set them down as lost and their values wiped out. What of the rest?

One thing deserves to be given your readers as the key fact to this great fire. The devastation has wiped away the bane of Chicago in the destruction of her old buildings, and these old buildings have in turn revengefully wiped out the heart of Chicago. Many a stately factory has before this been destroyed by its cotton waste. For the past thirty years it has been the pernicious practice of Chicago to save its old-time wooden structures to be moved again and again to temporary leaseholds, and encumber and impair the streets in their ricketty hegiras. This had caused the square that lay along LaSalle-street, and west to the river on Wells, Market and Franklin streets, to be thickly impacted with frame buildings, one behind the other on the same lot, filling many of the blocks so that a cat could scramble on the closely-ranged roofs from one street front to the other. Among these were old business buildings of Lake-street of the earlier day, the old stores and prairie taverns of Lake and South Water streets. Among buildings of this class burned was actually the old wooden "Grave's Tavern" that stood on Lake-street, opposite the late site of the Tremont House, where, in 1834, your CHARLES FENNO HOFFMAN attended his Garrison Ball described in his Winter in the West. There were old structures of the Fort, the lodging-houses that were new when Mark Beaubien was "keeping tavern like damnash." There was actually among the destroyed buildings on the north side Gen. SCOTT'S headquarters in 1831. All this was historical, but dangerous, and the destruction has fallen. I have given these particulars because the cause of the wide-spread havoc was the burning of twelve or thirteen of these solid squares of old fire-traps in the centre of Chicago, dried into tinder by the protracted drouth. The magnificent Pacific Hotel, whose loss Chicago will long lament was a pioneer improvement in this region where property has been held too good for improvements of a moderate class, and not ready for the ambitious future structures the owners, the solid citizens, designed for them.

You know from my dispatches what has taken place. I am to tell you, and the map will tell your readers what is left. For four miles north of the burned district, into the suburb of Lake View, on the lake shore, for three miles north-westerly to Holstein and the great rolling-mill and packing-house, and distillery district of the North Branch; two miles west to the City limits; four miles south-west to the populous and busy precincts of Bridgeport, with her rolling-mills and packing-houses; three miles and a half south-westerly to the great Union Stock Yards, below Egan-avenue, and beyond them into the great packing-house district of that quarter; four or five miles south of the fire district, to where I write, at Englewood, with the midway great railroad shops and bridge works, and then stretching south-easterly along the lake shore through Oakland, Kenwood and Hyde Park to South Chicago and its great enterprises; study this remaining area and see what remains of Chicago. Outside of all lies the Park and Boulevard section, the recent theatres of high speculation, now probably ended, for as an operator who has lost half a million in expectancies, said to me at breakfast, "What's the use of talking about six miles from the Court-house when you haven't got no Court-house."

Within these outposts above enumerated, understand that a large share of the area is given up to the homes of Chicago. There are many elegant residence quarters more permanently so than any destroyed. The residence sections of Wabash-avenue and Michigan-avenue that have been visited were by no means the choicest in that character, for they had begun to possess a mixed quality. On a large extent of Michigan-avenue not a new residence of the best class had been built in the past five years. As to the north side, the residence portion invaded was of a choice character, but many of the buildings were of the old-time class.

Set it down, therefore, that Chicago still lives. Her homes, her industrial enterprises are still largely intact. Very few of her manufacturing establishments were destroyed. The loss falls in her public institutions, her larger buildings, her centres of trade and finance, and upon an army of the lower class of tenants and bank and mercantile employes. With these losses many fine homes have gone, but this is all. Enough remains to build anew upon. Said a leading banker and large loser to me today, and through me to the NEW-YORK TIMES: "Young man, tell New-York to stand steady on the centre, and Chicago will rally on the right."

Meanwhile there is an appalling cloud of disaster out of which are beginning to come tokens of individual distress the whole country must hasten to alleviate. Later dispatches will give you the already massing and frightful details.

THE FIRE OUT AT LAST—EXTENT OF THE CONFLAGRATION—
THE BUSINESS PANIC ABATING

SPECIAL DISPATCH TO THE NEW YORK TIMES

The fire is out, thanks to the rain, having been already under control in all directions, because it has exhausted its fury. Not a bank is left standing, nor a public building, nor a newspaper office. In fact, hardly a business house of any sort remains. Five hundred of the largest business blocks in the city are in ashes; three to five square miles are burnt over, and are now smoking like a baffled tophet. It is already known that twenty or thirty persons have perished in the ruins of their homes. Four women were burned in the Arcade block. A thief was suffocated and burned while stealing from a jewelry store. Plundering was prosecuted with a lawlessness never before witnessed, and when pilferers were caught in the act the officers were compelled to release them, for the jail was burned. The streets remind one of the streets of Fredericksburg after the battle, presenting every phase of the bivouac. I saw a strong man sitting upon a wayside box weeping like a child, his wife meanwhile cheerily boiling coffee with some bits of the unlaid Nicolson pavement, and his children playing hide and seek among the cast out wares. It is rumored that Gen. SHERIDAN has ordered rations from St. Louis and tents from Indiana. Some car-loads of cooked food are expected from MILWAUKEE to-night. The panic of yesterday is quieted somewhat, and a few men begin to look to the future with courage. They think the East has confidence in Chicago and will come here with money. It is estimated that some thousands of men will be driven to quick assignment. We send to wealthy New-York the Macedonian cry—"Come over and help us."

POTTER PALMER, of CHICAGO, now at the East, was overtaken at Erie on Monday noon, with other Chicago gentlemen, by full advices of his disaster. He places his loss at a large figure. Indeed, in the single item of rents it will reach $250,000 per annum. But he instantly dispatched to his agent at Chicago, Mr. Phelps, to "Clear away the ruins of the Palmer House and prepare to rebuild at once, and push the work on the fire-proof hotel," the completion of which will be hastened several months by the disaster.

DISPATCH TO THE ASSOCIATED PRESS

CHICAGO, Oct. 10—Noon—The fire continued to burn all last night on the north side, but this morning is under control. It is literally true to say that there is nothing remaining of that side from the river north to Lincoln Park on the north, and from the North Branch of the river on the west to the lake on the east. This portion of the city, except along the main river, where there were business blocks, was occupied by dwellings. Two-thirds of the population of this district were German and Scandinavian. These people are now homeless, and are some of them in frame buildings on the north-west section, and others on the prairies, without shelter throughout the day. Yesterday a renewal of the fires on the west side was looked for, and a change of five degrees in the direction of the wind at any time would have led to that result. There would then have been no refuge for any. Everybody had their clothing packed ready to start for the prairie at any moment, but God averted this last possible addition to our disaster. At sundown the wind lulled, and at 3 o'clock this morning the rain, so fervently prayed for, came. It did not rain long, but the roofs of houses and the ground have been wet, so that now it is possible to have fires and cook food for the multitude.

A meeting of citizens was held in the First Congregational Church, in West Washington-street, which was continued throughout the night. Measures were concerted to protect what property was left, and to provide for the homeless. Messrs. RICHARDS AND CHARLES CRANE, of the North-western Manufacturing Company, have contrived a plan which is being put into execution, for providing water in case of fire breaking out at any time. The machinery of their works is being used for that purpose, and their engine and boilers are being used for pumping water from the river. Fifteen hundred citizens were sworn in last night as an extra police force, and the Secretary of War authorized Gen. SHERIDAN to employ all available troops for guard, and issued an order for 100,000 rations. Five hundred soldiers are on duty. This precaution was necessary, for as remarkable as it may seem, there were fiends who still sought to extend the disaster. Two men caught in the act of firing houses on the West Side were arrested and immediately hung to lamp-posts—one on Twelfth-street, near the river, and the other three miles away on Clayborne-avenue, North Side. This summary action has checked the thieves and murderers.

The arrival of firemen and engines from Milwaukee, St. Louis and other cities, has apparently restored confidence. The Cincinnati train arrived this morning with four engines, three from that city and one from Dayton. They were seventeen hours on the way, having to change the route twice, and then finally came via Piqua and Logansport. There was an inexpressible pleasure in seeing those experienced firemen go right to work in a business way where work was most needed. They are playing on coal piles to save whatever of fuel is possible, and preventing the further spread of flames. The vast plain is covered with people wandering about seeking the evidences of a wealth that has completely vanished in flames and smoke. A few business men with some nerve are seeking houses for business in the west side. Rooms that rented last week for $50 now readily command $6,000. There are not many of these, but enough to allow a few business men to start. The newspapers will be started again in a few days or weeks. Hon. JOSEPH MEDILL, of the Tribune, who is one of the heaviest sufferers, succeeded yesterday in leasing a brick building on Washington-street, at the Tunnel. He also purchased two single cylinder presses, used in a job office on the West Side, and has telegraphed East for paper and type, there being nothing left here. Mr. STORY, of the Times, will erect a rough one-story building, and begin the issue of that paper as soon as material can be procured. The Journal is provided for on the West Side. The Post, Republican and Staats Zeitung will also arrange for business as soon as practicable; but everything must come from elsewhere, there is nothing left. Water for drinking and household use is secured from the lake and the parks, and for horses from the river. There are a thousand people camped about the artesian well, four miles out, and perhaps as many more at the lake, and on Fullerton and Victor avenues, near the prairie. The people are being fed in the remaining churches, school-houses, in sheds and by the road-sides. It was cold and chilly this morning, causing great suffering but it is now clearing up again; but instead of this being welcome, the people are praying earnestly for more rain, so fearful are they of a continuance of the flames. This is the situation; further information will be sent as rapidly as received. Meanwhile, we give a report of the fire and its incidents, specially prepared for the Associated Press by those who witnessed and fought the flames throughout:

Late on Sunday evening, a boy went into a stable on Dekoven

street, near the river, on the West Side, to milk a cow, carrying with him a kerosene lamp. This was kicked over by the cow, and the burning fluid scattered among the straw. This was the beginning of the great fire. A single extinguisher on the ground, or active work of the Police in tearing down one or two shanties, would have prevented the spreading flames; but the engines were waited for, and when they arrived the firemen, stupefied by their exertions at the first fire on Saturday night, worked slowly and clumsily. Their efforts unavailed, the wind from the south-west blew a gale, rapidly the flames shot from house to house and board-yard to board-yard, until the district burned the night before was reached. Meanwhile the flames had crossed the river north of Twelfth-street on to the South Side, and made for brick and stone and business blocks, railroad freight depots and manufacturing establishments. The full extent of damage was realized for the first time; the Fire Department, already tired out, worked like heroes, and the Mayor and City Government, that had supinely rested, now began to exert themselves but the opportunity had been lost. The time when thorough organization could have blown up buildings, or prepared for the emergency was neglected, and it was now a fight for life, the wind blowing a stiff gale had possession of the flames, and the beautiful buildings—Chicago's glory—lay before them. Harrison, Van Buren, Adams, Monroe, and Madison streets were soon reached, the intervening blocks from the river to Dearborn street on the east being consumed. Three-quarters of a mile of brick blocks were consumed as if by magic. It being Sunday, proprietors and employes were at home, utterly unconscious of what was transpiring. Those who saw the flames supposed it was the remains of Saturday night's fire, and having confidence in the Fire Department, were unconcerned; but between 11 and 12 o'clock a rumor got abroad that the fire was in the business portion of the city. Then the people commenced moving. Horses were brought into requisition to take the proprietors and others to the conflagration. What a scene met their gaze! The Board of Trade, Court-house, Western Union Telegraph, and Associated Press office, and hundreds of other buildings were all a flame. The air was filled with live coals, which were hurled to the north and east

—a beacon of destruction. The fire-engines were powerless for saving. All that man could do was to blow up buildings, but this availed little.

The Times, Tribune, Post, Republican, Journal and other news-paper offices, the Western News Company block, Field & Leiter's establishment, the Drake block, recently built, FARWELL & CO.'S, all were soon in ashes. It seemed that no sooner had the flames struck a wall than they went directly through, and a very few minutes sufficed to destroy the most elaborately built structure, the walls melted and the very bricks were consumed. The wooden pavement took fire, making a continuous sheet of flame two miles long by a mile wide. No human being could possibly survive many minutes. Block after block fell, and the red hot coal shot higher and higher, and spread farther and farther until the north side of Lake-street was a vast sheet of flame from the river to the lake at one time so hemming the people that it was expected thousands must perish. Sherman, Tremont and other hotels were emptied of their guests, and a remarkable sight presented itself in the hurrying throngs with trunks, sacks, or bags on shoulders, fleeing amid flames for their lives. Those who could make for the remaining bridges, others got next to the lake and so south. One block in all the vast business section remained at daylight, viz., the Tribune block. The custom-house and Honore block in Dearborn-street had burned, and those who had fought the flames here thought at least this block could be saved. A patrol of men under SAMUEL MEDILL swept off live coals and put out flames in the side walls, and another lot of men under the direcion of Hon. JOSEPH MEDILL watched the roofs. At 7½ o'clock, this appeared safe and most of the men went to get rest or food. A number went to sleep in the Tribune building, but there was a change of wind. The flames reached Wabash, State-street and Michigan-avenue, and soon McVicker's Theatre caught fire. In a few minutes the Tribune was in flames, and at the last moment the sleeping men were aroused and rescued from the flames. By 10 o'clock in the forenoon this remaining block was in ashes. Now was to be seen the most remarkable sight ever beheld in this or any country. There were from 50,000 to 75,000 men, women and children fleeing by every available street and alley to the southward and westward, attempting to save their clothing and their lives. Every available vehicle was brought into requisition for use, for which enormous prices were paid, and the streets and sidewalks presented a sight. Thousands of persons and horses inextricably commingled; poor people of all colors and shades, and of every nationality—from Europe, China and Africa—mad with excitement, struggled with each other to get away. Hundreds were trampled underfoot. Men and women were loaded with bundles and their household goods, to whose skirts were clinging tender infants, half-dressed and barefooted, all seeking a place of safety. Hours afterward these might have been seen in vacant lots, or on the streets far out in the suburbs, stretched in the dust. These are the suffering lambs, whom Christ now calls on the rich world to feed and clothe. God help them, if the heart of man shall prove obdurate! One of the most pitiful sights was that of a middle-aged woman on State-state, loaded with bundles, struggling through a crowd, singing the Mother Goose Melody: "Chickery, chickery, crany crow, I went to the well to wash my toe," &c. There were hundreds of others likewise distracted, and many made desperate by whisky or beer, which from excess of thirst, they drank, in absence of water, in great quantities. Who spread themselves in every direction a terror to all they met. It is fearful to think of the loss of life. It is conjectured, with good cause, that near 500 have been burned to death. We saw four men enter a burning building, and in a moment they were overwhelmed by a falling wall. There was a crowd of men around the corner of a building trying to save property, when the wall yielding, some of them were buried beneath it. About twelve or fifteen men, women and children rushed into the building of the Historical Society—a fireproof building—for safety. In a few minutes the flames burst up, and they were burned to death. Among those who took refuge in this building was the venerable Col. SAMUEL STONE, eighty years of age, for a long time connected with the Society; also, JOHN B. GERARD and wife, Mme. DEPELGROVE, the noted teacher of music. It is feared that Dr. FREAR and family were also burned, as they were in the building, and have not been seen since. Mrs. EDSALL, whose husband was murdered last week, and who was suffering from an illness, was carried away for protection to a building which was afterward consumed, and it is feared she also perished. All the books and papers of the Historical Society, including the original copy of the famous Emancipation Proclamation, President Lincoln's, for which the Society paid $25,000, were destroyed. It is feared that a large number of children, inmates of the Catholic Orphan Society, on State-street, were also burned, as many of them are missing. On Chicago avenue, a father rushed upstairs, to carry three children away, when he was overtaken by the flames and perished with them. The mother was afterwards seen on the North-west Side a raving maniac. In the same neighborhood a family of five persons perished. The list of such fatalities is very long, and can only be fully verified after the smoke shall have cleared away. There are hundreds of families on that side who saved no clothing but barely their lives. Among these is the family of PERRY SMITH, formerly President of the Northwestern Railroad Company.

LATER

A careful survey of the insurances today shows that there were written on the property destroyed over two hundred millions of dollars; add another hundred million to this sum, and a fair estimate can be reached of the loss. All the leading merchants who have been seen express their determination to resume business at once. This includes heavy houses, such as John V. Farwell and Field, Leiter & Co. The latter saved from three hundred thousand to a half million dollars' worth of goods. Both firms have already established head-quarters on the West Side.

The Evening Journal and Tribune hope to publish small sheets to-morrow. At a meeting of the business men to day a spirit was manifested to at once set to work to rebuild the city and restore business. A special meeting of the Legislature is to be held to provide means for aiding the business men, and provide employment for the poor. Fears are entertained that the desperate distress of so many will create squads of pillagers, and that life will not be safe. To relieve these Gen. SHERIDAN is telegraphing for more troops, and special Police forces are being organized by the citizens. The only effectual remedy is to find employment for the thousands who would work if they could. The temporary office of the Western Union Telegraph Company is thronged by thousands anxious to advise friends. The operators are busy every moment, but as the number of wires available are few and the fires in the country threaten these, Gen. STAGER has directed that private (family) messages and Associated Press dispatches shall first go. The General press report will cover everything, as no pains or expense is being spared to render this reliable and perfect. Arrangements have been made by the Post-Office authorities, under direction of Col. WOOD, for sending, receiving and distributing all mail matter.

THE PRESENT ASPECT

Women and children are going around the burnt district, vainly seeking something to satisfy their hunger. They ask for relief, but there is none to give them. No one has provisions or money. What provisions there were in the city are now burned or eaten, and some few people have enough to last them for a day, but not longer. Provisions have arrived from Detroit, Cincinnati, Milwaukee and St. Louis, and are being distributed as fast as possible. Twenty-three dead bodies have been taken to a station on the North Side. At the present time it is impossible to know who they are. As night comes the want of gas is keenly felt. There are but few candles in the city, and no water except what is taken from the lake. Very grave fears of outrages by thieves on the west side are felt on every hand. Gen. SHERIDAN, who has been a hard worker all through the fire, is still calling for troops from different points to keep order. All business and work is suspended, and every one is intent on security, first, something to eat, and a place of shelter.

The suffering on the North Side is heartrending to witness. Fifty thousand men, women and children huddled together like so many wild animals, and in other places 17,000 Germans and Irish praying for relief, helpless children asking for bread, heart-broken parents who know not which way to turn or what to say, and nothing to do but await the distribution of supplies, which, at best, must be a slow proceeding, as there are parts of districts over which it is almost impossible to travel—present, indeed, a harrowing scene. Women in the pains of childbirth, and patients who have been moved from beds of sickness, to save their lives, which at the best were nearly spent, were all exposed to the rain of last night, and the cold raw winds of today. Several deaths have occurred at Lincoln Park, and three women have brought children into the world only to die. There are people who, in the bitterness of their souls, ascribe the calamity to God's judgment. A German said to me: "This a second Sodom and Gomorrah, and the curse of God is on it." Another night must be spent in Lincoln Park and the brick fields at Division-street, and yet another and another. Each train and extras are loaded to their fullest capacity taking people away, who, in many instances, have no place to go, yet they cannot stay here, and every train is obliged to leave five times as many passengers as they take away.

Every precaution is being taken by the authorities to guard the people to-night, and if morning comes without robberies and murders, they all will thank God and go forward with courage.

The Indianapolis Fire Department are here and doing good services. Springfield and Peoria have done nobly, contributing liberally. The expression of sympathy on all hands is most gratifying, but help must come.

THE PRESS REVIVING

The Evening Journal got out half a sheet tonight, and other papers will follow tomorrow, some presses having been found. The private residences of HORACE WHITE AND WM. BROSS, of the Tribune, were consumed, Mr. MEDILL, Mr. COWLES, and Mr. WILSON, of the Journal, also Mr. STOREY, were more fortunate.

INSURANCE COMPANIES AND BANKS

The general agent of the Etna Fire Insurance Company of Hartford announces that the Company will pay every dollar of its insurance. Meetings of citizens in the West and North Sides will be kept open the rest of the night. The Commercial National Bank will commence rebuilding on their old site to-morrow; meanwhile they re-open for business on West Washington-street. They opened their vault this afternoon, and all their books, papers, money and securities were in perfect order.

THE DEAD AND MISSING

There is a rumor that in a burnt blacksmith shop on Rush-street the bodies of fifteen men were found burned to a crisp, they having rushed into the shop to escape from the flames, which had surrounded them before they had discovered their peril. An immense number of people are missing, and for the purpose of aiding in the discovery of the missing ones a central intelligence office has been established, where are collected the names of all missing ones, and they are given to the Police.

BRANDS FROM THE BURNING

The large hotel in the West Division, just completed, has been taken by GAGE BROS. & RICE, late of the Sherman House, and they will open it in ten days. It will be known as the Sherman House. The North Division is swept clear from the Chicago River to Wright's Grove, a distance of more than three miles. But one house, that of MAHLON D. OGDEN, formerly WILLIAM B. OGDEN'S, remains standing in the entire district. A large portion of the population driven from this desolated ground are encamped on the prairie to the north where they have nothing but the canopy of heaven to cover them and scarcely sufficient food to satisfy their hunger. A meeting of the citizens of the State was held this evening, at which resolutions were passed recommending Gov. PALMER to call an extra session of the Legislature at once. Ex-Gov. OGLESBY was appointed to proceed to Springfield and lay the matter before Gov. PALMER. All the packing-houses in Chicago and many of the elevators remain uninjured, and these two branches of Chicago's best property will be but slightly interrupted. The directors of the Chamber of Commerce met today and resolved to proceed at once to the re-erection of their elegant edifice. Two companies of United States Infantry arrived here this evening and will be at once put on patrol duty.

THE AGGREGATE LOSS

ESTIMATES OF THE LOSSES BY A CHICAGO
MERCHANT—INTERESTING SUBDIVISION OF
THE PROPERTY DESTROYED.

The following is an estimate of loss by the Chicago conflagration, as made by a merchant of Chicago:

All reports say 10,000 houses burned of which probably 2,000 were business houses and 8,000 were dwellings.

2,000 business houses at $25,000	$50,000,000
8,000 dwellings averaging $4,000	32,000,000
Engines and machinery attached	2,000,000
TOTAL loss in houses alone	$84,000,000

Of business houses there were probably ten that contained goods and wares of the valuation of $1,000,000 each	$10,000,000
20 containing valuables of $500,000 each	10,000,000
40 whose contents were worth $250,000 each	10,000,000
200 with contents worth $100,000 each	20,000,000
500 with contents averaging $30,000 each	15,000,000
And remaining 670, averaging contents of $10,000 each	16,700,000
Furniture and other contents of 8,000 dwellings, averaging $2,000	16,000,000
Lumber-yards, railroad stock and water craft	2,300,000
Total loss in goods and wares, machinery, lumber, railroad stock and vessels	$100,000,000
Aggregate loss by the fire	$184,000,000

A FALSE REPORT OF A RENEWAL OF THE FIRE
—EXECUTION OF INCENDIARIES

ASSOCIATED PRESS OFFICE
NEW-YORK, TUESDAY, OCT. 10-8 P.M.

The report received at a late hour this afternoon and bulletined throughout the City that the fire had broken out again in Chicago in a quarter hitherto untouched happily proves untrue. Gen. PALMER, Vice-President of the Western Union Telegraph Company, on reading the report, telegraphed directly to Gen. STAGER, Superintendent of the Company, now at Chicago, for confirmation, and received the following reply:

CHICAGO, OCT. 10-4 P.M.

GEN. PALMER: A fire started in a small building on Thirty-first-street, but was speedily put out.

The incendiaries are busy, but seven or eight have been hanged or shot at sight.

(Signed)   ANSON STAGER.

THE FIRE NOT BROKEN OUT AGAIN
ASSOCIATED PRESS OFFICE

NEW-YORK, OCT. 10-10 P.M.

The following dispatch in answer to inquiries from this office, effectually disposes of the rumors of the renewal of the fire:

CHICAGO, OCT. 10-9 P.M.

The fire has not broken out again.

(Signed)

AGENT OF THE ASSOCIATED PRESS

REORGANIZING THE GOVERNMENT OFFICERS IN
CHICAGO

WASHINGTON, OCT. 11.-The Internal Revenue Office has sent to Chicago Mr. EDWARD TOMPKINS, of that office, to assist the revenue officers there in recovering or arranging their accounts and rendering any assistance in his power to the authorities. Nearly $1,000,000 worth of stamps were in the Collection Office at Chicago, and it is supposed they have been destroyed by the fire.

GEN. SHERIDAN'S DISPATCHES TO THE WAR DEPARTMENT

WASHINGTON, OCT. 10.-The Secretary of War has received the following telegram from GEN. SHERIDAN:

CHICAGO, OCT. 9.

The City of Chicago is almost utterly destroyed by fire. There is now reasonable hope of arresting it if the wind, which is yet blowing a gale, does not change. I ordered on your authority, rations from St. Louis, tents from Jeffersonville, and two companies of infantry from Omaha. There will be many houseless people and much distress.

(Signed)   P. H. SHERIDAN
                                             Lieutenant-General.

CHICAGO, OCT. 9.

To W. W. Belknap, Secretary of War:

The fire here last night and today has destroyed almost all that was very valuable in this city.

There is not a business house, bank or hotel left. Most of the best part of the city is gone. Without exaggeration, all the valuable portion of the city is in ruins. I think not less than 100,000 people are homeless, and those who had the most wealth are now poor. It seems to me to be such a terrible misfortune that it may with propriety be considered a national calamity.

                                             P. H. SHERIDAN,
                                             Lieutenant-General.

WASHINGTON, OCT. 10

Lieut.-Gen. Sheridan. Chicago:

I agree with you that the fire is a national calamity. The sufferers have the sincere sympathy of the nation. Officers at the depots at St. Louis, Jeffersonville and elsewhere have been ordered to forward supplies liberally and promptly.

WILLIAM W. BELKNAP,
Secretary of War.

REBUILDING THE CITY BEGUN

BUFFALO, N. Y. OCT. 10.—An order was received here today, from a merchant in Chicago, for 250,000 bricks, to commence rebuilding.

ACTION IN THIS CITY

Effect upon Wall-Street Yesterday—Decided Reaction in Stocks—Confidence Restored in a Measure—The losses of the Insurance Companies.

The effect of the fire in Chicago was most distinctly felt in Wall-Street yesterday, and was observed in the reaction which followed the announcement that the disaster was not as great as was at first reported. As soon as the full extent of ruin was known the various moneyed institutions of the City set at work to devise plans of relief, and hundreds of thousands of dollars were promptly subscribed and sent forward to the sufferers by the fire. Meanwhile the operators in stocks set at work to repair the devastation caused by the panic of the day before, and succeeded in sustaining the market against a further decline, but went further and advanced the prices of stocks that were on Monday greatly depressed. This required vigorous and determined effort, but they were successful and the market closed firm, and from four to five per cent, in advance of the opening prices of the day. The basis was thus established for a restoration of confidence, and the way is paved for an ultimate recovery of business. The operations in the Gold Room were significant. The market opened at 113¾ and closed at 114⅜. Early in the day the carrying rate ranged as high as $\frac{1}{16}$ of one per cent, and soon after noon it was changed to $\frac{1}{16}$th of one per cent, per day for the use of gold, showing an increasing short interest. The scarcity of cash coin had an effect upon exchanges, which declined from 109⅛ for sixty days, and 110¼ for sight to 109 and 110⅛, respectively. Money was too active during the day to permit a lock up of greenbacks, and it was thought likely that gold would be in favor of borrowers for some time. The reports from London showed that bonds were lower at the close of the market, and private reports gave still lower quotations than were made on the street. The holders of stocks have sustained tremendous losses, and at the last moment have thrown all their securities overboard and are now figuring to see where they stand. Some who have been persevering bears for some time past, will now endeavor to work down both stocks and gold, selling the latter recklessly with a view to keep prices low and panicky, and thereby realize on their stock investments. It will be understood that the loss on several millions of gold sales can easily be afforded when stocks can be purchased a few points below in consequence, and thus destroying any little reaction that may be made apparent. The decline in bonds yesterday was in consequence of the large lots that are thrown on the market by the insurance companies who have met losses by the Chicago fire, and who wished to be prepared to meet their liabilities.

Baseball
in Philadelphia, 1888

THE GAME WAS STOPPED

A CROWD OF 40,000 PEOPLE AT THE BALL GROUNDS

THE SUNDAY GAME OF THE BALTIMORES AND ATHLETICS
BROKEN UP AFTER THE FIRST INNING

PHILADELPHIA, May 20.—Sunday baseball playing was begun, or attempted to be, this afternoon at Gloucester. It was the first experiment of the kind in Philadelphia or vicinity and attracted not less than 40,000 people. Two-thirds of that number tried to get into the new ball park and the game between the Athletic and Baltimore Clubs was broken up in the first inning. There were no accidents of a serious nature, and the nearest approach to it was when a man who refused to give his name tumbled into the river from the guards of one of the boats at Gloucester. His son jumped in after him, but they were both speedily fished out without harm, except a good ducking and a thorough scare.

There was a tremendous crush at the ferry house between 1

From the *New York Times,* May 21, 1888.

and 4 o'clock, but the height of the pulling and hauling was reached prior to the departure of the 3 o'clock boat. The crowd then began to grow rapidly and a savage rush was made for the little ticket office. It was a mob, and the three or four policemen on hand were only in the way as they shouted "Get back there, will yer," to people who could not have stirred if they had wanted to. Hats were crushed, eye-glasses lost, and canes broken. As the Dauntless swung into the dock on her up trip about 2,000 people had been provided with tickets, while quite as many more stood in the streets waiting for a chance to get them. When the gates were thrown open there was a mighty rush for the boat. Down the in-cline of the movable dock men rushed helter skelter, cheering and shouting as if they were on a Fourth of July trip and it was to be their last.

The crowd did not stop on the way. It had journeyed from the 31 wards of Philadelphia to see a game of baseball, and as it was after baseball it would take nothing else. About midway of the trip the thousands coming from the grounds furnished the informa-tion that there would be no ball playing, and gave the advice not to buy tickets, as the infield was overrun with people. Such proved to be the case, and one-half the immense throng was just as much in a hurry to get away from Gloucester as it had been to get there. They ran back to the ferry, and the boats were packed until the last left at 9 o'clock, carrying back the thousands of dis-appointed ball lovers.

Manager Barnie took his Baltimore team from the Hotel Wind-sor in an omnibus. They went over the Kaign's Point ferry and drove to Gloucester. "We never would have got there any other way," said Manager Barnie. The Athletic managers and players were on the ground early. It was 2 o'clock when the gates were opened, but it was 3 o'clock before the big crush came. There are two roads leading to the ground. The one along the river is the shortest, and thousands went that way. Close to the ticket office is a big, wide piece of marshy land. Over this a bridge 16 feet wide and 100 feet long had been erected. Shortly after 3 o'clock, when the bridge was full of people, it gave way, and over 100 people were dumped in the swamp.

Over 10,000 people were inside the inclosure at 3 o'clock and they were piling in at the gate as fast as four men could take up the tickets. The crowd didn't all come in at the gate. Hundreds jumped over the fence, and hundreds more came in under the fence through holes burrowed in the sand.

The game began at 2:30 o'clock. There were two umpires. Neddy Cuthbert was behind the bat and Gaffney gave the base decisions. The batteries were Matamore and Gunning for the Athletics and Cunningham and O'Brien for the Baltimores. The crowd had been edging on to the players during the first inning. When the last Baltimorean was retired there was a grand rush, and in a minute the crowd had swallowed up the ball players, umpires, and managers. The game was over. Managers Sharsig and Barnie, the players, umpires, and police tried to get the crowd back, but it was no use, and the players left the field.

Just about this time the crowd on the outside broke down the big gate and rushed by the ticket takers. Pandemonium reigned. "We would only have been too glad to play the game through," said Manager Barnie.

"There were 16,000 people on the ground," said Manager Sharsig. "Next Sunday we will give them all seats."

Manager Barnie said the Athletics settled with him for 7,200 paid admissions. The Baltimores got one-third of the gate money, or $600, and the Athletics pocketed the other $1,200, besides $800 or more taken in for reserved seats.

The Big, Happy, Beating Heart of the Detroit Sound

by Richard R. Lingeman

AT NIGHT as I stand on the other side of East Jefferson Street in Detroit, the Ford Auditorium, a long, low, blue-granite-faced building with a vertical latticed metal front, suddenly looks to my wondering eyes like a gigantic hi-fi amplifier. A hallucination, no doubt, caused by my having spent two days at Motown Records, the big happy beating heart of the Detroit sound.

Those who think of "Detroit sound" as referring to the din of the auto assembly line intermingled with the muted wail of manufacturers announcing price increases on their 1967 models may be surprised to learn that in the pop record business the Detroit sound means the kind of music made by Motown Records, a relatively small company which sells more singles than any other company in the country.

What is more, Motown is a Negro-owned business, with mostly Negro performers and composers, whose musical style stems from what is called rhythm-and-blues music—in the past, a trade euphemism for a kind of music performed by Negroes and sold mainly to a Negro market. Due in great degree to the popularity

From the *New York Times Magazine*, November 27, 1966, copyright © 1966 by The New York Times Company.

of a Motown singing group called the Supremes, Motown's records have attained national, as opposed to racial, best-sellerdom; and the company has become sort of the compact giant of rock 'n' roll, standing in relation to the real giants as George Romney's Rambler once did to the Big Three.

Why am I going to the Ford Auditorium? Why, damn it, man, I am going to the Soul Show, starring Jackie "Moms" Mabley and also a rhythm-and-blues group called Smokey Robinson and the Miracles, which happens to be the very first of many such groups formed by Motown and has been with the company ever since it was founded in the late fifties by a young Negro auto worker and part-time song writer named Berry Gordy Jr.

A word about "soul," a vogue word among Negroes having had a number of transmogrifications these days. Soul can mean a mild manifesting of race pride and social solidarity—"our thing"—a shared emotional bond of unity and good feeling. In the early sixties among Negro jazz musicians, most of them conservatory-trained, advocating a return to the roots of Negro music for inspiration, a return to field hand chants, work songs, funky blues and gospel rhythms in what was a rejection of sophistication in favor of strong feeling. Some even felt compelled to eat "soul food"— deep South and ghetto dishes like ham hocks and collard greens, pigs' feet, pigs' knuckles and chitterlings.

A fraternal term, "soul brother," has had recent ominous manifestations, as in the Watts riots when Negro businessmen chalked it on their stores so the antiwhite rioters would pass them by. It also operates as a commercial thing, as when New York's WWRL calls itself "soul brother radio" and gives its predominantly Negro audience a steady diet of rhythm-and-blues music, an elemental, emotional kind of popular music with a strong, pounding beat, right down to an R & B version of the Pepsi singing commercial.

Now, in the pop music field, "soul" has entered the vocabulary as a loose description of the kind of music made by invariably Negro performers, many of whom record for Motown—performers such as James Brown, Otis Redding, and the Supremes, who are Motown's star vocal group and probably the leading girls' vocal group in the world, based on their record sales and international appeal.

Inside the austerely appointed auditorium, the Soul Show opens with a white Southern comic named Dick Davey, who is a sort of hip Bob Burns telling reverse Dick Gregory jokes slanted at the 90 per cent Negro audience. He tells of doing a show in Harlem ("They was real polite to me in Harlem. Kept calling me 'Mr. Charley' all the time.") and draws applause when he says he asked a colored dancer why she was enjoying herself so much and she replied: "Honey" (infectious laugh), "if you could be colored five minutes you'd never want to be white again."

Next come the Miracles, four catlike young men attired in bright red shirts with flowing sleeves. Robinson does the solo, singing in a near-falsetto voice, and the other three back him while performing intricate, whirling figures of choreography. The choreography is a great crowd pleaser in its own right, bringing frequent cheers, and has something of the unintentional camp quality that those Negro shows at the old Kit Kat in the Village had—as though they had been choreographed by George Raft in the thirties and never changed since. At one point, a buttery Pearl Bailey voice wafts down from the balcony: "When you get done singing, Smoke, you come on up here."

"Moms" Mabley closes the show with some wry jokes about crime in the streets—to borrow Mr. Goldwater's phrase—encountered while walking down "Saint Ann-twine" (St. Antoine) street in Detroit, and tells of the poor beggar who came up to her and said in a pitiful voice: "Moms, Moms, I ain't got any warm clothes. I ain't got nuthin' "—her voice shifts into menace—" *'cept this gun!*" She closes with a pitch for brotherhood to the tune of "Together":

> *If we do the right thing together*
> *We'll bring peace together*
> *No more black and white*
> *Only wrong and right*

—and so on. Such is the current state of soul, baby.

The offices of Motown (for Motor Town) Records are in a cluster of seven neat, middle-class brick bungalows with porches and green lawns, spaced among a funeral home, doctor's office, and private residences on both sides of a wide tree-lined boulevard in a middle-class, integrated residential section of Detroit. On a fine autumn day knots of producers, song writers, performers stand around, shooting the breeze. A group of colored school kids arrives and casually circulates among the groups, collecting autographs from their favorites. Only one of the Motown buildings jars the tranquility of the scene. It is painted a glaring white and bears a big sign: HITSVILLE, USA.

Berry Gordy and his company have been a mecca for Detroit's rock and roll talent, the majority of whom are Negro youngsters who grew up in the Detroit slums, ever since he founded the company on a song ("Way Over There") which he wrote and which the Miracles recorded and which became Motown's first hit, plus $700 borrowed from his family's credit union. The Motown complex now houses four separate companies: Jobete, a highly successful musical publishing company; International Talent Management Incorporated; Hitsville, USA, which owns Motown's recording studios; and the Motown Record Corporation, which issues singles and L.P.'s under a variety of labels, including Gordy, Tamla, Motown, VIP and Soul. In addition, the company has a burgeoning foreign business conducted by indigenous licensees and international distributors. The international flavor—symbolized by the globes on display in Motown offices—reflects the global scope of American teenage music today.

Though Motown is a predominantly Negro corporation, one sees a healthy sprinkling of white faces in every department and it is integrated at all levels of management. At the same time, it is still very much a family firm; there are presently 10 Gordys and in-laws now employed at Motown in a variety of positions. Gordy's sister, Esther, wife of a Michigan legislator and active in civic affairs, is vice president in charge of management and wields authority second only to Gordy in the company's affairs.

Motown began as one of a number of small R & B record companies which sprang up in Detroit during the fifties, partly in response to a demand for such music by Negro-oriented radio stations, which were also born at about the same time to serve Detroit's large (now over 500,000) Negro population. "On nearly every block in some neighborhoods," says Peter Gzowski of the

Toronto Daily Star, a close observer of the Detroit music scene, "there seems to be at least one small record firm, sign over door, Cadillac in driveway. Motown is the first of these firms to break into the big time."

The extent to which Motown has broken into the big time was, the week I was there, obvious for all to see: in the sales surveys that week, the company had three of its single records in the top five positions. Such a near-monopoly was unprecedented even for Motown, which has been, for the past two years, the leading vender of single 45 r.p.m. records in the nation. When one asks Motown's controller, Edward Pollak, about the firm's income, he declines to answer on the grounds of the 16th (income tax) Amendment, but the company will probably gross about $15 million this year, according to other sources.

Such success is reflective of a growing demand for R & B music among teen-agers who, of course, make up the bulk of single-record buyers. R & B music, once known as "race music," used to be considered music primarily for a Negro market (record-trade publications still maintain separate R & B charts, measuring air play by Negro-oriented radio stations and sales in predominantly Negro outlets). And since the strictly R & B market is limited, the name of the game is to score what the record industry calls a "pop breakout," i.e., a song played by pop "top 40" disc jockeys, and achieve ranking on the pop charts, which reflect sales in the broader mass market.

Motown's performers and composers, under the generalship of Berry Gordy Jr. have come up with a style of music that embodies a consistent "breakout" formula, yet which still does well on the R & B charts. Lately, other R & B artists in other cities—Memphis, Chicago, New York—are more frequently "breaking pop." As Dave Finkle, an editor of *Record World* magazine explains, "This is due in great measure to the sound of Tamla-Motown, which created a wide market so that R & B broke across the racial barriers."

Much of the credit for the spreading of the Motown gospel belongs to three herald angels known collectively as the Supremes, and individually as Diana Ross, Mary Wilson and Florence Ballard. "The Supremes were our big break-through," says Motown record promotion man Larry Maxwell, whose job it is to stimulate air play and sales of Motown Records. "A few years ago we couldn't make a WABC pick [that is, be selected for air play]," Maxwell recalls, "because they'd say, 'That's a blues sound.' Used to be you had 'good' music or popular music and you had 'race' music. Then you had rock and roll and you had rhythm and blues. Now Motown's bridged the gap between pop and R & B." Translated, that means that R & B was once not generally considered a pop sound, hence, no pop air play and no pop charts; now it is a pop sound, and the deejays will play it.

Of course, ever since Elvis Presley began twitching his hips, R & B has been a major influence on teen-age music. Elvis is supposed to have developed his singing style by imitating a Negro R & B performer named Arthur Crudup. The pop music that came to be known as rockabilly, a mixture of country music and R & B, has been called a "whitened" R & B. In other words, mass audiences would accept R & B only when filtered through white performers—including, recently, British performers, most of whom borrowed from Negro R & B performers.

In today's pop sound mix, the heavy reliance on electronic distortions has helped considerably to make the sources of pop music extremely eclectic. A long-time student of pop music, WMCA disc jockey Joe O'Brien, thinks R & B no longer has much meaning as either a term of classification or ethnic orientation. "These boundaries no longer mean a damn thing," he says. "You have whites out in Wasp areas buying just as much Negro music as they do white. Sometimes we play Motown records on WMCA before they do on WWRL. In today's pop music, any imaginative musician will use any style or sound. There is no longer even a straight 'white sound.' Everything is fair game—Latin, folk, country and Western, Viennese, schmaltz—you name it. Anything can be used because there's no longer a right way to make a record. Whatever works, works."

Today's pop record is a palimpsest of noninstrumental sounds; even an old hand such as O'Brien, who plays the stuff for four hours every morning, confesses that he can no longer identify the instruments used because of the use of such sound techniques as reverb, overdub and feedback. The biggest influences on contemporary pop music, O'Brien says, are Latin groups (such as the Joe Cuba Sextette), the Motown sound, and folk music (not traditional folk, but contemporary folk by such groups as the Mamas and the Papas and the Lovin' Spoonful, who, of course, write their own folk songs.) In such a climate the novelty and variety of R & B performers seem to be finding a hospitable teen-age ear.

Thanks to the Supremes and other Motown artists such as Stevie Wonder, Marvin Gaye, the Temptations, the Four Tops, and Martha and the Vandellas, as well as three of the hottest composers in the pop market, none of them over 25, named Brian Holland, Lamont Dozier and Eddie Holland (known in the record world as Holland-Dozier-Holland, or simply HDH—names with the solid ring of Merrill Lynch, Pierce, Fenner & Smith in the financial world), plus a number of other composers and producers of energy and talent, Motown has come to stand for a distinctive kind of R & B. It is so distinctive that it is known the world over as the Motown sound or the Detroit sound.

Roughly, that sound may be described as a sophisticated, slicked-up, unique R & B sound that is an amalgam of gospel harmonies, a blues beat, symphonic effects, electronic gimmickry and a "sweet" kind of rock 'n' roll. The lyrics usually convey a sort of inspirational message or hymn the yearnings of adolescent love in a direct and energetic manner that avoids soppiness. The lyrics of "You Can't Hurry Love" may be taken as an example:

> *I need love, love to ease my mind*
> *I need to find, find someone to call mine*
> *But mama said you can't hurry love*
> *No, you just have to wait*
> *She said love don't come easy*
> *It's a game of give and take . . .**

Gordy describes the music simply as, "a happy sound, a big happy beat with a good strong bass. Tambourines gave it a gospel flavor," he says, "but it doesn't have so much of that now."

* Brian Holland, Lamont Dozier, Eddie Holland, © 1966, Jobete Music Co., Inc.

Gordy—husky, taut, a Napoleonic head, shy engaging grin—is sitting at the desk in his paneled darkened office. With a turntable at his side and big speakers concealed in the walls, he monitors records, deciding whether they should be released. Much of his time nowadays, he says not too happily, is spent in meetings and reading countless memos, or else traveling with his artists on tours (he had just returned from the Far East with the Supremes). But he still listens to all the company's records at one stage or another.

An assistant brings in the newest Supremes and Miracles records, and Gordy places the Supremes on the turntable, cocks his head, and turns up the volume to about 100 decibels. He sends back the Supremes, saying it needs more work, commenting: "It's O.K., but not really the one." Gordy calls my attention to the "Bach counterpoint" in the lead-in to the Miracles and suggests that the title be changed from "Come Around Here, You're the One I Need" to, simply, "You're the One I Need."

"Most people think all rock 'n' roll sounds the same," Gordy says, "but that's not true. You have to be a creative artist to decide what people will like." To prove his point, he sends for the three current Motown hits and plays a little of each, pointing out the differences and analyzing each record in a terse esthetic which is encompassed in a few words such as "strong," "good rhythm" and "that song has a philosophy."

The Supremes' "You Can't Hurry Love," No. 1 that week, has that "good rhythm," and it is obvious from the fondness with which he says it that this is the heart of the matter. Lyrics are important, he indicates, praising the "philosophy" in the Temptations' "Beauty Is Only Skin Deep":

So in love, sad as I can be
'Cause a pretty face got the best of me
Suddenly you came into my life and gave it meaning and delight
Now good looks I've learned to do without
'Cause I know now it's love that really counts
'Cause beauty's only skin deep . . .*

---

* Eddie Holland, Norman Whitfield, © 1966, Jobete Music Co., Inc.

But most important is the sound and the successful merger of rhythm and melody. And, of course, each record must have a quality of novelty that will catch the listener's ear.

Without overpraising the musical values of the records (Motown's critics accuse its song writers of writing sounds rather than songs), one agrees with Gordy that each one is different and clever, distinctively styled and lathed to a shining chromium perfection. Perfection is another of Gordy's talisman words, and I am told that Motown will record a song 20 or 30 times and then "if it still isn't right, we'll record it 15 more times."

"A Supremes record will sell 500,000 almost automatically," Gordy says. "Kids buy their records without even listening to them. We are putting something into their homes sight unseen so we want it to be good."

Watching Gordy in the mastering room, where the producers are editing a final tape of a Supremes record, you sense, as he helps them solve a cutting problem by clapping and stomping out the beat himself ("That's strong. Fine. Right there."), that he has that big, happy Motown beat throbbing inside him like a coiled, twanging string. He frequently hums a little bluesy tune under his breath —wooo-woooo-wooo-wooo. *There's* the Motown sound, on a little tape recorder playing inside Berry Gordy Jr.'s head. Bim-bimbim-bimbim. Wooo-ooo-ooo-ooo. What more can one say?

But don't get the impression that Motown is a sort of hit-hazardous operation. Berry Gordy Jr., the one-time auto worker, has built himself something of a pop assembly line. He has attracted a lot of young raw talent and created an organization capable of nurturing and polishing that talent until they become smooth, well-drilled performers who are capable of holding a night club audience, as well as catching a teen-ager's ear for a couple of minutes.

There is at Motown, for example, something called an artists' development department, whose function is to take rock and roll kids and convert them into a viable night club act. This "finishing school," as it is known among the Motown performers, employs a galaxy of veteran showmen to train the kids to make the break from the sound studio to a live performance on stage. As one faculty member says: "Rock 'n' roll shows us the plum. Our job is to bring it in here and can it."

Canning it involves teaching that intricate Motown choreography and blocking, as well as broadening the repertoire so the businessman at the Copa will hear something like "There's No Business Like Show Business" as well as "Baby, Baby I Need You" with his $7.50 steak. Portly, genial Maurice King, an experienced bandleader, either conducts the night club orchestra himself or else selects the conductor and musicians—who play Motown arrangements, of course. Gordy insists on keeping the Motown style, King says, even in the case of standards. There is also a charm school in which girl performers are taught how to sit, how to hold a fork, how to walk, how to speak. "They learn how to behave both on stage *and* off," says Mrs. Ardenia Johnston, the smiling, maternal lady who teaches them, with something of a school marm's glint in her eye. "I just can't tell you what Motown has meant to these kids," Mrs. Johnston says. "Some of them would have ended up juvenile delinquents if they hadn't had this opportunity."

One of Motown's most charming and accomplished finished products is the group known as the Supremes. Since their first big-selling record, "Where Did Our Love Go?" in the summer of 1964, the three girls, still in their early 20's, have amassed a continuous string of top-10 hits (including six gold, or million-selling records), won a worldwide popularity among teen-agers, and appeared with great success on television and in night clubs.

Chic in their dazzling array of gowns (the girls call them "uniforms"), most of which are selected for them by Mrs. Harvey Fuqua of Motown's special projects department, the group is full of youthful exuberance and gives off a charming naiveté. They were praised by reviewer Robert Shelton as "unusually vibrant, exultant vocalists who soar with seemingly endless energy."

Diana Ross, the lead singer, has been compared often to Eartha Kitt, but she has a flexible, sweeter style of her own that can shift gears from a gospel fervor into a romantic ballad. Florence Ballard and Mary Wilson are posted in the background, adding a vibrant, close harmony, delicately tapping their tambourines against their hips, or chiming in with jokes from time to time. The Supremes have a hard, driving quality, too, deriving both from sheer energy and an intense competitiveness; though they will boost other Motown performers with company-girl correctness, they also will give their all to outstrip them when playing on the same bill.

Such was the case at a Forest Hills Stadium concert last August. The Temptations' flashy and well-choreographed act had drawn three encores and the singing of Stevie Wonder, the little, 15-year-old blind blues singer, had drawn enthusiastic ovations. It was a simple matter of pride to the Supremes to close the bill with the greatest applause of all and, as witnesses present will attest, they went out and gave the performances of their lives. Or, as Diana put it, "We got out there and worked like hell. I wasn't really nervous until I heard that crowd screaming. It was a big shock. The audience was so far away, you couldn't see them, and I worried about that. I wanted to see everyone. I was soaking wet when we finished."

It is sometimes said about the Supremes that they have a "white sound." Diana rejects the description. "The white sound means the commercial sound," she explains a little hotly, as if to say, "This is our sound, baby, not theirs." She gives credit to British pop groups for making R & B more palatable to American audiences, but adds: "They copied a Negro sound and sang a popular version of R & B."

The girls, who grew up in Detroit's slum ghetto, have been singing together since they were about 14. They gravitated to Motown and Gordy after high school ("Everybody was talking about him," says Diana); he started them dubbing in background on records and christened them the Supremes. They began to record, while learning as much as they could from other groups. "The Temptations would teach them harmony to get them off their backs," Gordy recalls.

For a time, they were at the bottom of the Motown pecking order and were known as "the girls." (Now another, newer, group is known as "the girls.") Success began coming their way after they were placed in the hands of Holland-Dozier-Holland, who wrote their first hit, "Where Did Our Love Go?," and just about all their subsequent ones; the producing team of Brian Holland and Lamont Dozier gave their records a style and identity they had previously lacked, emphasizing Diana's voice in the solos, with Mary and Florence contributing in the harmony.

Offstage, the Supremes are friendly, rather ordinary girls with a bouncing sense of humor; their conversation is studded with little in-jokes about one another based on what someone had written about them. Diana seems a trifle more mature than the others, displaying an earnest, serious manner and a cool professionalism. She is almost achingly thin (size 5) with fine, large eyes set in a feline face and she speaks in a hoarse June Allyson voice. Mary is small and nicely proportioned, demure in a tan suit and frilly blouse. In conjunction with the others she tends to fade into the background, which is deceptive because she has a distinctively droll sense of humor; when she smiles, her eyes crinkle into two horizontal crescents. Florence is earthier. She is usually known as "the quiet one," but she can be outspoken in an abrupt, flaunting way if the spirit moves her.

Gordy speaks about them in a bemused, detached manner. "We had some trouble with them at first. You must be very strict with the young artists. That instills discipline. But once they have a No. 1 record they tend to get more independent. They start spending their money extravagantly." In the case of the Supremes, in their first flush of success they bought new homes with lots of expensive furniture and moved in their families.

"After a year, they saw their mistakes and came to appreciate our handling of their affairs," Gordy observes. The Supremes' money, as is the case with many Motown artists, is invested for them in a variety of business interests, stocks and bonds. Though their yearly income nowadays is in five figures—record royalties are divided equally—they have been put on an allowance of $50 a week. "If I'd been strict when they had their first hit, it would have been bad," Gordy says. "They were growing up, demanding to live their own lives, so I loosened up on them. Now they're more sensible, and they seek and appreciate advice." His brow furrows as he adds: "I don't know what the next phase will be." Then, hopefully: "But now they're less mixed up, more relaxed about their love lives. They take more interest in learning about the world. It's amazing how they've educated themselves in their traveling."

I sense that keeping happy these volatile, ambitious girls who account for a sizable percentage of Motown's record sales is one of Gordy's important executive functions. Anyhow, he spends a lot of time with them on the road. "Every company has trouble with its artists," he says. "It's always the little things that blow up. If the little things can be cleared up before they get big, trouble can be prevented."

Next day, at Diana's home—a comfortable, two-story brick affair—we have coffee and doughnuts in a shiny kitchen that has an air of unopened newness and Diana muses that she has never cooked on the stove or even sat down in the kitchen, so rarely is she at home. Her mother, Mrs. Ernestine Ross, used to travel with the girls as chaperon, but now stays home to devote more time to Diana's youngest brother, Chico. When it is time to go, Florence and Mary are collected at Florence's home, which is diagonally across the street from Diana's (Mary lives down the same street). Then, with a minimum of fuss, the girls gather their luggage for an engagement in Las Vegas, pile into the station wagon, wave good-by and vanish.

Florence's oldest brother, Cornell, a husky good-natured chap who is an investigator with the Michigan Department of State's driver improvement program, takes me to meet Florence's mother. She is a stout impassive woman and Cornell kids her about becoming "more glamorous, more outgoing," now that her daughter is a singing star. "Why, you never used to leave the house—did you?" he asks.

"I'm going to the Rooster Tail Monday," Mrs. Ballard says, a calm, satisfied smile on her face. "I'm going to Puerto Rico in March with the girls. I want to go to New York, too. I've never been to New York."

Back at Motown, I say good-by to Gordy. We are standing on the sidewalk, the knots of producers, writers and performers are gathered as usual. Gordy answers a question about the white HITSVILLE, USA building, and explains that he used to live there. The company's grown a lot since then and is planning to build a new office building in Detroit.

Gordy worries about things like a shortage of executive talent, and outgrowing the present staff. "Yes," he says, "We've expanded from that one building. Now, of course, we've got . . . we've got—" He is stumped. "How many buildings do we have now?" So Berry Gordy Jr. pokes out a finger and begins counting the number of buildings at present making up his Motown record corporation.

A Full Day on the Job with the Mayor

by S. J. Woolf

THERE IS A new spirit in City Hall. The old corridors which for years have re-echoed to the leisurely tread of late-coming or slow-going Mayors are now filled with new sounds. Speed is the order of the day. Dead and gone Mayors, whose portraits in more or less stilted poses line the walls, would gasp in amazement—if their oleaginous eyes could see—at the present occupant of the office.

Artificial dignity has been cast into the discard; political pull has become a liability and youthful college professors have supplanted wrangling ward bosses as advisers of the city government. A friendly atmosphere has displaced gruffness; even the policemen who guard that corner of the building in which the Mayor's office is situated have stifled their growls and now smile at expectant visitors.

These are but a few of the changes which Fiorello LaGuardia has wrought. He has upset traditions, turned old routine topsy-turvy and instilled a spirit of energy in those surrounding him.

Short and heavy-set, he combines in his appearance the rugged-ness of a bulldog and the agility of an acrobat. His body is but a reflection of his mind. He is purposeful but not set, intense yet not

From the *New York Times Magazine,* January 14, 1934, copyright © 1934, 1962 by The New York Times Company.

close-minded. His rapid movements are no quicker than the working of his brain. He can read undisturbed with half a dozen people talking in the same room with him and he can jump from a problem of finance to one of education in the twinkling of an eye. He is typically Italian in appearance and he embodies all the emotionalism of the Latin. Yet he is reserved when one would expect him to be explosive, calm when one would expect him to be unrestrained.

The Mayor's day starts early. Soon after 8 he leaves his apartment on upper Fifth Avenue. It is not the smart section of that aristocratic thoroughfare in which he lives but that neighborhood in which the new ghetto merges with transplanted memories of Naples and Sicily. What chiefly distinguishes his house from countless others in the vicinity is the presence of the solitary policeman now stationed before its door.

I had an appointment to spend the day with the Mayor. He had suggested this when I had gone to ask him for an interview.

"I could talk from now until doomsday," he said, "and you would not get a clear idea of my job unless you saw me in action. Be at my house a little after 8 tomorrow morning and see what I have to do. I'll tire you out." And he did.

There is no way of announcing visitors at the house and the elevator boy, taking my word that I was expected, hoisted me to the sixth floor in one of those old-fashioned cars which resemble cages for wild animals.

The Mayor's apartment is a modest one. The mission style still holds sway and the hand of no interior decorator is in evidence in the furnishings. One of the bedrooms has been converted into a study. A desk stands beside a window which overlooks the northern end of Central Park. Bookcases line the walls and while I waited for him I glanced at their contents.

Lives of Washington and Lincoln, each in numberless volumes, and collected editions of their writings, together with Farmers' Bulletins and Congressional Records make up most of his library. There are also many single volumes on economics and government, but the usual sets of standard novelists are missing. Fiction is absent. The lighter forms of literature have no place in the Mayor's reading.

Mr. LaGuardia did not keep me waiting long. He bustled into the study, dressed in a baggy overcoat and a large black sombrero, and, after a word of greeting, we were off. His car has been fitted with a folding table, at which he can work on his way downtown. But he does not drive directly to City Hall. Each morning he takes a different route so that he can survey the city and see what is going on. As we traveled downtown the Mayor stopped his car several times to question policemen and street cleaners. We sped past a large market on the upper East Side; the Mayor pointed it out.

"I heard a short time ago," he said, "that this was the best-run market in the city; then I discovered that it was not a municipal market. To me that was a remarkable piece of evidence of the breakdown in the management of the city's affairs. With the proper administration there is no reason why municipal projects should not be run as well as, if not better than, privately managed ones.

"In order that they may be so run our house must be thoroughly cleaned. For four years or more I talked about the graft and incompetence in the city's management. Since I have taken office I have found that I understated the true condition of affairs. They are much worse than I said.

"The people have entrusted me with the job of putting their house in order. I have started. I have forgotten politics and personal friends. It makes no difference to me whether a man is a Republican, a Democrat, a Socialist or member of some other party; if I feel that he can bring something of value to the city, even though I may dislike him personally, I shall appoint him to the position in which he can be of help.

"I have a definite philosophy of government, which I propose to put into effect. It will be an experiment that I hope will be successful.

"For years the political leader has come between the people and the government. Men who have been members of a political party all their lives cannot see the harm in it. Thousands and thousands of our citizens have regarded Mr. Curry as the ruler of this city. He has been virtually a dictator. They have seen nothing strange in the fact that a private individual, not elected by the voters, was more powerful than their properly chosen officials.

"When they had legitimate requests to make they never thought of going to the man whom they had placed in charge. They sought the underground method of appealing to a district leader. If they wanted a position they did not apply for it in the regular way; they sought some one with political pull to get them the job, and if the pull was strong enough, the job was obtained.

"These people do not think this is wrong. That is their philosophy of government, and I should find no fault with it if the results had not proved disastrous. Tammany has been no worse than the Republican machine in other cities. Right through the nation we have seen municipal governments fall down because of this pernicious system.

"It is this system that I shall endeavor to change. I do not want the politician—and when I say politician I am using the term in the worst sense—I do not want him to stand between the people and their duly elected representatives. If a man wants a job in this administration the fact that he is sponsored by some one who for years has been feathering his nest at public expense will not help him to secure it. That sponsorship will not be a recommendation. I want to know what the applicant has done, whether he is capable and whether he will serve the best interests of the city.

"I do not know whether you realize fully what this means. My eyes are open to the dangerous position in which I am putting myself when I fail to recognize the demands of the bosses. They are going to fight for their lives. But I am going to fight for the life of the city."

We were passing under the elevated on the Bowery. Along the side streets we could see the teeming tenements. Unemployed men were numerous. There was a huskiness in the Mayor's voice as he called attention to a ragged woman picking decayed fruit from a garbage heap.

"Look at those slums," he went on. "With proper city management and the elimination of useless expenses they would never exist. This city can be made clean and beautiful. There must always be poor people, but there is no excuse for the vile conditions under which many are compelled to live. They have been forced to live as they do because of the thievery that has been going on for years. Politicians, growing wealthy, have maintained their hold by throwing out a few crumbs and posing as the friend of the downtrodden. For too many years the poor man has been fooled."

We reached the City Hall. Without waiting for his chauffeur to assist him, the vibrant Mayor was out of the car and bounding up the stone steps. It was not yet 9 o'clock. Clerks and stenographers were leisurely walking to their jobs, but the Mayor of the city hustled into his office. His secretaries greeted him.

"Send in two stenographers," he said as he took off his overcoat and hat. Adjoining his office is a washroom with a large clothes closet. At one time this closet was filled with well-pressed suits. Now only the hangers remain. Mr. LaGuardia disdained them; a hook was all he wanted for his overcoat.

The Mayor darted to his desk. From a pocket he took a pair of horn-rimmed spectacles. He unbuttoned his vest and began reading the mail piled on his desk. As he did so he dictated answers, short, gracious, but to the point. One stenographer took his letters. The other jotted down memoranda of things which the Mayor wanted to do—people to be called up and matters to be investigated.

Suddenly he stopped for a moment and rubbed his chin as he re-read a letter. He pushed his spectacles up on his forehead.

"Take this," he snapped. He began a letter with the name of a man prominent in Congress. "My dear—," he dictated. "I thought you knew that political pull was to play no part in my administration. I am sorry I cannot do as you wish. With kindest regards, I am."

By 10 o'clock the Mayor had attended to his mail and made several long-distance calls, then the first visitor was announced. For two hours Mr. LaGuardia conferred with the heads of various departments. He switched from one subject to another with no apparent effort. He spoke of parks with Robert Moses, and of transit plans with City Chamberlain Berle. When the Director of the Budget read him a report which went into detailed figures to be presented to a meeting of the Board of Estimate, the Mayor said:

"Cut those figures out. They're unnecessary. Don't you think the members of the Board of Estimate can subtract?"

One of his secretaries entered and told him there was a couple outside who wanted him to marry them.

"Yes, I'll do it," he snapped, "its part of my job. But no publicity and no photographs."

The pair were ushered in. The Mayor read the ceremony and sent the newlyweds on their way without stopping to kiss the bride.

By 11:30 various members of the Board of Estimate began to gather in his office. At 12 to the minute, he led them upstairs to the Georgian room in which the meetings are held.

Seated in the great chair on the dais, Mr. LaGuardia seemed very small, yet there was an air of dignity about him as he pounded with his gavel and called the meeting to order. As a presiding officer he combines authority with urbanity. He listened to objections with no display of anger and treated persons who interrupted the proceedings with firmness but consideration.

It took the board more than an hour and a half to complete its work; when the meeting adjourned he rushed downstairs and once more saw visitors. It was after 2 before we left for lunch. The Mayor had not realized the lateness of the hour and when he noticed a clock, he changed his plans, going to a restaurant on Fourteenth Street for a sandwich instead of to a club on Park Avenue.

I had asked for an interview, but except when we were driving down in the car I had found little time for questions. Seated at a bare table within a stone's throw of old Tammany Hall, I asked the Mayor whether he believed that Tammany was dead. He stopped eating and looked at me.

"Tammany," he replied, "is a cancer in the very heart of the city. It can only be eradicated by starvation. That is the method of treatment I propose—I want to starve Tammany by withholding all patronage from it. That, to my mind, is the only way to get rid of it.

"As in the treatment of cancer in the human body, all sorts of quack cures are suggested which will not work. Until the district leaders are deprived of their power—and their power consists of patronage—Tammany will always be a menace."

The Mayor looked at his watch. It was 10 minutes to 3, and the Armory Board was to meet at 3 o'clock. Again we were on our way. Back he rushed into City Hall, off came his overcoat and once more, unbuttoning his vest, he sat down at his desk. The Armory Board awaited him in one of the other rooms.

"Tell them to come in here," he said to his secretary. "This room is large enough to hold them all, and hereafter we'll meet here."

He arose to greet them and stood very erect, buttoning his vest. Several serious men entered. They were worried over technicalities in regard to the Building Code, but the Mayor straightened matters out and they departed, satisfied.

His Honor then swore in a few new appointees. After that the Board of Education arrived for a meeting that lasted an hour.

By this time it was dark. Through the windows could be seen men and women on their way home from work, but the head of the city had still an hour and a half to go. More letters to dictate and more visitors to see. One caller was Milo Reno, leader of the farm-holiday group, who wanted the Mayor to put the unemployed to work making goods to be exchanged for food products from the West. Mr. LaGuardia said the plan was not practicable; as he spoke he was very thoughtful. When Mr. Reno had left, the Mayor turned to me and said:

"There is something in these people's dissatisfaction. Farmers are burning food and here in the East people are going hungry."

The Mayor did not want to see the City Hall reporters because he had decided that on days on which the Board of Estimate met there was plenty of material for the papers without his giving an interview. But when his secretary told him that the reporters had not yet adjusted themselves to the new edict, he agreed to receive them.

I have seen Presidents and Governors and Mayors hold newspaper conferences but I have never seen any one answer questions more fully or more frankly than Mayor LaGuardia. There were no "off-the-record" remarks, there was no parrying with words. He spoke briefly and crisply. There was an atmosphere of cordiality in the group which was not in evidence during the last administration.

At 6:30 the Mayor was ready to leave for home. Roughly speaking, he had held thirty or forty conferences, yet, except for his ruffled hair, he was as fresh as when he had started in the morning.

"We'll call it a day," he said as he sat back in his car. But he did not relax. He is constantly tense.

"Now you have seen a day in my life," he remarked. "At the present minute our principal problem is one of finance. Until our budget is balanced we cannot really get to work. The city has been trying to borrow itself out of debt. That is an impossibility. The reason I proposed the bill which we sent to Albany was that I felt that it was impossible for a number of men to agree upon any way of cutting down our expenses.

"Were the Board of Estimate to pass upon the reduction, each Borough President would want the reductions to be made in a borough not his own. I have no desire to be a dictator, nor have I any desire to take from the city's legislative body any of the functions which belong to it.

"We are living in unusual times. The entire world has suffered and the city has suffered doubly because in addition to the general state of affairs it has had to contend with corrupt and incompetent administrations. Extraordinary circumstances demand extraordinary actions. What I have proposed is purely an emergency measure, similar to measures which the Federal Government has found itself compelled to adopt.

"We must find money to run the city. We have to devise means to provide relief for thousands of our citizens who are in distress. It is essential that our expenses be cut down. Unless we reduce them we cannot raise any more money. There are thousands of useless jobs which are taxing the city's payrolls. I have seen department after department in which there are employes who do not work one hour a day. In some cases they come in for fifteen minutes and then leave.

"No private corporation could live with a padded payroll; every corporation has been compelled to make cuts in the salaries of even those employes who are essential. The city has made some cuts, but these are not sufficient. We must go further.

"After the budget has been balanced we can go to work. We can start some of the projects of which I have long dreamed. It seems too bad that my administration had to start with the city in its present financial condition, because this only delays the beginning of those projects.

"With Federal and State help, we are going to put about 200,000 men to work. Funds for materials for them to work with must be increased; I do not believe in employing them to dig ditches to keep them busy.

"The State parks are an example for the city; slum clearance must be pushed forward; our streets, which for years have been a disgrace, must be kept clean; our hospitals must be efficiently managed; politics must find no place in our educational system. There is no reason, in a municipality such as ours, why a man or woman who really wants to work should go hungry.

"I have a four-year job ahead of me—a tough job. I told you on the way down this morning that what I proposed to do was to carry on an experiment. I am not sure that the people are ready to discard the dangerous middleman in the shape of the professional politician. I am not sure that they are willing to ignore the district leader and the political boss. I am going to try to give them a government by the people and for the people, but I am fully aware that in endeavoring to do this I am committing political suicide. If I succeed in making this city a better place in which to live, I shall feel that the result justified the sacrifice."

"Any functions tonight?" I asked as I left him.

"No," he replied. "I am going home, have something to eat, read a little, and by 10 I'll be in bed. Being Mayor in the daytime is a man's size job. I shall cut out all public dinners, and even smokers.

Occasionally, when there is a meeting of people from other parts of the country, I shall attend it. This, I feel, is a part of the Mayor's duty. Occasionally, I said; that means perhaps once a month. Sometimes I shall go to a concert, sometimes to the theatre, but not often. Most nights will see me in bed early, getting ready for the next day's work."

Crump of Tennessee: Portrait of a Boss

by Harold B. Hinton

ON THE north side of Adams Avenue in Memphis, between Third and Main Streets, stand four structures of great importance in the lives of Shelby County's more than 300,000 citizens. Reading from east to west, toward the Mississippi River, they come in this order: the Shelby County Courthouse, the central police station, Fire Engine House No. 1 and the offices of E. H. Crump & Co., investment bankers.

The two main entrances to the ionic-columned courthouse are flanked by symbolic figures of justice, authority, liberty and wisdom. There may be some local doubt as to the distribution of justice, authority and liberty among the four buildings, but there has been very little as to the abode of wisdom. For the past twenty years it has been considered suicidal in Memphis to question the political wisdom of Edward Hull Crump, the 72-year-old investment banker whose name has become synonymous with the Democratic party in Shelby County.

Despite a recent flare-up of opposition from the CIO and assorted critical groups throughout the State, Mr. Crump today stands at the height of his power—absolute master of Memphis and Shelby County and the dominant political figure in all Tennessee.

Mr. Crump has been in politics since the turn of the century. Then young and red-haired, he had worked so hard as a clerk in a Memphis harness shop that he had become its owner. But the rising merchant was not satisfied with the outlook for the harness business; he was concerned about the horseless carriage. Unlike certain other early converts to the automobile, he did not invest his money in the industry. Instead, he dropped the harness business for politics, and eventually got himself elected Mayor of Memphis.

Although Mr. Crump is not currently much interested in official titles, he has been elected to public office, including that of United States Representative, some twenty-three times. He says he has taken an interest in 102 Shelby County elections and never got a trimming. There are those who say that his memory must be slipping, but they admit that he has very seldom backed a loser. His admirers claim that the boss of Shelby County came to the fore through the same qualities and circumstances that have kept him at the helm all these years. They say there was no one else on the scene, and there is still no one in sight, equipped with Ed Crump's concern for what he considers the welfare of Memphis.

He is a wealthy man, but enemies as well as friends say that Mr. Crump has been careful to make no personal profit from his connection with public affairs. His enemies shrug this off by adding that he doesn't have to chisel. Advertisements on billboards around town describe E. H. Crump & Co. as "the South's largest insurance writing agency," and other insurance men think that statement may be correct. It is emphasized that the Crump firm does not write any county business. In addition to the insurance company, he owns a soft-drink bottling plant in upstate New York.

With the passage of years and many political feuds, his hair has turned white, and he wears it long, managing to resemble an old-time pilot on the river that he loves. He affects enormous hats and fine clothes. He neither drinks nor smokes. He is affable and likable when he wants to be, and these days that is most of the time.

At the zenith of a long and arduous political career Mr. Crump alternates between the detachment of an elder statesman and the shrewdness of an experienced ward heeler. As he has grown older and more secure, he has tended to leave day-by-day political details to subordinates in his fabulous organization, and his subordinates remain notably eager to please the chief. The story goes that the boss, as witness to his great fondness for birds, founded the E. H. Crump Audubon Society. As witness to their fondness for Mr. Crump, his lieutenants promptly identified themselves as bird fanciers also, even to the extent of feeding the feathered creatures in public places.

While, to the visitor, there is a certain Graustarkian air about his kingship, to him and to most inhabitants of Memphis (they would resent being called subjects) there is nothing comic about it. Memphians say that not a sparrow falleth here but Ed Crump knows it. And there are those who believe that the hairs in the heads of Shelby County's voters not only are counted but are recorded in a card index in the sheriff's office. Certainly, Mr. Crump is always prepared to discard the detachment of royalty whenever he feels it necessary.

Even now there is no matter too petty for him to handle himself, if it strikes his attention. He was anything but detached when his ticket, headed by Senator Kenneth D. McKellar, was campaigning for the recent primaries. He tired himself out and, after his ticket swept the State, went off to Saratoga for a rest.

In some respects Ed Crump cannot be classified as a political reactionary. He has always opposed the Ku Klux Klan. He supported Franklin D. Roosevelt for President all four times and has made something of a trademark out of his opposition to public utilities under private ownership. In the course of his opposition he has frequently inveighed against "Wall Street's" dire influence on Memphis and once did epic battle with the Commonwealth and Southern Corporation, a public utilities holding company, over local rates.

Under Mr. Crump Memphis has acquired ownership of its waterworks, electric power system and gas plant. To commemorate that day in 1934 on which Memphis voters approved municipal ownership of the electric system, he had the name of Maiden Lane, a little street between his office building and the firehouse, changed to 6th of November Street. His admirers say that Mr. Crump, well read and widely traveled, was inspired to this change after noting that the streets of European cities are often named for the dates of decisive events.

Although an early supporter of the Tennessee Valley Authority, Mr. Crump this year decreed that the city of Memphis should not reduce its power rate by the 15 per cent by which most cities served by the Authority cut theirs. This decision sprang from his present devotion to the idea that users of gas, light, power and water should be charged enough to pay the entire costs of local government. There will be no taxes, in the ordinary sense, if he carries his theory to fruition.

This may or may not be a good way to finance a municipality. The point is that Ed Crump decided it was a good way, and Memphis had better like it.

Beyond doubt, Mr. Crump thinks of himself as Shelby County's benefactor. In the fashion of autocrats he has come to believe that what he thinks is good for Memphis must be good for Memphis. And he ridicules the idea that there is any element of danger in the iron-clad control which he and his organization exercise. In his view, a dictatorship for Memphis is all right if it is benevolent. As proof of his machine's beneficence, he points to the city's low fire insurance rates, low crime rate, prizes for traffic safety and generally efficient administration.

Possibly Mr. Crump's own concept of his role in Shelby County was best expressed in a full-page newspaper advertisement published back in 1927 when he was involved in a bitter political feud: "My whole desire and purpose is for Memphis to progress, to have every opportunity for growth, and for its people to be happy in their pursuit of everyday business, and for the same spirit to reign in their home life. I am deeply conscious of my responsibility to exercise my privileges as a citizen of a free republic, and this I intend to do so long as I have in me the independence of a man."

Mr. Crump is a frequent advertiser in newspapers and an inveterate writer of letters, usually denunciatory, to their editors. He takes newspaper opposition to heart and his style is not distinguished by understatement. A recent letter to the *Nashville Ten-*

nessean, which Mr. Crump has regarded as his arch-enemy ever since he and a former publisher, Col. Luke Lea, contended for State leadership years ago, opened with a reference to a "trio of mangy bubonic rats." The trio was identified in the next sentence as the paper's publisher, editor and political writer. Toward the current publisher of the *Tennessean,* Silliman Evans, Mr. Crump entertains a dislike as strong as that he once held for Colonel Lea. Mr. Evans is proud to list himself among Mr. Crump's opponents and sees the master of Memphis as a Tennessee-wide political menace. An editorial in the *Tennessean,* published the day after Senator McKellar defeated Edward Carmack, declared:

"Boss Crump is no apparition, no vague something-horrible-that-may-happen. He is the something horrible that has been happening to Tennessee too wearisomely long, the leaden weight, the distasteful power, whose long-ensconced political nuisance must be thrown out, not only because it desecrates a people's government but because it insults and offends a people's inborn self-esteem."

After the recent campaign the *Chattanooga Times* also expressed alarm over Mr. Crump's State-wide influence:

"There has been no effort this time to conceal the fact that Mr. Crump of Memphis speaks as State boss. Protests of citizens who dislike dictatorship in any form are likely to be met with the statement that 'Mr. Crump gives good government in Memphis,' therefore might do well as State dictator. Memphis seems to have good government if one overlooks the fact that the very essence of good government is missing there—the right of the citizen to vote freely and without fear for any man he chooses, and the right of the citizens to choose their candidates for public office rather than to be told by a political machine who those candidates will be."

Labor organizations as well as newspapers have found themselves in disagreement with Mr. Crump, and the CIO in particular has felt the weight of his displeasure. It was at the time of the 1937 sit-down strikes that Mr. Crump decided that the CIO would be a bad thing for Memphis. He said as much in advertisements, and when, despite these warnings, CIO organizers ventured into Memphis to unionize the Firestone plant, they had a singularly rough time of it. As survivors of the struggle recall it today, they were never beaten by uniformed policemen, but uniformed policemen never interfered when a CIO man was set upon.

During the war, which started an industrial and a union boom in Memphis, Mr. Crump apparently concluded that the CIO wasn't such a bad thing for his city after all. In 1942 the Mayor of Memphis even made the welcoming address to the State CIO's annual convention—an address that never would have been delivered without Mr. Crump's approval.

The current Crump feud with the CIO seems based on political rather than social or economic grounds. He insists that labor unions have no business mixing into politics. This summer the CIO's Political Action Committee made the mistake of mixing into politics on the opposition side; the PAC endorsed Mr. Carmack against Senator McKellar. According to political observers, the master of Memphis worked his head off during the campaign not so much because he thought his slate was in danger as because he wanted to put the CIO in its place.

He succeeded. In Shelby County Mr. Carmack polled 4,800 votes, Senator McKellar 50,000. What the PAC cannot understand about these results was that the CIO's estimated 30,000 members in Shelby County had all promised to vote for Mr. Carmack.

Mr. Crump's critics were saddened by the campaign's outcome; his followers seemed merely convinced anew that he is the source of all political wisdom. Memphians in the more prosperous categories are particularly inclined to take Mr. Crump at his own evaluation as a public benefactor. A well-to-do cotton merchant put it like this: "Somebody has to look after all these things, and we are all glad to have Ed Crump do it. He loves it and he is good at it. We feel we are lucky in having a high-minded citizen who is willing and able to do these things for us."

In the minds of his Shelby County followers, Ed Crump is associated with all the good things about Memphis, and his organization is blamed for such defects as the system is admitted to have. An admirer may bring himself to say that "the organization is ruthless against opponents"; he will never say that Mr. Crump is ruthless.

As an example of "organization" ruthlessness, one admirer cited the sad case of a Memphis businessman who had been the Shelby County manager of a losing candidate for the Governorship. When the State Legislature met following that election, it adopted a bill, proposed by the Shelby County delegation, increasing by something like 1,000 per cent the license fee for curb markets in all Tennessee cities with a population of more than 250,000. There is one such city in Tennessee—Memphis. At the time there was only one such curb market—belonging to the campaign manager of the unsuccessful candidate.

Usually, in business circles, things do not come to such a pass. The machine is so well organized that a mere hint of opposition on the part of a merchant may bring an immediate, quiet but effective boycott. Hotels will not entertain a convention unless the "organization" concludes that its purpose is non-subversive, by Crump standards.

The Achilles heel of the Crump machine, if it has one, seems to be the police force. It is deemed efficient and honest, but it appears to have become over-zealous, if not tyrannical. The widow of a former county official and a personal friend of Mr. Crump was saddened the other day when her long-employed chauffeur told her he was leaving Memphis because he couldn't stand the way police treated Negroes.

He reluctantly told of the incident that had led to his decision. Along with four or five other men he was waiting to get his hair cut in a Negro barber shop when a policeman came in.

"What are all you niggers doing here?" the chauffeur said the policeman asked.

The head barber assured him that the men were simply waiting to get their hair cut, just as numerous white men were waiting in other parts of town. "Go on, get out of here and go home," the policeman is reported to have said, chasing the customers out of the shop.

It was suggested to the chauffeur's employer that occurrences like that might be frequent in a city so thoroughly bossed as Memphis.

"Mr. Crump had nothing to do with it," she said indignantly. "It was the organization."

Conceivably, the stern ways of the police may some day convince neglectful Memphians that forgetting about civic problems, on the theory that a beneficent overlord will take care of them, may not be an ideal situation. But the majority seem much more troubled about what will happen when the leader dies. In the citadel of the leader's power, friends and foes alike agree that the machine is impregnable in Shelby County as long as Ed Crump lives. They are equally agreed that there will be all kinds of confusion when he disappears from the scene.

His two sons, both of whom are with the insurance firm, seem completely indifferent to politics, and there is no heir apparent among his lieutenants. Whenever they can bring themselves to contemplate Shelby County without Ed Crump, his supporters are quite discouraged. They groan mentally at the thought of the scramble and uncertainty that will ensue with his passing. They seem anything but eager to assume the burden of responsibility they have avoided during the long years of the Crump regime.

His supporters, including the "right people," might worry more if the leader's health were not so robust. Every time he returns from an annual check-up at one of his favorite medical refuges he confounds wishful thinkers with reports of boyish blood pressure and other evidences of constitutional fortitude which would be the envy of a man half his age. Whatever the future brings, the master of Memphis now seems more than capable of holding his own.

The Political Boss: Going, Going—

by Leo Egan

FIVE SHORT YEARS ago Carmine G. De Sapio was being described
as a miracle man, one who was giving new life, new vitality and
new power to urban Democratic political machines. Today his
status is in jeopardy.

Ironically, it is the reputation he acquired as he was clawing his
way to the top five years ago and his subsequent efforts to live up
to it that are responsible for his present predicament. He was billed
as a new type of political leader, a streamlined, modern, Madison
Avenue version of the old-style machine boss, endowed with all
the virtues and free of all the liabilities of the famous political
leaders whose sun had set.

What Mr. De Sapio and those who hitched their wagons to his
star overlooked was that the American electorate had had its fill
of political bosses, old-style or new. Voters were looking for public
officials who made their own decisions. They were fed up with the
likes of John P. O'Brien, New York Mayor in 1933, who couldn't
tell whom he was about to appoint because he hadn't gotten "the
word."

A Tom Dewey or a Fiorello LaGuardia or a Dick Daley

From the *New York Times Magazine,* January 8, 1961, copyright © 1961
by The New York Times Company.

(Mayor of Chicago), who are their own bosses, the electorate can respect and support, as it has proved time after time. But, given a choice between men they suspect of being controlled by others and men they regard as independent of such influence, their preference is for the independent, as they demonstrated with the election in 1950 of Vincent R. Impellitteri as Mayor of New York and in 1951 with the election of Rudolph Halley as President of the City Council.

Mr. De Sapio failed to appreciate this fundamental fact at Buffalo in 1958 when he forced the nomination of District Attorney Frank S. Hogan as the Democratic candidate for United States Senator, over the combined opposition of W. Averell Harriman, then Governor, Mayor Wagner and Herbert H. Lehman, then Senator. Now he is paying dearly for his mistake. Except that he flaunted his strength, he might still be the most powerful figure in the Democratic party in New York State today.

The mistake De Sapio made at Buffalo was one that Charles F. Murphy, his illustrious and wily predecessor as leader of Tammany and de facto boss of the Democratic party in New York State, carefully avoided. Unlike De Sapio, "Mister" Murphy (he was never called anything else by Tammany members) preferred to work in the background and was not above deception at his own expense to achieve his ends.

The late Senator Robert F. Wagner, father of New York's present Mayor, had a favorite political story dealing with "Mister" Murphy's talent for self-abasement. It concerned the selection of John F. (Red Mike) Hylan, then a County Judge in Brooklyn, as the Democratic candidate for Mayor in 1917, when Murphy was at the height of his power.

"Is Hylan a man we can trust and do business with?" Murphy asked John H. McCooey, his Brooklyn lieutenant, Senator Wagner recalled.

"He certainly is," Mr. McCooey attested. "Do you want to meet him?"

"No," replied Murphy. "I want you to ram him down my throat."

And that is what McCooey did. Civic groups were organized to demand Hylan's nomination. Democratic clubs in Brooklyn passed resolutions commending the good Judge's independence of Tammany. Finally a "reluctant" Murphy threw in the sponge and accepted Hylan as the Democratic candidate for Mayor.

At Buffalo, De Sapio rammed District Attorney Hogan down the throats of elected Democratic officeholders instead of allowing them to ram Hogan down *his*.

The New York District Attorney is a widely known man of spotless reputation. By nominating him De Sapio hoped to induce voters of moderate views who had left the Democratic party over the prior fifteen years to return.

Nevertheless De Sapio's display of naked political power at Buffalo marked the apogee of his political career. It convinced a new generation of voters, without any experience under old-style political bosses, that there was no difference between old-style and new-style bosses.

This impression was heightened by De Sapio's physical resemblance to the motion picture and television stereotype of a sinister character. It is a resemblance attributable to his need for wearing tinted glasses because of an eye ailment (iritis), his taste in clothes (he likes the sharp kind) and his distinctive hair style (it usually looks as if he had just left the barber's chair after getting "the works").

Actually the resemblance between Carmine De Sapio and the more famous political bosses of the past is far more apparent than real. The meat on which this Tiger has fed since he came to power as leader of Tammany in 1950 has been so bland his predecessors would have spurned it in disgust.

During all his years as Tammany's boss, De Sapio has not had a single city franchise to sell. He hasn't licensed a single gambling establishment or brothel, so far as any records show. Nor have repeated investigations turned up a single instance in which he has shared the profits of a city or state construction or purchase contract.

In these respects his record presents a marked contrast to his better-known predecessors as political bosses in New York and elsewhere, most of whom amassed fortunes by engaging in just such activities.

William Marcy (Boss) Tweed, the classic example of a political boss, helped make the very name of Tammany a symbol of political corruption by the personal profits he obtained from politics.

A hulking 300-pounder, Tweed was one of the "Forty Thieves," as the city's Aldermen were known in his day. He supplemented a private profit from the sale of traction franchises with a share of the profits from contractors responsible for the building and furnishing of the famous Tweed courthouse which used to stand behind City Hall. He died in the old Ludlow Street jail.

Richard F. Croker, another of De Sapio's illustrious predecessors as the leader of Tammany, amassed enough money in nineteen years as the city's political overlord to retire to England and take up horse-breeding and the life of a country squire. One of his claims to fame was that he voted seventeen times on a single election day when he was twenty-two years old. At the age of seventy-three he married a Cherokee Indian girl who survived him.

"Mister" Murphy, a benign-looking gentleman who advanced the political careers of Senator Wagner, Alfred E. Smith and Jimmy Walker, likewise waxed rich as a political leader. It was frequently charged, but never proved, that a large part of his fortune was attributable to his success in obtaining a franchise for the Pennsylvania Railroad to build its tunnels under the Hudson and East Rivers. A relative had the general contract for the construction work.

The practice of licensing underworld characters to engage in illegal activities prevailed until relatively recent times. Jimmy Hines, an ex-blacksmith who carved out a tidy little political duchy for himself on the West Side, was sent to jail for licensing the late Arthur Flegenheimer, better known as Dutch Schultz, to run a policy bank.

In Murphy's day it was an open secret that some district leaders under him were granting extra-legal "licenses" for the operation of gambling establishments within their territories. Big Tim Sullivan was reputed to have granted the license for Arnold Rothstein's famous place, where many of the city's better-known theatrical and financial figures frequented the gaming tables.

The licensing arrangement was relatively simple. For a share of the profits, the licensor would see that the licensee was not unduly disturbed by the police. It was, of course, understood that a few token raids would have to be made on occasion and that certain small fry might have to go to jail from time to time. The inconvenience of such incidents was kept to a minimum.

Democratic and Republican political machines in other cities and in other states operated on substantially the same principles and in much the same fashion.

Among the better-known ones were the Boies Penrose and William H. Vare machine (Republican) in Philadelphia, the Frank ("I am the law") Hague machine in Jersey City, the Pendergast machine in Kansas City and the Crump machine in Memphis, Tenn.

In all instances the success and continued operations of these profitable organizations depended on remaining in control of the government. This was accomplished in a number of ways.

Arriving immigrants were helped to obtain jobs, then quickly naturalized and persuaded to vote for their benefactors. Needy families were given food, clothing and coal at Thanksgiving and Christmas and the breadwinner directed to employment. Those who ran afoul of the law found a friend in the machine's local representative who could persuade the judge to be lenient.

Thousands of voters were placed under obligation to the machine for minor favors. The advent of the automobile proved a bonanza. Ticket-fixing enabled the machines to put the drivers in their debt.

If the votes that could be coralled in this fashion were not enough, because of some outbreak of public indignation over the way a city was being run or the way taxes were mounting, there was always the possibility of stealing an election through use of repeaters, floaters, ballot-box stuffing and disorders that would dissuade anti-machine voters from casting their ballots.

The repeater method was probably the most widely used device for stealing an election, because a repeater could always be depended upon to vote right. Floaters, who were registered in colonies, were usually men of relatively low intelligence and often mismarked their ballots. The colonizing system, nevertheless, was frequently employed. There are many authenticated instances in which fourteen to twenty unrelated men were registered from a single room.

This is why rooming-house operators are still required by law to file lists of their tenants with the Police Department and boards of election well in advance of election day.

Ballot-box stuffing was used only in cases of dire emergency because, from the very nature of the operation, it became clear as the boxes were opened that fraud had been committed. In the case of repeaters and floaters this fact was not obvious; it took an investigation to establish that people who were not entitled to do so had been permitted to vote.

For most of a political machine's operations, control over the police force was essential. A license for gambling or vice could only be good as long as the police cooperated. This cooperation was achieved in two ways: through control of assignments and through a sharing of the "license" fees.

During the Seabury investigation, John F. Curry, then leader of Tammany and the dominant Democratic leader in the city, testified publicly that he regularly visited the Police Commissioner once a week and gave him "recommendations" for transfers and promotions within the department. A detective who interfered unduly with a mid-Manhattan licensee might find himself back in uniform patrolling the lonely beaches of Staten Island the following week.

Control over specification writing and inspection services in agencies responsible for construction contracts and municipal purchases was also essential. A former Borough President of Queens was convicted of conspiring with some subordinates to require the use of a particular make of pipe in all sewer construction. A supplier who was making short-weight deliveries had to have the cooperation of an inspector who would overlook the deficiency. Generally such an inspector would be one who owed his job to the dominant political machine.

The decline of city political machines started with women's

suffrage and the curtailment of immigration in the early Nineteen Twenties.

Although slow to exercise their vote at first, women were more outraged than men at the alliance between political leaders and the underworld; they contributed heavily to reform movements designed to put an end to it. The Cable Act, setting up immigrant quotas, slowed the arrival of new candidates for naturalization to a trickle.

The effect of these two developments was greatly magnified by other events of the early Nineteen Thirties. The great depression called for measures beyond the financial resources of the machine, and so Government took over the functions of providing relief to the needy and of steering breadwinners to the jobs that were available.

The end of prohibition cut off a big source of underworld revenue and sharply reduced public toleration of law evasion. Municipal revenues were hard hit and city treasuries found themselves unable to satisfy the needs and desires of the machines. City charters were revised to reduce the opportunities for favoritism in the making of purchases and the award of construction contracts.

New York was harder hit by the cumulative force of these developments than many other cities. Fiorello LaGuardia's reform administration was installed in City Hall to root out the evils disclosed by the Seabury investigation. Under direct orders from the White House, Tammany was placed on a starvation diet with respect to Federal patronage.

In other places like Jersey City, Memphis and Kansas City the anti-machine tide was slower in making itself felt, but its march was inexorable. As an institution the political machine was doomed and, in time, this fact became clear even to Frank Hague, Ed Crump and Boss Pendergast. Machines still persist in a few small cities, but even in these it is questionable whether they can outlive their present operators.

By their very nature, political machines run counter to what is fast becoming a fundamental American ethic: choices between candidates should be based on their merits or the merits of their programs. In the case of machine voters the merits of the candidates or their programs are the least of the considerations entering into a choice. Far more important is the desire to discharge an obligation or the lust for power and office.

Despite the setbacks he has received, De Sapio has continued to court the good opinion of the public. Even though the jobs are unsalaried, he obviously likes being leader of Tammany and Democratic National Committeeman for New York and won't surrender either place willingly.

The attraction of both offices is the power and position they give. John Adams once wrote that any man who can control more than his own vote is an aristocrat in a democracy. One who can control as many votes as the leader of Tammany becomes, by this definition, a first-flight aristocrat. By his control or influence over nominations and appointments he can advance or retard a political career. He is a man to be reckoned with, one whose goodwill is important. And De Sapio likes being important. It is a safe speculation that his political power is also an asset in the insurance business that provides his personal income.

In modern society, the political boss of old is being replaced by the expert in public relations, by the people who can create illusions and translate the intricacies of government into simple, understandable general principles, by those who know how to manipulate symbols.

Mr. De Sapio, on the basis of his record thus far, is not such a man. Rather he is a politician's politician. Other politicians respect and admire his handiwork. They welcome his counsel. In an earlier age, he would have been unbeatable. But this is the sixth decade of the twenty-first century. Times have changed. That is why De Sapio's back is to the wall.

Allen of Atlanta Collides with Black Power and White Racism

by Reese Cleghorn

MAYOR IVAN ALLEN JR., a brisk, silver-haired man of 55, turned his car off a main thoroughfare in Atlanta early one morning a few days ago, headed down a dingy street lined with ramshackle houses, and cruised slowly along looking at the yards and rain-rutted vacant lots. He waved as he passed a cluster of well-dressed Negro children on their way to school. In a moment he was chatting with a man he had stopped beside the street, asking how the garbage pickup had been and how things were going in general. Then he drove on, out of the Summerhill community of poor Negro households back toward his office at City Hall.

Only a few days earlier, bricks, bottles and gunfire had torn the air of Summerhill. Mayor Allen had been jeered at and toppled from the roof of a car as he tried to calm the crowd, and the sharp smell of tear gas had spread through the streets in the wake of Atlanta's first slum riot in the pattern of 1966.

From the *New York Times Magazine,* October 16, 1966, copyright © 1966 by The New York Times Company.

On that day the Mayor had won praise throughout the nation for his courage in rushing to the scene and facing a mob. He had seemed a beleaguered, symbolic man of the times, a Southern politician of a new kind who had championed civil rights and fought the mob spirit in whites, and who now had moved into a mob of Negroes to preach law and order. Vice President Humphrey said immediately afterward: "If there is a hero on the domestic scene today, it's Ivan Allen of Atlanta."

But Summerhill was still there. Other Summerhills in Atlanta, slums and semi-slums with all the ills that fester in the open wounds of American cities, were still there, too. All seemed to make hollow the dramas of momentary heroism and even the concerted slum blitzes of the kind Mayor Allen had been engaged in for months. Atlanta's Mayor thus may be a symbol of another kind, too—of urban America's struggle in 1966 to get a slippery handhold on its greatest problem, the slums, even as violence is erupting there and a white backlash hardens politicians against solutions.

In Allen's case, this may be the meeting of the irresistible force and the immovable object. Atlanta's chief executive has been referred to by waggish admirers as "our Mayor a go-go." Pre-eminently a man of action, he is so outspoken that his best political friends cringe at times. One of those times was three years ago, after the major Atlanta hotels had agreed to a limited form of volunteer desegregation. Then Allen heard that one hotel manager was secretly trying to undermine the agreement. He strode into the hotel for a finger-wagging lecture during which he referred to the manager as "a little punk."

Another such time came on Sept. 29, and the whole country heard about it. Lester Maddox, an ultra-segregationist who once had forced Negroes to leave his restaurant at pistol point despite the 1964 Civil Rights Act, had just won the Democratic nomination for Governor of Georgia in a primary in which many Republicans had voted. Allen, a strong Democrat, called a press conference and, with a face reflecting his indignation but a firm voice, declared that "the seal of the great state of Georgia lies tarnished."

"It is deplorable," he said, "that the combined forces of ignorance, prejudice, reactionism and the duplicity of many Republican voters have thrust upon the state of Georgia Lester Maddox, a totally unqualified individual, as the Democratic nominee for Governor." The state would not be surrendered, he maintained, to "the rabble of prejudice, extremism, buffoonery and incompetency." He would not vote for Maddox, he said, and added: "It is high time all Georgians put aside their prejudices and begin to realize that a large segment of our population that is Negro is entitled to full rights and privileges as American citizens."

Some of his political friends deplored that thunder from City Hall, directed at a man who had won half a million votes and might sit in the Governor's chair. But a close associate of the Mayor's said later with a touch of wonder: "If you think that was a strong statement, you should have seen what he was going to say before we toned him down."

Mayor Allen is the perfect personification of that great American phenomenon, the civic shaker and the business mover. He is a former Chamber of Commerce president whose son is now head of the Jaycees. He is the son of the founder of the firm, but a millionaire through his own business acumen. He is of the social élite, but prefers a dove hunt to a party. One friend of long standing calls him "Jack Armstrong grown up."

Ivan Allen is very much like Atlanta, a comparison he would like. He is successful, optimistic, young in spirit, and disdainful of anything that stands still. His reflexes are those of a businessman, and when he seeks to "sell" a civic idea he instinctively does it by talking about why it is good for business. He is open and direct, and only partially sophisticated, a man who takes his wife to a good seat at the opera without knowing who the soprano is, a moving center of attraction with great poise, confidence and almost perpetual animation.

As you talk to him in his modest City Hall office, he props his feet on the simple table that is his desk. Then he brings the feet down with a semi-stomp and walks restlessly around the visitors' Kennedy-style rocking chairs, clapping his hands occasionally while talking. He stops at a closet and pours a Coke. In a moment he is beside you again, patting you on the shoulder to emphasize a point, and in another moment he is gently swinging a golf club (under wall stickers that say "LBJ for the USA" and "Atlanta Braves").

During Allen's five years as Mayor, Atlanta has built an $18-million stadium and brought in major league baseball and football; started building a convention hall–auditorium complex and a huge, privately constructed cultural center; pushed through a downtown expressway interchange that joins three interstate highways; and taken the first steps toward a comprehensive reorganization of city government. The city's economy has continued to boom, with great bursts of high-rise construction and an unemployment rate often less than 3 per cent. Greater Atlanta's population, now one and a quarter million, continues to grow by about 35,000 a year.

The Mayor helped engineer desegregation of city parks, swimming pools and other public facilities and, after the Student Nonviolent Coordinating Committee and other civil rights groups brought the always-necessary pressure through demonstrations, he led the behind-the-scenes efforts that began desegregation of restaurants, hotels and theaters before this was required by national law. When Congress began hearings on the Civil Rights Act of 1964, Allen went to Washington to ask passage of a public accommodations section, the first major Southern political leader to do so.

All of this had made Allen seem a "do-something" Mayor and the representative of a new breed on the Southern political scene.

When Senator Abraham Ribicoff's subcommittee on urban problems held hearings this summer, two mayors who went before it seemed to personify the great contrasts among big-city mayors in America. One was Sam Yorty of Los Angeles, who vexed some of the Senators because during the Watts rioting he had remained aloof, never even going into the troubled area; before the committee he seemed to be justifying a kind of City Hall detachment on grounds that Los Angeles' Mayor, with limited powers under a "weak-mayor" system, must not try to do too much. The other was Allen of Atlanta, which also has the "weak-mayor" system.

Senators who had acidly scolded Yorty heaped praise upon Allen and his city.

By the time Atlanta had its disturbances in September, small brushfires compared with the Los Angeles holocaust, Allen had already come to his own conclusion about Yorty's aloof handling of the Watts situation. He had decided Yorty was wrong, and had been thinking about what he might do.

At City Hall on the afternoon of Sept. 6, Allen was beset by a series of crises that seemed to summarize the worst problems of all big-city mayors. Firemen were on strike for more money. The firemen's pickets and antiwar pickets were crossing paths at City Hall. A walkout of carpenters had halted major construction throughout the city. Aldermen were in session wrestling with the necessity of raising taxes $4-million a year for the lackluster business of building sewers. Then, late in the afternoon, word came that a riot had started at Capitol and Ormond Avenues.

A Negro auto-theft suspect had been shot but not critically wounded by an officer trying to arrest him. A garbled story of the event spread. (One version was that the man had been killed while handcuffed, and another had it that a Negro child had been shot. A sound truck operated by Snick, which has headquarters in Atlanta, had gone through the streets excitedly calling for mass protest in the streets and raising the cry of "Black Power!" Soon crowds were in the streets and bricks and bottles were flying at motorists and police.

Allen strode out of City Hall as soon as he heard. He and one unarmed police officer who is his driver and bodyguard headed straight for the trouble spot. When they arrived, fewer than 20 policemen were there, without riot equipment and unable to cope with the milling crowds. When Allen's car had gone as far as possible, he got out and walked the remaining distance to the center of the disturbance as the sounds of turmoil increased. ("That was the longest 100 yards I ever walked," he said later.)

Down Capitol Avenue he moved with his driver and, shortly, another nonuniformed and unarmed officer. Angry shouts swirled around them. Taking charge and checking the police, he began striding rapidly up and down the street, passing repeatedly through clusters of people. "Everybody, go to your homes," he said. "Let's go home. Come on, let's go home."

For about an hour Allen personally broke up street groups. At one point he seemed on the verge of success in persuading a throng to go with him to the nearby stadium to talk. He was buying time. In the meantime, police were gathering in force, equipped for trouble.

As dusk was falling, Allen, looking tired now and with the blue lights of police cars playing on his face, climbed to the roof of an automobile and tried to speak through a megaphone. The crowd jeered. A bushy-haired young Negro in a faded blue sweatshirt grabbed the megaphone and yelled: "Atlanta is a cracker town. It's no different from Watts. The Mayor walks around on plush carpet and wears $500 suits and eats big steaks, while we eat pig foots and chitlin's."

By now the crowd was beginning to rock the car, and Allen jumped to the street, falling to his knees. He was quickly up, and walking through the crowd again with the same message: "Let's go home. Everybody go home. I've told y'all, if six of you will come to my office we'll talk. . . ." No one was listening.

In moments the block was torn by gunfire, some of it from police shooting into the air, some from armed Negroes. Big chunks of broken pavement began to fly at police and others. "Who's the man with the pistol over there?" Allen said, pointing to a bystander with a holstered weapon. "Go get that gun." The police did. "Cut loose with that tear gas," the Mayor said. The gas guns were fired. With a handkerchief to his nose, Allen moved into groups, still asking them to go home.

By now Negro ministers he had summoned were on the scene but no one seemed to listen to them. One asked Allen whether he had been hurt. "Man," the Mayor said, "you know they can't throw anything as fast as I can run." Finally someone asked him to leave and let the police face the perils of the night. "Listen," he said, "if anything is going to happen here tonight, it's going to happen over me."

The disturbance slowly died. Sixteen people had been sent to hospitals, some 75 arrested. But no one was dead. Some cars had been badly damaged, many windows broken and a one-story frame building burned. But there had been no looting, no one had been shot by police, and the streets were still.

Five nights later more disturbances began in another Negro slum area, when a white man drove in and shot two Negro youths, one of whom died; later a man was arrested and charged with murder. The Mayor returned on two of the three nights of trouble to play the same role. This time the police were better prepared and the area was quickly sealed off. Again, although a dozen storefronts were smashed, there was no looting, and no fatalities except the one that had touched off the trouble.

The Mayor's obvious bravery in the midst of very real danger moved many people. To his wife, a retiring, Atlanta-born patrician who takes no part in public affairs, these were quiet hours of desperation. To his friends, there was genuine concern that he was taking unnecessary risks.

But the bitter segregationist enemies, who have hated him all along, were not touched. A white butcher told an Allen friend: "I see your Mayor's chillun are getting out of hand. I hope they kill that bastard one of these nights." A huge number of telegrams and letters poured into City Hall commending the Mayor, but some reviled him as the cause of the trouble. One said now he could enjoy being "amongst your black buddies."

Allen believes he did what he had to. "I didn't know anything to do but go to it," he said. "Any elected official who had taken the position I had as a champion of the civil rights crusade—and I think I have been that—has been severely criticized by many white people. I would have been branded as willing to do one thing about civil rights but unwilling to take a stand in moments of crisis. This was the other side of the civil rights struggle."

There was another aspect, too. "Every Southern police force is looked on by many Negroes as a head-knocking, billy-swinging operation," he said. "I wanted to be certain that there was restraint by the police force. Any group of men has a breaking point. But I wanted top elected officials to be there in defense of the police, too."

Why had it all happened? Allen blamed Snick, whose members had been on hand to arouse tempers on both scenes of trouble, and the "white thug" who had shot the Negro boys. "I think this was the backwash of the civil rights crusade, in which a group of ex–civil rights crusaders were just drunk for power, that's all," he said. "And to tie the present Snick group in with the basis of the civil rights movement is preposterous. The whole idea of the civil rights movement was that under law and order and with the help of the courts, full citizenship should be provided for all American citizens. The move of Stokely Carmichael, Snick's leader, on this and other occasions was to grab an incident and promote it into a riot."

Could it have been prevented? "All these things could have been prevented if we had done all we should have done all along," he said. "It's a question of how far to go back in history in explaining the conditions that exist. Negroes all along have been economically at the bottom of the ladder, and in great numbers almost devoid of education, certainly in the South. If full citizenship had been there all along we wouldn't have had these conditions. . . . I guess considering the hate on the extreme ends of the Negro and white communities—and I emphasize extreme—and the large numbers of transient people moving in, we were lucky to have gotten by as long as we did without this."

Many Negro leaders agreed with him on the immediate cause. The Atlanta Summit Leadership Conference, an organization embracing scores of Negro organizations and most of the city's top Negro leadership, later commended the police department for its effectiveness and restraint. Snick was roundly condemned by a number of Negro leaders, including others of the militant leadership. John Hood, a Negro state legislator representing one of the troubled areas, said of Snick's sound-truck harangue the first night: "I think the whole thing could have been avoided if the truck hadn't come in here."

But the city's shortcomings in coping with the most deep-running ailments of the slums were strongly denounced, too. The Atlanta Council on Human Relations said: "No one group, including Snick, can be held responsible for the disturbances in Atlanta

. . . the basic responsibility lies with Atlanta's lack of concern over miserable conditions in the slum areas." A minister of a downtown white church which has involved itself in the problem said: "One of the problems is that the Mayor and City Council don't know or understand this [slum] community."

Allen, who is inclined to consider criticism of Atlanta criticism of him, smarts under words such as these, especially when people note that the city built its status-symbol stadium in the area of some of its worst slums. Allen feels Atlanta has moved rapidly on its slums in the past several years and that, given the burden of a century of callousness and limited public funds now, his administration has made notable progress. "It's amazing how much we've done in those areas," he said. "Does anybody realize what Atlanta would be like if Negroes, 44 per cent of its people, had been living in one ghetto? How would it have been then? We've been working like hell to improve these conditions."

He cites urban renewal projects that have cleared big areas that formerly were slums; a map of these does suggest the magnitude of the substandard ghetto that once was. But much of Atlanta's urban renewal clearance has been for commercial projects and public facilities, such as the new stadium and convention hall–auditorium, rather than for low-cost housing. As in many other cities, urban renewal has cleared slums but often has only sent the displaced poor into other, more crowded slums. Physical improvement is apparent in Atlanta, but human betterment is less obvious, and this is the nut of the problem that Mayor Allen, perhaps with mayors all over the country, is now coming to.

His reputation as a get-things-done man now is put to the test by the slums, and they seem to be his greatest exasperation. He lectures his fellow businessmen about living with blinders. "They need to quit riding the same streets, associating with the same groups of people and enjoying the same personal advantages, and get out on the side streets and back roads of the city," he says. "Nobody wants to do business with the poor, even our great civic associations. Anybody who thinks you can't save most of those people does not have the spirit that made this country great."

Atlanta has a sizable Negro middle class, but many members

of it appear to be subject to the same criticism Mayor Allen makes of his prosperous white friends: they have no contact with the slums and are unfamiliar with the frustrations, pressures and turbulence there. Although residential segregation still is prevalent in Atlanta, prosperous Negroes are as far from the ugly realities of slum life as are middle-class whites.

Allen often is exasperated with his own officials in City Hall, too. Last spring, he gathered nine department heads and took them on a tour of the slums. "I just want you to see some of the things that have added up to four and a half years of frustration for me," he said. In one street, he pointed to two dead dogs. Nearby he noted a porch that had collapsed. Moving along the street rapidly with the others in tow, he pointed to trash in vacant lots, abandoned cars left beside the streets and houses that should not be occupied, fussing alternately at the sanitation chief, construction chief, building inspector and the others. He has since led other tours, and occasionally has brandished a personal check with the warning that if a department head could not find money to do a particular job he would personally pay for it—and then embarrass some officials with the canceled check.

Last summer the Mayor began a concentrated program of city services in four slum areas. Some of the results are impressive. A visitor to one slum commented to a resident that in a 10-minute period a street sweeper and a street-washing machine had gone by. "They come all the time," the Negro resident said. "Before this summer we hardly ever saw one."

Allen himself is cognizant of this. "It's worth something just to expose city vehicles and show people we are working for them," he said. "The tax dollars which are supposed to be spent equally for citizens have been used almost exclusively for the benefit of the white man. We have got to catch up in areas we have neglected for 100 years. I think that in American cities in general the Negro areas have been slighted on services."

Allen is candid and emphatic about where he expects help to come from. He believes the states have abandoned the cities to the Federal Government, and Washington has come to their aid with good programs and no strings except logical ones of economy and efficiency attached. He knew this, he says, after two years in office.

"I suddenly realized that although I had a fine personal relationship with our Governor, there had not been a single state program sent across my desk that would help our city with its worst problems, and I was daily receiving from the Federal Government programs that would help us. Tell me where there are any programs of vision, of real planning, and the funds to back them up, from state government!" State governments have abdicated most of their responsibilities, with the notable exception of education and highway building, he says. He expects them to recover in time, but he thinks cities now must look to Washington.

This year Allen persuaded a local private foundation to pay for a study of all Federal programs that might benefit Atlanta, with an analysis of what aid is being overlooked and how it can be obtained. Then he added to his office a director of government liaison who works primarily on Federal programs. Atlanta has been effective at tapping these sources of aid. "The only reason Atlanta has been able to keep from being swallowed up by the great forces of social change has been . . . a positive and expeditious program of Federal assistance by the United States Government," he argues. "And what is called 'Federal encroachment' has been the 'Federal salvation' of Atlanta."

Those words clash sharply with the political music coming most often these days from a region where Barry Goldwater ran strongest in 1964 and where further reaction seems to be the theme for 1966. A Southern politician who bears down hard on problems of Negro poverty and slum life, denounces the "indifference" of the states, renounces the South's anti-Federal political refrain, and speaks of a "Federal salvation" for a Southern city—obviously such a man is cut from different cloth.

Personal difference does not, of course, entirely explain Allen's stance. The 44 per cent Negro population in Atlanta not only gives the city serious poverty problems, but also gives Atlanta politicians, through heavy Negro voting, some freedom to move toward solutions.

"The Negro vote in Atlanta is basically an anti-status-quo vote," Allen himself says. "It helps to counter-balance the stand-still influences. The strongest local influences, I think in every city, are generally negative, against change." But it is Federal action that Allen seems to regard as the absolutely essential antidote to municipal paralysis. "About the only way you can bring change is to get across the idea Uncle Sam is paying for it."

That is from the perspective of one whose power is derived in substantial part from "selling" his former business compatriots. The office Allen holds is, on paper, one of little power. The city's department heads have as their bosses not the Mayor but the Board of Aldermen and its respective committee chairmen. Nor does the Mayor have a substantial political organization, except on Election Day. There is no substantial patronage distribution to reward the faithful, and thus no machine. The at-large election of aldermen and school board members militates against the evolution of ward bosses. And, because all officials are chosen in "nonpartisan" elections, party organization is virtually irrelevant to city affairs. All of this leaves the Mayor as little more than a kind of master of personal influence.

For more than 23 years Allen's predecessor, William B. Hartsfield, held power because he had the support of business and financial interests, racially moderate white middle-class sections of the city, and Negroes. Hartsfield was widely known for his strong leadership in Atlanta and his policies of racial moderation. When he decided in 1961 not to run again, Allen moved in as the leader of this same alliance, and his power has been derived from the same sources as Hartsfield's. He has great influence over the Board of Aldermen because it, too, is largely responsive to these forces.

Negro votes have made the difference: on a number of occasions Atlanta's moderate leadership has failed to win half the white votes. Allen argues that in his first race for Mayor he did receive more than half the votes, but other observers doubt that. In 1965, on the heels of his victory in bringing major league sports to Atlanta, he was re-elected by a landslide vote of about 70 per cent; but a closer analysis revealed that even then he had won only 51 per cent of the white votes. "Atlanta has always been on the verge of being Birmingham," a Negro leader says. "It has been very different from Birmingham, but without Negro votes it wouldn't have been."

These votes have made it possible for Allen to take the positions he has taken, which are quite different from those he once took. Those who know him best see the change as sincere and genuine, and not just a calculated response to the complexion of Atlanta's electorate. But the fact is that without the Negro votes the change in public posture would not have come. Almost all Southerners of Allen's generation who now have insight into the sickness of racism and consequently are called "liberal" have had to come to their new positions through deep-running changes in their thinking. Allen explains his change by saying, simply, that he "developed a social conscience late in life."

Allen grew up in Atlanta with the attitudes of most well-bred Southern boys of financially comfortable families. At Georgia Tech, he studied commerce and won the student body presidency. His father, who had dabbled in politics and served as a state Senator, is said to have wanted him to be Governor. After college Ivan, Jr. went into the family business, the Ivan Allen Co., an office-supplies firm, but he had a political interest even then. In 1945, when he returned from Army service, he became executive secretary to Governor Ellis Arnall, whose liberal administration was a bright interruption in an era of racist demagoguery. (Allen supported Arnall in the latter's comeback attempt this year, but the former Governor was buried in an avalanche of segregationist votes Sept. 28.)

In 1957 Allen made a try for Governor. It was characteristically measured and realistic. Armed with a program for advancing Georgia industrially, he traveled the state and made 65 speeches. But he saw that the response, while friendly, was not enthusiastic. He never paid the fee to enter the race formally. Few people then thought that a man from Atlanta had any chance, anyway.

In that almost-race, Allen went through the ritual required of all hopeful Southern politicians in 1957. He said he was a segregationist, and he talked, at least minimally, about "preserving our Southern way of life," which meant white supremacy. In looking toward a campaign in the midst of the racist tempers that had flared in the wake of the 1954 Supreme Court school decision, he said school segregation should be preserved.

Earlier, he had taken another position, privately, of the kind many segregationists were taking publicly in those days. He wrote segregationist Governor Marvin Griffin, suggesting that the state might finance the departure of Negroes who would leave Georgia. That letter suddenly emerged in 1961 when Allen was running for Mayor. Allen's friends heard his enemies were going to make it public, and there was momentary panic because it seemed clear Allen had to have Negro votes to win. A senior Negro political leader was called in and handed a copy of the letter. He slowly read it and then laughed. "Mr. Allen," he said, "don't worry. We Negroes don't like anybody better than a reconstructed Southern white man." The letter did not become an issue after all; but Allen had found it was, indeed, possible for a Southern politician to change.

He is not notably an introspective man. But he is tormented at times by the obstinacy and unconscious racism of many of his peers. His close associates say that as he frets over what to do about Atlanta's slums he is concerned that many of his city's more comfortable people are caught in the backlash of the civil rights movement. Many seem to be digging in against Federal solutions, Negro leadership and progressive white leadership. One dramatic sign of this was Maddox's startling victory over Arnall for the Democratic nomination for Governor; both Maddox and his opponent, a conservative Republican, Congressman Howard (Bo) Callaway, have exploited the backlash.

Allen is fearful of what the political trend of 1966 means for a city which must meet the ugly problem of the slums. "A terrible reaction has set in," he said. "For 30-odd years this country has been making progress. We may have to have another economic purge, a real depression, before people come to their senses. A whole generation has forgotten there is anything but rising prosperity, and what poverty means. A great many politicians are taking advantage of the convenience of racism."

When the Southern Negro Moves North

by Robert Coles

SINCE THIS CENTURY began, and particularly in the last three decades, millions of Negroes have abandoned the rural South to go
North. Voteless, only recently declared "free," incredibly poor and
heavily illiterate, they were nevertheless hopeful enough to risk a
long trip into strange and not always friendly territory.

Had Northern cities received hundreds of thousands of immigrants from Europe in the past few decades no doubt all sorts of
emergency provisions would have been made to help settle the
newcomers, make them welcome, provide food, clothing and
shelter for them, and enable them to find work. Southern Negroes
obtained no such courtesy, and what recognition they did get was
calculated to remind them that white Americans may fight among
themselves but in the clutch know how to stand together as a race.
Called "in-migrants" rather than immigrants, the newcomers were
quickly made to know their "place."

Still, for a few years it had all seemed clearcut: America was
divided into the oppressive South and the promising North, a "land
of freedom," or a place "up there where it's better," as I've heard
rural Negroes from the Mississippi Delta put it. When the civil-

rights struggle of the early nineteen-sixties came along, that seemed to offer even more hope. Whites flocked South to help change things faster, and in 1964 I heard this from a Negro in Alabama:

"I wish I had left here a long time ago. When my brother went up to Chicago I told him he was a fool for going there, because it's the same all over, a little better here or there, but not really, only the frills. Now, I figure I was wrong. These whites keep coming down here, and I guess they must like us; and if they do, then it must be better up there, where they live all the time."

He never did leave Alabama; and now he has little reason to envy his brother up North, though he lets you know how mean and hard life is for him. Recently he told me: "We went up there, a lot of us colored people like my brother and his family, and it was the way I first said it was, it was a hoax if you ask me. It's as if you've been cheated—you know, led down the wrong road.

"Now my brother says *I'm* the one who is lucky. I live poorer down here, but up there they don't live at all. They have more money than we can get down here, but they're packed tight into the buildings and they can't do anything, not even dream of going North, the way I do when it gets rough. It's bad, real bad; and they hate it."

Apparently they do—hate and resent the Northern sanctuary that has turned out to be little more than a new and different kind of hell. In June of this year, as riots broke out yet again in one Northern city after another, an interesting and carefully done report from Brandeis University's new Center for the Study of Violence offered evidence that "a high proportion of Southern-born Negroes living in the ghetto increases the possibility that a city will have a riot"—particularly when they feel themselves aggrieved, insulted, put upon and in general reminded of the "old days." My own work with individual families in a Boston ghetto confirms that finding almost daily—to the point that at times I have wondered not why we have riots regularly each summer but how so much anger and frustration manages to stay under reasonable control most of the time, week after week.

One family I have come to know rather well after three years of visiting can be called the Carrolls. They now live in the very center of a Boston slum, in a building that has been condemned again and again for its rats, its faulty plumbing and heating systems, its poorly lighted halls, its garbage-strewn yard that takes up the slack when two—exactly two!—cans become filled with the refuse of 10 families. The Carrolls have lived in that building for five years now, ever since they came North from Marengo County, Alabama.

Why did they leave? What has happened to them since they came to Boston? Why did two young men in the family take part in a serious riot that took place in Boston early this summer? I ask these questions not to "answer" them with all sorts of sociological and psychiatric "explanations" and "conclusions," eagerly awaited by a public that wants things simplified and generalized. The obvious "answers" are that the Carrolls left to improve their lot; they eventually became disenchanted in Boston because they remained poor, still put down and looked down upon by the white man; and they rioted because they are sick and tired of losing, of wanting, of traveling, of searching, of being pushed aside and scorned.

All that is true, yet the whole truth is more complicated and I fear both more ambiguous and more horrible.

Mrs. Carroll, for instance, never wanted to leave Alabama. She is 40, the mother of eight children, two of them in their early 20's: "I was born down there, and I wanted to die down there. I never could picture us going up to a place like Chicago, or here in Boston. There would be the people you knew and grew up with, and suddenly they'd be gone, and you'd hear they were up in Detroit making automobiles or something; but my Daddy had a good deal going with 'the man.' He would work in the field, like everyone else, and he could pick his cotton faster than anyone in the county, people would say; but he used to take care of the missus, too. He did errands for her, and if they wanted someone around, real fancy-like, to open the door and take their coats and things like that—well, Daddy would do it. When I was a little girl I heard someone say to my mother that my Daddy was a 'house-nigger' who was sent to spy out there in the field, and that was why he was there, to make sure the others did their work.

"Well, I know that wasn't so. Poor Daddy didn't get a cent

more for going up there to the House, just some of the food they had left over, and it wasn't fixed the way we like it, I can remember that. But when they started getting the machines in, and telling the colored people, one after the other, that they'd have to be getting off the land, then we figured we had it pretty good, because 'the man' came over and said we could stay—'until forever and a day' were his words.

"And that's how I thought it would be. And a lot of other colored people down there felt like me, too. We knew we had it real bad down there, but to tell the truth we didn't want to leave, if we could help it. A lot of us had relations up there, and they'd write and tell us it was different—oh, yes, we sure knew that— because you were in the city, and there wasn't the sheriff to beat you up if you waited a second before obeying a white man. And you could get more relief money, and the big city hospitals took you in if you were real bad sick, whether you had a dollar or not.

"But we also heard it was bad up there, worse even. They'd write and say they were glad to be out of the South and up there, but they wished they could get out of where they were, too, and come home. 'Now I ask you,' my mother would say, 'where will they go next? Move to the North, maybe, where there's ice and snow all year long, and where no one hates the poor colored man because there's no one around, period?'

"That's the way I thought, just the way she did—until I got married. I was 15, and I started worrying about feeding my babies. And my husband Fred, he started looking to the future and wondering what we'd be doing 10 years ahead, and if we could even stay alive that long. But we thought we'd try, where we were, like all the people that had before us, right in Marengo County, down there—and we did. We lived through 10 years and more even, and we lost three children that might have lived, but the others did stay alive with us—and you can see I have eight—even if it's hard to know what tomorrow will bring. (Usually, nothing is what it brings!)

"Well, it was five years ago we left, and I'll tell you how it came to be. My sister's husband, he was in the war—the Korean war it was—and hurt there so bad he was on full retirement when he came home. He'd have to go into the V.A. hospital all the time for treatments, and then they would send him up to Washington for a doctor to look him over and maybe operate on him. And his brother was in Boston or nearby I think, and he went to visit him after the doctor said he could go, because there wasn't any more a hospital could do. And when he came home he said Boston wasn't so bad, and we should go see. He said he thought they're better to colored people in Boston than in New York or Chicago, and there were less of us there, and you get polite treatment most of the time.

"We didn't know whether to believe him or not. I wanted to stay and my husband said, no, let's go. He was working on the land alongside my Daddy, and he was helping clean the House, and 'the bossman,' he said my husband could take over when my Daddy would pass on—so no need to worry about work. That was O.K. by me, but not for Fred. He said he wanted to try it up there, and we could go back if we didn't like it.

"So, we agreed to go on trial—for a vacation, I kept telling myself. I'd say it out loud, to make Fred hear, and not forget. We told Daddy we'd be gone a while and he said good-by like it was forever. I said it wasn't—we'd be back. He said, no, we wouldn't. Fred said we'd see. We told them up at the House that we had sick relations to see up there, and they needed our help. I don't know if they believed us or not. They said we could come back if we wanted, and they wouldn't burn our house down for one year— but after that we'd have to stay away. I said we'd be back in a month or so; but I was wrong, as you can see."

She has never returned, though she has sent her children back on various occasions to visit their grandparents and other relatives in Alabama. The children are put on buses, with food and token presents and waved off. I saw a boy and girl go a year ago, right after school was out. For all the world they might have been going back to Ireland or Germany or Italy—to see the homeland their parents had left, yet still kept in mind. "You tell them we may come back yet," I heard Mrs. Carroll say as the bus left. She spoke those words in a quiet voice—as if she were uncertain enough not to shout, but definitely moved to declare something, perhaps only an impossible yearning.

They will stay in Boston, the Carrolls and others like them who have steadily come into Northern cities in recent years. Maybe it is presumptuous of me to be so sure, yet *they* are. "What can we do, go back? I tell my husband I'd *like* to, but we know it's worse there, even than here. Here my husband has to stay away and hide so we can get the welfare check; but down in Alabama they don't give a lot of us a cent, and if you speak back to them, you're a poor insurance risk, I'll tell you."

Mrs. Carroll spends her days taking care of her children. She has no friends at all. Her husband comes and goes. He is not unfaithful to her, but only if he is gone can they qualify for relief. From what I can gather the social worker is particularly sensitive and flexible: "She knows he's around—I can tell—but she don't ask too many questions. She's better than the last one, who kept at me all the time, asking this and asking that, and wanting to know about everything, until I told her she was worse than my four-year-old girl, with her questions. I said, 'Don't you ever get tired of asking?' And she said I was being rude and ungrateful, and I said she should go bother someone else with her asking, and I didn't care if we starved to death. So she called me a lot of names, and I told her I was going down to the Mayor's office and report her. And believe it or not, she got switched. I didn't do anything. All I knew was that a new worker came. I guess I scared the old one, or maybe she just got worried, finally. That's what she needed, to worry herself and not make us worry."

Mr. Carroll cannot keep as busy as his wife. She has eight children to tend. He cannot find work. He is essentially illiterate. He is no loafer, though; he tries. When he first came to Boston he immediately called on relatives, his wife's brother-in-law and a cousin of his own. He came North first, found a three-room apartment near his cousin, put just about everything he had into the first month's rent ($60) and sent for his wife and children, who came by bus. He borrowed everywhere, in Boston and Alabama, to pay for their tickets. He got a job helping his cousin, a janitor's assistant I suppose the "position" could be called.

"It wasn't bad," he recalls. "At least I was doing something, and it wasn't like back home in Marengo County where you worked for nothing and all the time, like you were a pet. (They'd be good to you if they liked you, but if they didn't you might as well be dead.)

"It was old buildings, like a lot of them in Boston, that I had to mind, and I took care of the garbage and tried to keep things clean and if someone had something wrong I reported it and they sent people right over to fix it. But then they sold the buildings, and the new 'bossman'—well, he was a company and had a 'janitor service,' they called it. So I was let off, and my cousin, too, and ever since then it's been hard, real hard—and touch and go. I'll pick me up a job washing dishes and they'll get a dishwasher. I'll try sweeping out the movie theater late at night and in the morning, and they'll get a company to come over with machines.

"I joined some group they had, part of the war on poverty, and they wanted to get us in shape, they said. That was last year. They told us to keep clean, and be careful of what we wore and everything like that, you know. I told my wife they could sink me in a tub of lye if they wanted, so long as I could get a job out of it. They had us talk in the right words, and we were supposed to get real good jobs.

"But it never worked out. They told me I needed more education, and being from the South it would take a long time, and they could only help people who were further along than me, so I had to drop out of the program. I had good 'initiative,' they said, but too many strikes against me—out of my past, they said. Well, a lot around my street are like me—and there isn't one of us who can get a good job. They only want our wives, to clean the white man's home and take care of his kids. And my wife has eight of our own. And the city, they only want to give money to the women, and only if the man leaves home, so they can call the woman a 'dependent.'

"So that's how I'm doing—real bad. I sit around and go look

for a job and hide when the welfare lady comes, even the good one.
I play cards. (I've learned since coming up North.) I get me a
beer or two, and when the welfare check comes in I settle with the
bartender. I'm not supposed to do it, but a man has to have something to do, just like his wife and kids, and I don't allow myself
more than two beers a day, and mostly one; and I don't smoke. I
never could. Mostly I just meets my buddies and we try to get out
of the way of our women."

Mrs. Carroll has a lot in her way, apart from her husband. She
is up at 5:30 in response to her infant's crying, and she is the last
one to bed, about 11 o'clock at night: "All day long it's go, go, go.
It's different here, different than down South, because there's so
little room. Three rooms for 10 people. Beds piled up. There's the
rats to keep away and they bite, and they don't give us screens
that work, so it's a picnic the mosquitoes have. I have to worry
about food, where it's coming from. There's always something
short, always. And clothes, they're the worst to find. They cost a
lot and you really need them up here. You have to have shoes for
everyone.

"With me it's just trying to keep us all alive. You don't have
friends up North, you just see a lot of people, but you don't know
them one bit. A lot of the time I wish I was back South, but I
know my kids have it better here—maybe. They can go to the city
hospital if they falls sick, and we see more money here—even on
relief—in a month than Daddy saw all year. You use it up fast,
and you need a lot that you have no money to buy, but at least you
don't starve, and we was near to it, I do believe. And we was
more afraid, that I sure know.

"Up here I feel like I was on the moon, or a strange place
somewhere. I mean I'm still not sure how to go about things. You
don't know the store people and they insult you with their remarks
as bad as they do in Alabama. You don't even get to know your
next-door neighbor too much. Everyone is to himself, and it's only
the kids who meet other people.

"I'm locked in here sunrise to sunset, except that I never see the
sun, like I used to, and I've forgot what it looks like, and the lake
we used to go visit. The only time I get out is to get the food, or

take myself and the kids to the hospital. I never see a tree or hear a chicken or see a bird. The other day I woke up dreaming there were some chickens running through my house, and of course it was the old place, down there.

"The kids would never go back even if I wanted to, which I don't really, I guess. The little ones are already used to it here, and the big ones, they'd be killed down there for the way they talk. The way things are going, they may even get killed up here, I'll tell you. At night, when I have a little time to clean things up I hear them talk to one another in bed, and believe me it's terrible what they pick up on the street. Up here the colored man lets it all out of his system, that's what I believe. They been beating on him and lynching him ever since the beginning, and he goes from South to North and he feels at last he can talk back, the young colored do. I try to tell my kids to be good and watch their behavior, but they don't listen. They're not afraid, like I was. They've gone from Alabama, they say, and I'm still there, they tell me."

The Carroll children are indeed most in touch with Boston—with its aged, crowded schools, its dense and growing ghetto, its nervous, angry police, and its threatening white backlash that may determine who becomes the city's next Mayor. Their mother's life is in the home; if the children are quiet she watches television and cooks. (The living room is a bedroom with a television set; even the kitchen has a bed in it; and then there is the bedroom itself.) The older children, however, ignore their home. They eat and sleep there, but little else. They wander all over their neighborhood, and have no interest in falling back on memories, on nostalgic reveries, to deal with the kind of life Boston offers. Nor do they feel their parents' fear or restraint.

"Why should we?" the oldest one, a man of 22, recently asked me. "Why should we beg and bow and scrape? What did it do for us, ever? The more you 'yes' whitey, the more he kicks you, pushes you, takes things from you and slurs you. That's it. That's it."

His words frighten his mother. She cannot account for them, for what has happened in a few years to him, for what is happening before her eyes every day to her younger children:

"They tell me they're ashamed of us, and they want to tear up the certificates we have that say they were born in Marengo County, Alabama. They say we never should have lied down before the white people and let them walk all over us. I try to explain, but it does no good. Even my seven-year-old boy, he's all mixed up. One minute he tells me he wants to be a policeman and he'd shoot down all the niggers who tried to cause trouble. Imagine talk like that! Then, the next minute, he says he's going to kill a white man one day, he just knows it, and when he does it'll be about time. I scream him down and I hit him sometimes. I've got to. But I don't understand. I don't. We were brought up to live with the white people, because you have to, and now my children want to be away from them, and get rid of them. Maybe you can up here, where they live outside the city and we're inside, but they're still on top, I know that, and no matter what the kids say, that's true."

Her two sons took part in the riots that seized the Boston ghetto this summer. Why? How did they get involved? Their mother cannot answer these questions. To her they were "two quiet boys." They had never taken part in any civil-rights activity in Alabama —as some children and young teen-agers in the region had—nor have they done so since their arrival in Boston. Years ago they were both called "proper" by the Southern schoolteacher who taught them in a two-room, rural school. ("It wasn't the best school, but they're not so good up here either," was Mrs. Carroll's way of making a comparison. "Actually, I think the school build-ings here are twice the age of those we had in Alabama.")

It didn't take long for the "proper" boys to change: "First, they were kind of made dizzy by the street. They'd want to stay inside, or they'd come back from outside full of stories of what they saw; there'd be drunken men, and people on dope, and there'd be a lot of sex, and just a lot of people standing around, and they'd see knives and things. Guns, I guess, too. You know, in the country it's not like that. We have a lot of bad colored people in Alabama, but they're not living all together, with no place to sit or take a walk, and with nothing but the sidewalk to rest on and the police to hide from.

"Well, my kids began to forget about everything they once knew

—just like that! The streets grew on them, and they'd come and tell me all the stories, and then they stopped. That's when I knew they were *really* changed—it was all second nature, and they were all just part of the scenery down there, I guess. So when the riot came, they joined like everyone else."

Her sons don't quite put it as she does. The oldest youth speaks bluntly and sarcastically. He asks me as many questions as he answers: "Why do *you* think we riot? Don't you know? You must by now, or you're pretty slow on the draw, pretty slow. We've had enough. They push you so far, then you can't let it go further. That's it. In Alabama they keep us down with guns. Here they say we're 'free.' But if we try to act free, then they pull their guns, anyway."

I knew him well enough to risk asking him what he meant by "acting free." Well, he meant acting like "whitey." "Look. You're upset by something, so you go raise your voice and get it stopped. We're told we can't. That's what they taught us in Marengo County; be quiet, obey the 'bossman,' and wait until heaven for your kicks. Here they teach you in school about that 'equality' stuff, and Washington and Lincoln and how they freed us, and everyone is the same—American. Then you look around and you see what a lot of lousy lies they peddle to you.

"In the South you couldn't look around much, or they'd take care of you for life—I mean they'd kill you. Well, up here they say they're not going to kill us. Maybe they should. If they killed us, every one of us, they wouldn't have their trouble any more. But if they don't kill us, we're human, we're men, and we'll catch them in their lies, and it's only natural we'll try to get ours. That's what you're supposed to do in America, isn't it—get yours?"

That is that. I hear it again and again from him when I stupidly try to ask—once again—what angers him, and how he became involved in the rampant violence that destroyed so much of his own neighborhood: "First of all, it's not *our* place. We came there, and they soak us for rent. Whitey owns the place. It's *his* place. And besides, we're trying to get ours, like you have yours. We hear a fight and, man, we rush to the scene. We figure, this is our chance to do something. Sometimes I see the cops go by, and I wish I was them, I wouldn't mind the uniform and the car with the siren and all that. But I know the cops are here to keep their eyes on us, and they won't do a thing for us but shoot us."

Like his younger brother, he can identify for a moment with the police, the armed white man, the only white man he really knows today. I've even heard him echo his parents' sentiments—"maybe it's better down South." But he knows it "really" isn't better in Alabama, and he knows he can never be a white policeman or, in view of his "educational background," a Negro one.

When I ask him what he'd like to be and do, I hear this: "Maybe a pilot, or a president of something, or an official of some kind. But, no kidding, something even half good, even half good; something that I could hold in my hands and know it'll stay there, like anyone else's job."

Good Gracious! Living in the Decibel Arms

by Mary Anne Guitar

HAD ANY New York apartment dweller been listening recently, he would have realized that a new knight-errant was riding to his rescue. Commissioner Harold Birns of the city's Department of Buildings told contractors and builders that he intends to eliminate, or at least control apartment house noise by instituting and enforcing a new building code. If that New Yorker had wanted to let his neighbors in on the good news, all he had to do was stand in the middle of his luxury living room at 2 o'clock some morning and announce in a voice barely louder than a whisper: "Commissioner Birns is going to save us." The words would have flooded the entire building, echoing and reechoing through air conditioning ducts, air shafts, laundry chutes and even through the walls, and shaking just about everybody out of bed.

"The authors of the present code," Commissioner Birns said, "had no concept of the cacophony produced without limit by a disharmonic symphony of radios, television, hi-fi sets, washing machines, air conditioners, fans, laundromats and dishwashers which now thoroughly inundate our apartment houses. They could not contemplate the sounds of surging waters in hidden bathrooms

From the *New York Times Magazine,* December 1, 1963, copyright © 1963 by The New York Times Company.

heard by persons in hallways or rooms in neighboring apartments, nor did they consider the disruption caused by loud, boisterous or discordant neighbors or the pitter-patter of little feet at 3 o'clock in the morning."

The modern Manhattanite could certainly agree. Things have come to such a pass that a tomato juice company even advises its customers to sing soothingly while pouring so that the plop of juice into the glass doesn't frighten neighbors in the next apartment. Harassed by a constant whirring, whistling, banging, clattering, clanging, crackling, snarling din reverberating through the building, the city dweller today cherishes visions of older, quieter days in soundproof, pre-war buildings.

Were those old buildings really all that quiet? Yes, builders grudgingly admit, but they quickly add in their own defense that they can't afford that kind of construction any more. The older buildings actually contain more "structural mass" than the new ones. Everything in them is thicker—the doors, the walls, the floors.

Builders use less bulk than they used to. By cutting an inch here and there on subflooring, insulation, plaster and other necessities, the builder can reap a sizable bundle of extra footage to redistribute where it pays off—in rentable space. "You can ask, 'What's another two inches; why not put more material between the walls and the floor?' " says a builder, Frederick Rose. "But if you lose one room on a floor, the whole building may become economically unfeasible."

Mr. Rose, an articulate crusader for less noisy apartments, frankly admits that in this competitive age, "I'm just a builder who builds as noisy a building as anybody else." He thinks a good part of the problem comes from overcrowding. "In the old days," he says, "we didn't have these one, two, three-room apartments. A family lived in a five or seven-room apartment and there was space to take care of the sound. Now we have as many as 400 apartments on a half acre."

High ceilings, once the hallmark of Manhattan apartments and still a sign that peace and quiet reign, have all but vanished. In prewar days, a builder would cheerfully put in 10 floors in the same space where today, he will jam 12.

Architect Robert Bien thinks that the new building materials have actually accentuated the noise problem. These new light-weight materials may be just as strong as the old aggregates, but they transmit sound much more readily. "Ninety per cent of the new buildings," says Mr. Bien, "are made of re-inforced concrete. They are monolithic in the sense that the structure is continuous and the sound is more easily transmitted. In the older steel frame buildings, the sound was broken up and isolated. The structure of today's buildings is like a drumhead. You can imagine what happens to it under the impact of high heels."

Even the layout of the apartments abets the noise problem. Long, narrow living rooms are placed side by side, effectively transmitting sound to neighbors; the bigger and wider living rooms of yesteryear were not such useful sounding boards. "The most ingenious architect," says Mr. Rose, "finds it impossible to avoid placing one tenant's kitchen next to another's bedroom, or a bathroom near a living room." Architect Bien adds, "We used to have entrance halls, foyers, galleries. Bathrooms and kitchens were positioned on the outside rim of the apartment. Today, they are inside rooms and you can be walking down a hall and hear somebody's tub filling or the bacon frying."

Actually, the apartment dweller's modern decor is partially to blame for the increased noise, though perhaps not as much as the building itself. In the old high-ceiling era, thick carpets, plump upholstered chairs and sofas, heavy draperies all helped absorb sound. Today, the interior decorator stresses a "slim, spare line," and nobody can claim that oiled walnut or teak soak up noises the way velvet and plush did. Windows are no longer covered; now they are "treated" with shutters, blinds and synthetic fabrics that boom noises back into the room, and ricochet off the plastic plants now in fashion. The whole effect is disastrous.

Disastrous may even be an understatement if one can believe the stories apartment dwellers tell about themselves and their neighbors. A favorite concerns the wife who had a long conversation with her husband one evening, only to find that she was talking to the man next door.

There was the young couple who abandoned the charm of an old Victorian brownstone in Brooklyn Heights for a gleaming modern building in mid-Manhattan. For the first few nights in the new apartment, they were vastly amused and entertained at the arguments of couples in adjoining apartments. "You could hear everything without even putting a glass to the wall. Then we realized they could hear us."

Another young couple recently moved into a sparkling new building on Central Park West. It didn't take them long to discover that the newness was all on the surface; what was beneath this tinseled façade was another matter. The water, which usually ran as a trickle, was a rich, rusty red; the elevator worked sporadically and unreliably; the kitchen sink backed up to such an alarming extent that if they didn't leave the stopper in the drain when they went out, the sink would overflow with the backwash from neighbors' garbage disposals. Worst of all was the noise. They could hear everything above, below and on all sides. Fortunately, the couple above proved compatible so they turned their mutual pipes into a two-way communications system. When one of the women wanted company, she simply went over to the kitchen sink and, bending down, whispered: "Would you like to go shopping?" Back would come the reply: "Meet you downstairs in five minutes."

The woman downstairs, however, proved a recluse of sorts, or merely someone who liked privacy and quiet; she swathed her pipes with cloth bandages in desperation against receiving unwanted messages all day long.

And then there is television, perhaps the worst noise maker of all. By the middle of any evening, the sets in nearly every apartment are glowing, and the sound is scrambled into an indigestible mixture of Dr. Rose Franzblau, Groucho Marx and Cochise. More than one startled lady has been suddenly awakened in the middle of the night with the conviction that William Holden has just walked through her bedroom door, only to find that he's merely appearing on the Late Show three apartments away.

Light switches are a constant harassment for tenants in new apartments. One young career girl in a mammoth "village" on the upper West Side had to stop reading after midnight because the switches sounded like cannons when she turned them off. One night she forgot. "Suddenly it was 3 A.M. and I had three lights to turn out. I wouldn't dare do it because it would wake everybody up." Pulling the sheet over her head, she dozed off and on until dawn, when she could snap off the lights without creating a panic. One of her neighbors has an electrician brother who solved her problem. He installed mercury switches for her. "She's the only one on the floor who can stay up late."

Just how far the noises travel is aptly illustrated by the story of the young bachelor who was anxiously expecting a telephone call. He left his apartment to dash out for a minute and had reached the elevator at the end of the corridor when he heard his phone ring. He raced down the hall, pulled out his keys and was just opening the door when he heard the lady next door answering the phone.

And there is the long-suffering husband who called to his wife from the bathroom one morning, "What time is it honey?" From upstairs came the answer: "Eight-thirty." From downstairs came the answer: "Eight-fifteen." And from down the hall his wife kept calling over and over, "What is it, dear, what did you say?" Dr. Samuel Rosen, an ear specialist, says that studies in Germany revealed that family turmoil and unhappiness increased as noise grew worse, and any number of husbands and wives can so testify.

What can be done to make New York apartments into, as Commissioner Birns desires, "a refuge, a peaceful nook where man can escape the alien contraptions which incessantly seek to attack and destroy his nervous equilibrium?" The Commissioner has turned to the Polytechnic Institute of Brooklyn to study the problem and help prepare the new code which it is hoped will conquer the problem of noise carried through the air—such as voices, music and the like—and noise carried by the structure itself—such as vibrations. Thickening the mass of the walls may prove one answer; more insulation another. Some experts talk about a European solution: when installing the floor, a concrete floor is laid, then a layer of sand is added, then a layer of cork and finally a layer of wood.

Until the new code is drawn up and put into effect, which won't be until the spring of 1965, it's going to be up to the apartment dweller himself to find the answers, maybe with a little help from builders.

Builders may be concerned, but they haven't done much. Many of them live in quiet sylvan spots in Scarsdale and other suburbs, and, weary of jokes about their construction methods, frequently snap: "Couples buy a new car and expect it to fall apart after a year. Why do they expect more of a new building? Anyway, they ought to test out the building before moving in just as they'd test-drive a car."

The picture is staggering: couples walking around Manhattan with sound-testing equipment, taking a decibel count of every apartment. There is, certainly, a simpler way, and some New Yorkers wouldn't think of signing a lease without trying it out. They merely carry a radio along with them, turn it on in the bedroom and then go into the living room and close the door. If they can hear the radio through the walls, they are probably going to hear the neighbors next door, too.

Another infallible test is to go apartment hunting in the evening, when the building is turned on. The sounds that pour into the vacant apartment are pretty good signs of what is going to be lived with.

For those couples already in a building and nearly deafened by the noise, carpeting can help. Some leases now carry in fine print the requirement that all floors be covered by wall-to-wall carpeting, thereby obliging the tenant to provide the soundproofing equivalent of subflooring.

Other solutions range from oiling the neighbor's dishwasher to wearing sneakers around the house. The tenant can invest some real money and hire an acoustical engineer, who might advise soundproofing the walls. This, of course, presents a problem: in new apartments, such a step would reduce the already minimal living space; in the apartments of the affluent, there is liable to be expensive custom-made wallpaper, moldings and door-frames.

Builder Rose and others in the field think soundproofing should be mandatory in all new buildings. It could be offered as an option, he says, where a $200 a month apartment would cost $215 with soundproofing. But he thinks that if the whole building were soundproofed, the tenants would just absorb the extra cost as they have the cost of air-conditioning, dishwashers and other now "standard" accoutrements.

Perhaps the best solution, though, is merely to soundproof oneself. The human ear represents the least amount of area in the room. You could simply stuff pieces of cotton in your ears and hope for the best. Before long you may not even need the cotton. Dr. Rosen believes that "the background noises that assault civilized ears must have some deleterious effect on our hearing." Having created the problem we may have, unwittingly, discovered an antidote to it. We may, in the end, just turn a deaf ear to what's bothering us.

Part 3

TOWARD
THE FUTURE ,
OF CITIES

AMERICANS HAVE weird attitudes toward time. They care little about the past; Henry Adams observed that no other people has ever been so indifferent to its own history. They cannot get absorbed in the present, for they are looking at their watches to be sure they are not late for the next engagement. ("Time is money" was a bit of folk wisdom in the United States long before the Civil War. This phase of the national character was pinned down by Henry James in *The Ambassadors*. Given American conditions, time in fact *was* money.) They do not see the future as an infinite vista. For Americans the magnet lies two hours from now, tomorrow, the next day. Exceptions, partial exceptions, do exist: the top executives of Standard Oil of New Jersey and DuPont ponder the nature of the world in 2000 A.D. and the place in it of their corporations. But they are not typically American.

Jane Addams was able to take the long view. Before the nineteenth century ended she knew that while many immigrants and poor people might need help, they did not want to be saved; they had to be left with the feeling that they had saved themselves. The same perception seems to be animating the rehabilitation of a once degraded district in Philadelphia.

If such projects are to make gains in the foreseeable future, self-help is indispensable, but it will not suffice. Aid from governments and from private organizations will also be needed. For example, many corporations have a policy of transferring executives from one location to another every three or four years. This forced mobility of manpower is not going to help the companies in the long run, and it is cutting the heart out of cities. The same indictment can be made against higher education; a college instructor gets ahead by moving from one school to another—as many as five or six times. If the pertinent arguments in the Introduction to this book are sound, such practices must be pared down.

As to government programs, aspects are explored here by the late President John F. Kennedy, by former Senator Joseph S. Clark, and by the director of the Metropolitan Museum of Art, Thomas P. F. Hoving. Their expositions leave many questions unanswered. Which level of government should finance what? Which should have what kinds of control? How much money should a national government or a state government spend to promote the influx of tourists into a localized area? How much should be spent by the municipality itself? To give one example, Montreal seems more a place in which one could live the good life than any spot I have seen. Women on the downtown streets are extraordinarily attractive—and to some men that matters. Several of the new office buildings, sponsored by banks, are superb. Even though Toronto chauvinists boast of a shopping center called the Colonnade, they prove only that they have not seen Place Ville Marie in Montreal. And how can one describe Parque Mont Royale, at most a ten-minute drive from the center of the city? Montreal also staged in 1967 a splendiferous world's fair. One result of all these charms is a city government with a fiscal crisis.

To such straits have the city planners and "urban renewal" brought us. They cut a swath across the North End of Boston, one of the few ethnic neighborhoods left in any big city. A few blocks away they put up the Government Center, thus increasing the weight of the bureaucracy riding on every citizen. (It used to be said that in Europe every peasant carried a soldier on his back.) And for their own convenience they build expressways from the heart of the city to their homes in the suburbs. All is done for this evening's performance; the dilemmas of later years we will to our descendants.

The few men who have tried to look at the distant future of cities have been free-wheelers. Foremost among them in the United States stand Frank Lloyd Wright and Lewis Mumford. The opinions of each man emerged in writings over a period of forty years or more. We should not try to simplify genius, but let me here associate one proposition with each man.

WRIGHT: Whoever shapes your physical environment—your home, your school, your factory, your office—shapes your life and shapes your character.

MUMFORD: Just as a city must fit into a larger unit, into a region, so a city must consist of semi-autonomous units, of neighborhoods, and they will cluster around churches, around shopping centers, around gymnasiums and parks and schools, and the neighborhood will control these functions for itself.

The House That Jane Addams Built

by Lloyd Lewis

FOR SOME WHIMSICAL reason, the great Chicago Fire in 1871 failed to lick up the two-story brick Hull mansion on Halsted Street. That fact is of especial interest this week when Hull-House is celebrating its fiftieth anniversary.

The Hull mansion was the big house of the neighborhood, even then an anachronism, standing amid squalid, small and flimsy cottages. A pioneer subdivider, Charles H. Hull had built it in 1856, away out on the prairie a mile from State Street, and, for all his realtor's optimism, had expected it to afford him life in the country for a good long time. But immigrants from overseas, thundering in upon the city after the Civil War, had crowded the West Side as by magic, and when the fire broke out, a stone's throw from Hull's house, the region was crammed with rows of tinder-box dwellings that went with a flash and crackle.

After the fire, hurriedly built houses rose again, and the foreign-born came back, bringing with them new thousands of cousins from Europe. Through the neighborhood, as it absorbed the endless flow of immigration, labor agitators grew commoner and

From the *New York Times Magazine,* May 19, 1940, copyright © 1940, 1968 by The New York Times Company.

louder as the Seventies passed. Voices of protest rose higher and hoarser as the panic of 1873 smashed down.

To the jobless newcomers were added the thousands of workmen who, two years before, had come from all over the Midlands to help rebuild the burned city. Carpenters and masons, who had then earned $10 a day, now became "tramps" or worked as unskilled "lumber-shovers" in the wholesale yards for 75 cents a day. And when even this wage was threatened with a cut, they struck and paraded under signs, "Bread or Blood."

Up and down past the Hull mansion, where owners had given place to "roomers," went many parades, many shouting or merely muttering groups of the discontented during the decade that followed. Albert R. Parsons, Confederate veteran, union organizer, eloquent stump speaker for workingmen's rights, went past, heading in 1877 for the "Black Road," that somber near-by cinder path to the huge McCormick reaper works where strikers were demanding the eight-hour day and where police, militia and strikers were splashing blood. Railroad workers were striking, too, and coming home to their shacks, around the Hull mansion, at night with bandaged heads. Over along the lake to the east and south, there were rich folk, the old Yankee families, leaving town in terror.

Eight years later blood was splashing again on the "Black Road" and again laboring men, striking against wage cuts in another national panic, were shooting and rioting, or listening to Parsons orate under flags of red and black. And the tenants of the faded Hull mansion could have sat on the big front porch and heard the dynamite bomb go off the night it exploded in Haymarket Square, ripping the life out of seven policemen and nobody ever knew how many spectators at the workers' mass meeting.

The old house had become part saloon, part furniture storage warehouse and part cheap tenement four years later when a 29-year-old woman named Jane Addams walked past it, came back, turned in, examined it, and rented it because it was just the place she wanted.

What she wanted was a house here in the eternal storm center of Chicago's labor world, here in the region where "dynamite," actual and spiritual, seemed to be forever stored. Cultured, college-bred, Midland born and reared, by no means poor, a "career girl," Jane Addams was just back from England, where on a tour she had been stirred by the same socialistic gropings that were agitating young George Bernard Shaw. More concretely, she had been moved by the sight of Toynbee Hall, where, in the midst of London's Whitechapel miseries, Oxford University men were trying to educate the minds and assuage the pains of the wretches who clustered there.

With a friend, Ellen Starr, Miss Addams had decided to establish something like Toynbee Hall in America. They chose Chicago because its slums were wretched, its immigrant problems enormous, and because both of them had been college freshmen at Rockford, Ill., a city near Chicago, and knew Chicago.

They had, in their brief survey of Chicago slums, come to know the Halsted Street section well, and to see that here their experiment should be made. Dirty children crawled up and down rickety stairways and out over the gutters; housewives in strange head-dresses threw slops into the street, which was jagged with broken paving; rank odors came from garbage piles; stables befouled the air, thieves hid in dismal groggeries, and the rest of the city turned its head away.

The native-born had passed from the neighborhood, and the more affluent of the foreign-born, too. The poor, the unskilled, the toilsome and unlettered among the immigrants gravitated here because living was cheap. Even on the edge of the section, where living conditions were somewhat better, there was need for something like Toynbee Hall's educational work.

Chicago had, in a scant half century, grown from a muddy trading post on a marshy slough known as "Stinking Creek" to a roaring commercial city of nearly 1,000,000 inhabitants and would within a few months take second place among American cities.

A full 68 per cent of the inhabitants were foreign-born, while of the remaining 32 per cent a great many were second-generation Irish or Germans. The "restless, often reckless" Yankees who had built the city were now in the minority, but they had the privileges and the power. They owned the banks, the factories, the real estate, the big stores, the utilities, the newspapers; ever since the strikes and bombs of the Seventies and Eighties, the majority of them had lived in distrust if not in terror of the great mass which they employed.

Social and industrial leaders not infrequently told each other that if these "foreign Communists, Socialists and anarchists" were to have their way with these labor unions, "we'll all be hanged." The word "Communist" had had a vogue after the French Commune sensation in the early Seventies, but was rapidly giving way in 1889 to the more popular "Socialist."

A Democrat whose father had been a friend of Abraham Lincoln on the Illinois prairie, Jane Addams began with much more concern over low wages paid workers than over what political party was responsible for them. Her words and acts, across her life, make it clear that she thought betterment was to come through social rather than political action. That she and her co-workers put pressure upon politicians now and again—pressure that made the solons squirm and scurry—is widely apparent upon the records of reform legislation in the United States, but the chief characteristic of their work was social adjustment of the alien poor to American life.

When Jane Addams rented the old Hull mansion the unskilled laborers around Halsted and Taylor Streets were earning from $9 to $12 a week, and little children were coming home with pennies earned at the rate of 4 cents an hour in sweatshop toil.

Miss Addams was mad about this, but not boiling—she was too tolerant to boil even when hammering the hardest at the "oppressors" of her people—as on September 14, 1889, she and Miss Starr moved into the Hull mansion, and, with one housekeeper to help with the domestic duties, opened the first "social settlement house" in America, though the term wasn't applied to the venture for some years to come. Their aim, they said in the incorporation papers of Hull-House, was "to provide a center for a higher social life; to institute and maintain educational and philanthropic enterprises, and to investigate and improve the conditions in the industrial districts of Chicago."

Aristocratic friends, members of the old Yankee ruling class of the city, had advised Jane Addams not to make this plunge into the slums. They said it would make her inacceptable in the homes of the "best people." And as she and Hull-House fought their way down through the next twoscore years, there was always to be heard a protest—sometimes a blast, sometimes a growl—about their perilous fostering of radicalism. That certain reactionaries always wanted "to run Jane Addams out of town" was true from 1889 until her death in 1935.

But she remained socially eligible and able to hobnob with the city's rich; she went everywhere in those pioneering days, enlisting money and influence. And she could talk well, as William Jennings Bryan had discovered in 1881 when, representing Illinois College in a debate, he measured words with a Miss Addams representing Rockford College.

Miss Starr also was eligible in the fashionable sector, which had by the Eighteen Nineties shifted from the West to the South Side. Another Hull-House resident, Mary Rozet Smith, daughter of the oldest local aristocracy, went about sweetly dragooning donations from the groaning industrialists.

Often in subsequent years wealthy donors would writhe when Mrs. Florence Kelley, one of Miss Addams' first recruits, went campaigning against sweatshops, or when she clubbed legislators into passing a child-labor law, or when Miss Addams disturbed the even tenor of life by agitating for garbage removal to save children's lives. Such things were all very well and should come in time, but Hull-House moved too fast.

The warfare was bitter. When Governor Altgeld died in 1902 nobody but Clarence Darrow and Jane Addams spoke at his little funeral. Altgeld had moved all the power of the Governor's office to help Miss Addams and Mrs. Kelley in their fight to get humane laws for the protection of women and children in factories and sweatshops, and had stood with them for that radical proposal, the eight-hour day.

Since the turn of the century the fame of Hull-House has become world-wide. The strenuous T. R., with his zeal for reform, poured hosannas upon Miss Addams and the whole social settlement movement, which by that time had become important in most of the large American cities. A whole school of settlement houses had grown up in imitation of Hull-House, and the University of Chicago had, by its marked friendship, given Miss Addams' idea high academic and scientific approval.

Some of the university's most celebrated professors gave time to the settlement's citizenship, poetry and English-language classes; for early Hull-House had arranged to give quarters to a certain number of "residents," persons who paid their own expenses and gave their leisure time to the manifold projects of the institution.

The influence of Hull-House upon many of its residents of the past fifty years has been highly apparent. It is to be seen in the social-mindedness of Harold Ickes, John Dewey, Professor Robert Morss Lovett, Frances Perkins, Walter S. Gifford, Gerard Swope, W. L. Mackenzie King, Prime Minister of Canada; Julia Lathrop, social settlement authority; Sidney Hillman, union-labor leader; Harriet Monroe, the poet; Francis Hackett, the novelist; William L. McInery, the editor; Stuart Chase, writer on economics; Alice Hamilton, the scientist of the Harvard Medical School; and Ramsay MacDonald, British statesman, not to mention less-famous educators who dot American colleges and high schools.

The days of the settlement's unorthodoxy are now long gone. Chicago hears about the Hull-House Theatre and its amateur dramatics now more than about Hull-House radicalism. Under Miss Charlotte Carr, who took the directorship in 1937, the settlement goes its busy course, teaching a myriad of things to a myriad of persons, and escaping criticism from the conservative forces of the city.

In its first year Hull-House counted 50,000 persons entering its doors, most of them curious at first, then gradually gaining confidence. Last year over 320,000 persons were served, and more than 30,000 visitors were counted. Now it is estimated that an average of 1,500 persons enter Hull-House daily.

First to arrive on a typical day are the lusty-voiced Negro girls training for household service under a WPA domestic science project. To the rolling tunes of "Wagon Wheels" or "America the Beautiful," they are wielding their mops and brooms by 8 o'clock, wiping away the dust of yesterday's myriad of footprints.

Close on their heels come the white mothers, bringing their babies for a morning's play in the pre-school nursery maintained by the Mary Crane League, or to be examined in the health service clinics which the league maintains at Hull-House.

While these groups assemble, a constant stream of people flows past the information desk, where a trained worker sits all day answering questions and endeavoring to help. First come men from the neighborhood's several flop houses, asking suggestions as to how to spend their time until the shelters take them in again.

Other neighbors come to ask about the labor laws, the relief laws and the tenement laws, about personal problems, how to find a missing son, how to get a divorce, what to do about a fire escape that won't work, why the milkman did not deliver milk this morning, or piteously how to make arrangements to bury a child.

Others in trouble call on the telephone. Upstairs in her office Miss Carr and her secretary take care of still another stream of people.

By mid-morning at least one group of tourists has come to Hull-House and must be shown through the settlement, for it has often been said that, after the stockyards, Hull-House is a Chicago visitor's first stopping place.

At 1 o'clock the library opens, and older boys and girls without jobs come in to spend the afternoon with books. Adult classes in art begin, too, at 1 o'clock, and the workers' education classes get underway.

From Monday through Friday this department has an average of ten classes every day, the first at 9 o'clock in the morning; during the evening hours several meet simultaneously. A typical day's schedule includes four classes in English and citizenship, two camera clubs, a class in lip reading, another in creative writing, one in speech improvement, another in beginning economics, and a discussion of current events.

Hull-House really becomes a beehive of activity after school hours. From 3 o'clock until 10:30 in the evening there is hardly a nook or corner which is not occupied by a class or a committee. Boys and girls pour into the game rooms, the gymnasium and the clubrooms, the music-lesson rooms, the art department, the printing shop, where they publish their own newspaper, the *Hull-House Star*.

In the afternoons junior clubs share the settlement's clubrooms with mothers' groups. One of these is the Stop-Light Mothers' Club, so named because it was organized to campaign for a stop-light at one of the neighborhood's busy intersections, in order that children could come to the settlement by themselves. They obtained the stop-light many months ago, but they have found other things to campaign for, so they have kept their organization alive.

Theatricals attract both children and adults to Hull-House for nightly rehearsals. Just now the major activity of the older group is the creation of "Halsted Street—1940," a living newspaper of community life.

Hull-House, amid its new and manifold activities, is still hammering away upon its old subject of sanitation, with committees of neighbors helping to spread the gospel. The awful slums are still there, but they are not so awful as they once were, and pressure from the United States Government is helping.

One reason why the world hears less of Hull-House today than it did twenty or forty years ago is that the Federal power has now taken over, on a national scale, the social betterment campaign. But Hull-House is still there, just as it was when its flag was the only one in the dawn's early light.

An Antibiotic for the Slum

by Mary Roche

PHILADELPHIA

IF YOU BOARD a northbound trolley at Independence Square, fifteen minutes of swaying and jerking and a few more minutes' walk will bring you to the corner of Eighth Street and Fairmount Avenue. There is not much there to charm a tourist. It is as drab as a hundred corners in Southwest Chicago, South Boston or the eastern bulge of Manhattan Island. But you can hardly miss the big white sign on the side of the corner building.

"LIVE IN PHILA'S FIRST REDEVELOPED NEIGHBORHOOD," says the red-letter headline, and reading on you come to "Work is your down payment."

That announcement, and the project it describes, is the Philadelphia Quakers' answer to a problem that is haunting city officials all over the United States—how to stop a slum. Slums are growing faster in most cities than new housing can overtake them, so that, compared to the staggering job to be done, the size of the Quaker project is minute. But, like William Penn's "Holy Experiment," it is demonstrating a new idea—one that might be applied on a

From the *New York Times Magazine,* October 25, 1953, copyright © 1953 by The New York Times Company.

larger scale to the rehabilitation of blighted neighborhoods anywhere in the country.

The Quaker testing ground is one square block. One hundred years ago about twenty-five well-to-do families lived there in fine brick houses with handsome marble doorways and spacious, high-ceilinged interiors. Just five years ago it was peopled by 114 families living in squalor. Today the block is cleaned up. Half the houses have been converted into clean, airy, cooperative apartments, and construction on the other half will soon begin. Already twenty families have moved in.

The first fifty-two apartments called for down payments of $700 to $1,200, but only two families could produce that much in cash. The rest are working it off in sweat and sore muscles. They have joined the construction crew and are putting in 800 to 1,000 hours of spare-time labor in return for a stake in their own homes. In forty years they or their children will own the property.

Work on the houses started only sixteen months ago. But it had taken the Quakers years of patient negotiating before they could get going. Their prompting spirit was Francis Bosworth, executive director of the Friends Neighborhood Guild, a settlement house, and this year's recipient of the Philadelphia award for outstanding civic service. Ten years ago, when Mr. Bosworth took over direction of the settlement house, he made a realistic protest: Why go on struggling to keep neighborhood youth out of jail when we ignore the primary evil—their wretched housing? The Guild board saw his point, but effective attack called for civic authority and working capital.

Meanwhile, a national Quaker organization, the American Friends Service Committee, had been guiding a self-help home-building project among fifty unemployed miners in Western Pennsylvania and thought of trying a similar experiment with urban housing. In 1947 the committee approved a proposal from the Neighborhood Guild, and the two agencies joined forces.

They enlisted the cooperation of the City Planning Commission and the Philadelphia Redevelopment Authority and applied for approval of the Federal Housing Administration. But the self-help

and cooperative features of their plan were posers for F. H. A.
The Quakers were also determined the housing should be interracial, though that might make it seem undesirable to some Negroes as well as to some whites.

After three years of conferences and waiting, the F. H. A.
agreement was signed. It took just twenty-eight Philadelphia
lawyers to do it.

One of the biggest snags had been the fact that F. H. A. does
not insure a cooperative until it has signed up members. Yet all
the Quakers had to show prospective self-helpers was a dilapidated
slum and a set of blueprints. Some of the neighborhood's less edu-
cated residents were convinced the whole project was a skin game:
"Whoever heard of working 800 hours and not getting paid a
cent for it?"

But those with imagination and faith signed up and went to
work with crowbars and hammers anyway. They carted away 450
double truckloads of debris. When they had completed the demolition schedule in one house, the contractor's men moved in and
the self-helpers moved on to the next. As prescribed by city code,
all major structural work, as well as plumbing, wiring and plaster-
ing must be performed by skilled workmen. When their jobs are
done (as they now are in nine houses, comprising about forty-five
apartments), the self-helpers come back and finish up. The self-
helpers' work amounts to 10 per cent of the whole job.

They sand and refinish the century-old floors (most of which
were still sound even after decades of abuse). They lay asphalt
tile, scrape the paint from old woodwork, paint the walls and
ceilings. A workshop has been set up, where they are building all
the kitchen cabinets. Outdoors, men are doing miscellaneous
masonry work, pouring cement and laying concrete for steps and
walks in the large center court, which will be landscaped to serve
as a recreation area and tots' play yard.

The sight of people doing so much work around their own
homes is hardly unusual today, with householders all over the
country going in vigorously for do-it-yourself improvements. But
most people who do their own remodeling already own the houses

they are fixing up, or at least a substantial equity in them. This group is doing the work first, in order to earn the equity. Their work is, as the sign says, their down payment.

Like any other building crew, the self-helpers do each job according to the contractor's schedule, regardless of progress on their own apartments. Thus some already established in their new quarters are now helping to finish their neighbors' homes.

They are a heterogeneous group—a retired restaurant manager, a young Negro school teacher, laborers, white-collar workers, housewives, all working together, with children all over the place. Only a few had any skills to start with. Most of them had to be taught each new operation, and ordinary safety measures as well. George Gerenbeck, the Quakers' project manager, can remember some grim moments. One girl, on her first day of work, shoveled a pile of trash out the window and hit the F. H. A. inspector on the head with it.

But, little by little, individuals have become adept at particular jobs. One girl, equipped with steel wool and a buffing wheel, became an expert at refinishing doors and now does that job exclusively. Another has developed a knack for laying asphalt tile and takes pride in showing off her work in other people's apartments (her own hasn't been started yet). As a group, their efficiency has just about doubled since they began, Mr. Gerenbeck says.

The biggest problem is time. Everyone has a full-time job except some of the housewives—who may have three or four children to look after. (One mother of five has a full-time job, too.) Sometimes the wives can squeeze in a few self-help hours on weekdays, but the family bread-winners have to work evenings and week-ends. Ten hours a week is what most of them average. Some devoted their summer vacations to the job.

Their "pay," or the credit they earn for an hour's work, is based on the contractor's estimate of the labor cost for the whole job if done by skilled workmen. Thus, if he estimates $5,000 to build all of the kitchen cabinets and it takes the self-helpers 5,000 hours to build them, each one who works on that particular job is credited at the rate of $1 an hour. But if it takes them longer (and inevitably they are slower than skilled workers) the hourly rate drops correspondingly.

No one pretends that a self-help plan is the most efficient way of creating new housing. It is slow. The general contractor, a Quaker himself, and a sincere advocate of self-help, admits that delay, caused while subcontractors waited for the self-help crew to catch up, cost him $4,000 to $5,000.

But the long-term benefits compensate for the lack of speed. Self-help makes home ownership possible for people who have difficulty saving enough for down payments. It promotes good neighbor relations. Working side by side with the family downstairs, Gerenbeck says, has done much to promote interracial understanding and to break down barriers between laborers and white-collar people.

In the Quakers' opinion, a self-help program is the best insurance there is against the ill fate that haunts all redevelopers—the sliding backward of a cleared slum to the old litter and filth. People won't abuse their new quarters if they have a financial stake in the property and have put their own sweat into improving it. Already the visitor can see this. Though construction work is still going on, the courtyard and hallways are neater and cleaner than those in most public housing projects. And private housekeeping in most of the apartments would put to shame the owners of many an expensive modern house.

The new apartments range from one- and two-bedroom units on the first and second floors of the three-story houses to three-bedroom layouts occupying the whole top floor. Monthly payments including heat, utilities and amortization, run from $50 to $85, or about $15 a room, which is no higher than the old slum rentals were with the cost of coal-stove heat added. Originally the upper floors in most of the houses were built on two levels. Hence the new top-floor apartments have a split-level plan that gives them the spacious air of a duplex. Some have as much floor space as a six-room house.

Indeed, more space is almost invariably the first reason given by the cooperators for preferring their new homes to whatever they had before. In the larger apartments the dining area is always part of the kitchen rather than part of the living room. These large dining-kitchens, with two or three big windows and the kitchen facilities confined to one wall, make an attractive kind of family room, while the living room is kept as a show place for company like the "withdrawing rooms" in early American houses.

The architect, Oskar Stonorov, took care to save as much as possible of the pre–Civil War architecture, though he has designed nothing but modern houses for the past twenty years. Chosen by the Quakers as "the most socially minded architect in Philadelphia," he lived up to their hopes by concentrating on economy, practicability and the human needs of the occupants, rather than exhibiting his talents for original design. As a result, many details defy the textbooks.

For instance, a Victorian molding along one wall may stop abruptly at the corner because the section on the adjoining wall was dilapidated and had to be ripped off. No attempt was made to restore purely decorative features, but often materials like wide floor boards and iron railings torn out of one house were salvaged for repairing another. Whenever it was necessary to add something new, however, the choice was always modern. Thus a Victorian roof cornice overhangs a large picture window; a modern steel casement faces a gingerbreaded, over-hanging bay; a modern flush door painted a dazzling red is framed by a stately marble doorway.

The owners like these features. They also like the freedom to choose their own colors. There are as many different schemes as there are apartments—some of them good, all a joy to those who chose them. In most apartments, color has made the kitchen unit so attractive that no one wants to hide it.

The Quakers were not so unrealistic as to suppose that the rehabilitation of one block could change the character of a whole blighted neighborhood. Their contract with the Philadelphia Redevelopment Authority guaranteed that general additional measures would be taken in almost twenty-five blocks surrounding theirs. One of the most important was to persuade the Reading Railroad to speed up its conversion to electric engines and Diesels —a Reading re-fueling station across the street from the Quakers' block had for many years blanketed the whole neighborhood with a pall of smoke. Today one can see blue sky from the newly landscaped corner of Eighth and Brown Streets.

Another block facing the Quakers' site was cleared by the Redevelopment Authority for a lower-middle-income housing project which is now complete and occupied. Three more blocks are being cleared for subsidized public housing. A three-block buffer strip between all these properties and the railroad has been cleared for landscaping as a green belt, and at one end another whole block is being converted by the city into a supervised playground. As a result, things look a good deal different from when architect Stonorov surveyed the site five years ago.

The Quakers have no permanent financial stake in their housing project. But they have spent some $60,000, which they plan to absorb as "the cost of pioneering." It went mostly for overhead, supervisory services and legal fees caused by the fact that there was no precedent for them to follow. They are confident these expenses will not recur when they proceed with three more blocks earmarked for rehabilitation after the first one is finished.

The Quakers' experiment embodies a number of lessons for redevelopers of slum areas in other cities.

It proves that when old houses are structurally sound, it is cheaper, quicker and better to remodel them than to tear them down and put up new ones. At an average cost per apartment of $9,300, including land, the Quakers have created clean, modern dwelling units for considerably less than the cost of new public housing in central urban locations.

It shows that slum clearance as well as new housing can be financed as a cooperative under F. H. A. Section 213, and that such financing can also cover a self-help program. This is the first "213" project in the country to have either of these features.

The Quakers hope it will convince private investors that they can safely put their money into run-down neighborhoods if a sound plan has been devised for rehabilitating them. The 90 per cent long-term mortgage on their cooperative will be taken over by a venerable Philadelphia savings institution that is scarcely known for taking wild-cat risks.

Other cities can also take note of the fact that this slum-clearance program involves no tax exemption. The State of Pennsylvania under its urban redevelopment law covered about one-third of the "land write-down"—that is, the difference between what the Redevelopment Authority had to pay for the slum property and its resale price to the Quakers. The City Council appropriated the rest but expects to get it back eventually in higher taxes and also in savings on the proverbially high cost of city services to slum areas.

Finally, one of the most significant achievements of the Quaker experiment is the change in the racial pattern of the block. Formerly 97 per cent Negro, it is now about one-third Negro, two-thirds white—which is in line with the make-up of the surrounding neighborhood.

The Quakers do not offer their plan as the complete and final answer to slum clearance. It is designed primarily for neighborhoods where the structural condition of old houses is still sound enough for economical remodeling, even though human living conditions have sunk to squalor. (However, the self-help and cooperative features will apply to one new building of nine apartments to be erected on the second half of the Quaker block.) There are still blocks and blocks of slums in Philadelphia and in other cities that must be completely demolished before they can be redeveloped. The Quakers offer their plan as a means for stopping the *spread* of a slum by rehabilitating the "twilight" areas surrounding the hard core of blight. Any such project must be integrated—as the Quakers' was—with a larger plan that will attack the hard core itself. Their contract with the Philadelphia Redevelopment Authority guaranteed that several additional measures would be taken in about twenty-five blocks surrounding theirs.

As practical citizens, the Quakers like to point out the structural, financial and civic merits of their experiment, but they are far more gratified by its human merits. Their aim is to rehabilitate people as well as houses. Helping a man to help himself, they believe, bolsters human dignity, while out-and-out charity more often than not diminishes it.

Francis Bosworth sees the biggest problem in any slum as the continual flight of neighborhood leadership. Settlement workers concentrate on helping neighborhood youth, he points out. But the most talented and enterprising youth move away and rarely want to come back. The self-help housing project has already brought a few back, and it has also attracted new leadership from other sections.

"To clean up a slum," Mr. Bosworth contends, "you have to attack the 'slum spirit,' to rouse it from apathy and despair. We try to stir up people's discontent. If they point to falling plaster, we say: What are you going to do about it? In time, discontent turns into thoughts of action. Then we can help."

He is convinced a housing program is a means as well as an end —"an antibiotic for the slum."

Think Big About Small Parks

by Thomas P. F. Hoving

MORE THAN A century ago the park movement of the United States was born in New York City. Like many progressive movements of the 19th century, it was a blend of moral vision and businesslike foresight. Without a carefully planned profusion of parks and open spaces, warned Frederick Law Olmsted, creator of Central and Prospect Parks, a city "would be devoured by its own ugliness and rapidly experience economic decline."

Five years after Central Park was inaugurated, land values in the vicinity had more than quadrupled. Land values are rising still —along with ugliness. Essentially, we're a noncaring, littering people, monumentally unconcerned with our environment. But despite the dizzying pace of change nowadays—in art, politics, culture—the nature of our parks has remained the same, lifelessly suspended in time like the pyramid of Cheops.

With the vanishing of large open spaces in the heart of the city the time is long overdue for a redefinition of our concept of a park and the role of the Parks Department.

Parks today must serve more diverse community needs because our community is more diverse. They must be used not only as

naturalistic havens of repose and relief from urban congestion—
"lungs," Olmsted called them—but to advance the urgent social
goals of our own day. That means the Parks Department cannot
sit back on its haunches with faceless serenity, parrying questions
and complaints with form letters while the needs of the public are
ignored.

A great deal of New York's available open land now consists of
small parcels, many of them junk piles, garbage heaps and slum
backyards. Nothing helps destroy a community like a stinking lot.
Yet thousands of these plots, owned by the city or privately held,
are in middle-class and slum areas where the need is crucial for
new parks and recreation facilities. These garbage-filled useless
spaces can be cleared, bought or rented for temporary use. Then,
reclaimed as joint ventures by local community groups—block
associations, religious and social organizations—and the Parks Department, the vacant lots can be filled with purpose: to put the
parks where the people are.

The apparently impressive statistics on New York's park land
are misleading. According to the figures, more than 17 per cent of
the city's area—some 37,000 acres—is set aside for parks and
recreation space. But 9,000 of these acres are under water (6,000
consist of polluted Jamaica Bay). Only 14,500 acres—roughly 7
per cent of the city—is park land located in the immediate environment—much less than in San Francisco (14 per cent) or Los
Angeles (11 per cent) and slightly less than in Chicago and
Philadelphia.

More than half our recreation space is peripheral, underutilized
and relatively inaccessible (East River Park, stretching from 15th
Street almost to the Battery, is a beautiful place to see from the
highway, but it is hard to reach without a local guide). And the
rest is unfairly distributed. A study by the Community Council of
Greater New York in 1963 divided the city into 74 defined communities; it showed that only nine of the 74 areas contained over
53 per cent of the total recreation acreage. Furthermore, the
number of playgrounds in an area had little relationship to the
local population. Riverdale and Tremont in the Bronx, for example, each have 12 playgrounds. But Tremont has approximately

25,000 youngsters, three times as many as Riverdale. Outrageous.

Vest-pocket parks, carefully spotted in an over-all plan, can help correct such inequities. Easily accessible in the heart of congested neighborhoods, they can be as large as a block or as small as a lot. Equipped with facilities that meet the community's needs and desires, they can be places for kids to play or the elderly to relax. And as a spur toward the creation of active community groups on which the success of the antipoverty program depends, the small-parks program can help speed the broader social and economic reforms that the war against poverty is all about.

I know of nine residential vest-pocket parks that have been built or are underway now under a variety of sponsors: one in the Bronx, three in East Harlem, three in West Harlem, one in Brooklyn and another at 29th Street and Second Avenue. This last was to be a temporary parking lot on land the Triborough Bridge and Tunnel Authority hopes to use as part of a mid-Manhattan expressway. Now, through the generosity of Robert Moses and the New York Community Trust, it's going to be a temporary park, at least for five years. In addition, William Paley of C.B.S. is demolishing the old Stork Club on 53rd Street off Fifth Avenue for a generous $1-million gift of an elegant plaza that will perpetuate the memory of his father. And in lower Manhattan, at Broadway and Howard Street, the Franklin National Bank is planning a branch office in a landscaped setting, giving office workers and shoppers a better place to rest than the fenders of parked cars.

Beginning this summer, I hope we can start 20 more neighborhood vest-pocket parks in a year-long pilot project to determine the best way to go ahead with a more extensive program. We'll probably make mistakes, but we're going to be flexible, so we'll learn. Assuming all goes well, we plan to step up the pace of building small parks during the next four years. And not one of them will be the mirror-image of another. We've had enough of the "swing, slide and sandbox" stereotype, the black-topped, link-fenced asphalt prison, the standardized architecture that has made the W.P.A. style the longest-lingering art style of the 20th century.

During the period from the thirties to the sixties, Robert Moses was a marvel at acquiring land for parks and developing hundreds of new facilities. Most of the city's park land we owe to him and Mayor Fiorello LaGuardia. But Moses and his successor, Newbold Morris, were slow to react to new trends and novel designs and wary of the small-park concept. Curiously, it was Jacob Riis, in 1897, who originated the notion of vest-pocket parks as secretary of a city Committee on Small Parks. "Any unused corner, triangle, or vacant lot kept off the market by litigation or otherwise may serve this purpose well," the committee declared. "There are such corners and lots to be found around the city, the property sometimes of the municipal corporation, and these could be used to advantage and without expense."

Now it is true, of course, that the revival of the vest-pocket idea was a European postwar phenomenon. Bombed-out building sites in London and Amsterdam, for example, were imaginatively converted into small neighborhood parks. In this country, Karl Linn, now a professor of landscape architecture at Long Island University, originated several vest-pocket parks in Baltimore, Washington, D.C., and Philadelphia. Linn, then at the University of Pennsylvania, persuaded Philadelphia city officials to turn over municipally owned tax-delinquent land for the creation of what he called "neighborhood commons." Adults and teen-agers helped build the playgrounds, using stone, wood and other salvage material from old building sites. The telephone company donated some old poles and huge cable spools.

Some of these experimental projects failed. Organizing a neighborhood, especially one that has been neglected and has neglected itself, is a very tough proposition. But where vest-pocket parks have proved successful, they belie the scorn of those critics who condemn the idea with such words as: Parks under one acre in size will be ridiculous undertakings. They are difficult to design, unfeasible to supervise, impossible to maintain. In short, nothing more than a passing fancy.

Dropped as blockbusters, statements like these land like duds. For though it would be foolish to ignore the obstacles to vest-pocket parks, it is even sillier to exaggerate them.

At the risk of candor (always somewhat perilous for a public official), allow me to raise some realistic problems about small parks and suggest some realistic replies.

Acquisition and Construction

One thousand vest-pocket parks—a Utopian projection—would add only 140 acres to the city's present park acreage, an increase of 0.4 per cent. Two hundred small parks would cover only 28 acres. In relative terms, the cost seems astronomical for a few more green specks on the map. In fact, however, the cost of acquiring and developing 200 parks would be about $7.5-million spread out over the next four years. And measured against the capital budget of the Parks Department—$25-million this year and a total of some $100-million over four years—the outlay would be less than 10 per cent of the entire capital-budget package. Moreover, these estimates do not include financial aid from the Federal and state Governments and private philanthropy, which might be expected to total $2-million or $3-million.

The cost of urban land is normally staggering; a plot of 10,000 square feet can cost $1-million or more. But the parcels we seek in residential areas may have limited commercial value, because of their size or location. We figure we can buy and develop vest-pocket park land at a cost to the city of about $3.50 a square foot. And, of course, the city now owns thousands of plots that can be converted to usefulness for considerably less, since the cost of acquisition would be eliminated. At last count, the Department of Real Estate had 24,455 pieces of unimproved property under its supervision and control. Many parcels consist of land taken over for nonpayment of taxes, or buildings condemned as uninhabitable. Some parcels are being held for possible inclusion into larger plots for a future school or other municipal building. On 119th Street between Park and Lexington Avenues, for example, a large city-owned plot on which seven buildings once stood has remained fenced-in and vacant for 25 years while the city considers whether to build a new police station on the site. And for 25 years the community has been fenced out of a possible park.

Construction costs would be held down in two ways. Where

feasible, the program will use available community labor (exceptional skills are not essential) hired through local anti-poverty agencies, thus providing on-the-job training as a bonus. Construction-union labor could be enlisted as supervisors. Second, since design standards and specifications have not significantly changed in the Parks Department for 30 years, the use of new materials and modern building methods ought to provide whopping savings —to say nothing about the joys of anticipating some creative architecture.

Small parks on prime land in the heart of Manhattan is another story, of course. Shoppers and strollers can bow in humble gratitude to William Paley and Franklin National's bank-in-the-park, but frankly, more oases like these are a matter of pot luck. Hopefully, other generous enterprises like these will share a slice of their profits with the rest of us by endowing parklets; private foundations, too, have an opportunity to "go public" in a bountiful way. For the immediate future, though, more plazas in prize commercial areas is a matter of gentle persuasion, not hard-nosed planning—except in special cases. The 34th Street Armory, for example, is due for demolition, leaving a half-block site. The land cost is $2.3-million and the city should make every effort to spend it and create a park. The opportunity is too rare to pass up.

Maintenance

Preserving vest-pocket parks in decent condition once they are built will be the most serious problem we face. And it will take lots of money—about $2-million a year, with small prospect of outside contributions from government or foundations for this unglamorous purpose. But the need for funds to maintain the small parks—preferably by unemployed members of the neighborhood—is as great as the need for the parks themselves. This will mean that our budget will have to be increased. Considering the extent and value of Parks Department holdings in this town, it is ridiculous that our departmental expense budget is less than 1 per cent of the entire city's expense budget.

The attitude of our city fathers has traditionally been: "Build it, forget it." Building parks gets great press notices, but three months later the parks are a mess. As a result we're light-years behind in adequate maintenance and staffing; we have 400 vacancies right now, but no money to fill them. Unless the situation improves I'm afraid we're going to consider closing down some parks and putting up signs that say: "Sorry, No Staff."

Though the basic need is money, better designed parks will help, too. So will curb cuts on the streets, enabling Parks Department trucks to clean the playgrounds mechanically, and a few mobile, giant vacuum cleaners such as they have in Washington, D. C. To use our available manpower more efficiently, we're trying a new system of maintenance crews who travel as a group from park to park, doing all the repairs at one time instead of piece-meal over a period of months. Sort of a blitzkrieg in reverse.

Ultimately, of course, the maintenance of the vest-pocket parks will only be as good as the community that wanted the park in the first place. We don't intend to stick a playground where nobody asked for it. But we are hopeful we'll get the cooperation born of enlightened self-interest.

Security

Up to a point, more recreational facilities help reduce crime. But dozens of scattered small parks, even hundreds of them, are no panacea for social ills. Crime is a horror in the city. Does that mean we should not develop our remaining open space? Looking at it that way, we'd have to shut down Bryant Park, a favorite playground for drunks and degenerates. No one has seriously suggested that alternative, as no one has suggested closing a school because kids are shaken down in the bathrooms.

For the umpteenth time, let it be said: we need more police, better lighting, additional scooter patrols. On the other hand, an active block association *will* help patrol its own turf. A pleasant park will attract people, and there *is* safety in numbers. And proper supervision will prevent the place from becoming a hang-out for toughs and hop-heads who prey on passers-by.

Recreation Supervisors

Another major new money item. Cost? About $1.5-million a year for some 250 additional people, organized in teams, since the small size of the parks would make a single stationary supervisor impractical. Federal antipoverty funds and foundation grants might help offset the cost, but the city's contribution is overdue anyway. The parks now have about 450 recreation supervisors, roughly the same number they had 20 years ago. This is a thoroughly disgraceful situation.

Red Tape

One of the biggest stumbling blocks to the creation of vest-pocket parks—quite apart from policy objections—has been the frustrating complexity in getting them started. City-owned land cannot be released and used under the existing bureaucracy without the approval of five agencies: Buildings, City Planning, Fire, the Corporation Counsel, and Gas, Water Supply and Electricity. Those aren't all. The Budget Bureau will not approve spending funds without assurance that the life of the park will be longer than five years (though many "temporary" sites, such as 29th Street and Second Avenue, are often in neighborhoods desperately in need of playground space). And actually to obtain the money, the Department of Parks must hand in a complete set of plans and specifications in order to let the job out for bids, a needlessly time-consuming procedure that holds up the acquisition and clearing of land.

A newly created Bureau of Vest-Pocket Parks in the Parks Department will concentrate on cutting through this snarl of red tape. In addition, it will coordinate all efforts, public and private, to set up vest-pocket parks, working closely with the City Planning Commission to make sure that neglected neighborhoods get their fair share of park land and are not passed over just because they don't know how to wave a big political stick. It will also help private groups with the insurance problems raised by the use of volunteer workers on city-owned land, which has been serious enough in the past (with premiums costing anywhere up to $1,000 a year) to scare off some private groups from building vest-pocket parks. If necessary, the Parks Department may have to pay the premiums directly out of its own capital budget if the cost means the difference between having a park and not having one, or between shoring up a community or letting it decay.

Early this year I helped open a vest-pocket park in the Bedford-Stuyvesant section of Brooklyn. Since it was the first such experiment in this congested, rundown area of more than 400,000 people, and one of the first new small parks in the entire city, its short, happy history makes a revealing case study of what can be accomplished.

Bedford-Stuyvesant has 378 vacant lots, many of them city-owned, so filled with decaying refuse and junk that they are no small hazard to health and safety. There are also 346 abandoned buildings, extremely dangerous but very tempting to children, who use them as indoor playgrounds for lack of real recreation space. Add to this depressing inventory more than 60 burned-out tenements that kids also play in.

Having drawn up this catalogue, the Central Brooklyn Coordinating Council—an affiliation of 84 community groups in Bedford-Stuyvesant—decided to do something about it. In November, 1964, more than 500 community representatives attended a conference out of which there came a recommendation to begin a demonstration project showing how vacant lots in residential areas could be converted into sitting areas and "tot-lot" playgrounds.

The city leased three back-to-back vacant lots connecting Quincy Street and Lexington Avenue, between Lewis and Stuyvesant Avenues. With the help of the planning department of Pratt Institute, the project received $10,000 from three philanthropies: the Avalon and New York Foundations and the Rockefeller Brothers Fund. M. Paul Friedberg, a well-known landscape architect, designed the park free. Most of the work was done by neighborhood residents. Five landscape workers, out of work with the end of the normal planting season, cleared the land and helped build the equipment. Neighborhood kids joined in, too, sweeping up, carting off junk and painting part of two colorful abstract murals on facing brick walls that border two sides of the park. Supervising the job were students from Pratt's Community Education Program, headed by Ron Shiffman.

Five weeks after they started, the 10,000 square feet vest-pocket park was finished. A pair of tree houses sprouted on the tops of two sawed-off, sick oak trees. The kids reach the tree house by pole or ladder. For swings there are rubber tires, suspended by chains from leftover lengths of pipe. Foot-square timbers, planted in the ground at different heights, make wonderful stepping stones. Instead of the usual slide and ladder, the slide was built into the side of a platform in the shape of a pyramid with steps; it is safer than a ladder, and a comfortable place for the children to watch, squat and talk. The benches are movable, large slabs of wood on a base, and when adults aren't sitting on them, they become part of the play equipment.

Perhaps because children of the community were involved in the Quincy Street playground from beginning to end, there has been almost no vandalism. The rails on the tree houses have been broken, but that may be because they weren't sturdy enough.

Maintenance has been the biggest problem, as we expected, but nothing at all on the scale that pessimists anticipated. There is no carpet of broken glass, no beer cans or fractured furniture. It's not spotless either—middle-class cleanliness people might object—but what are some scraps of wind-whipped newspapers compared to the filth that preceded the playground?

Quincy Street is not only a success as a vest-pocket park; as a pedestrian walkway connecting two streets it is a link in what is planned as a series of connecting, mid-block open spaces that will make Bedford-Stuyvesant a little more livable at the modest price of $1 a square foot.

Last month Mayor John Lindsay turned the earth for the city's latest vest-pocket park, on 123rd Street between Lexington and Third Avenues, another example of cooperation between an active community group and the Parks Department that I hope will be widely imitated. The project was proposed by the East Harlem Tenants Council. The city demolished several rotting, condemned buildings, cleared the 3,000-square-foot plot, and will rent the park to the Tenants Council for $1 a month. Matching Federal and city antipoverty funds will finance most of the $34,650 needed for construction, staffing, insurance premiums and architectural fees. And the community itself is raising $500 for games and other equipment by asking $2 from each family in the immediate area.

Scheduled to be finished in 10 weeks, the park will be a two-level, open-air community center. The first level will include a clubhouse, complete with kitchenette for light cooking and baking, tables for dominoes and checkers, a tot-lot with a fountain, a mothers' "gossip corner" and a quiet area for the elderly. Active games will be separated from the more passive activities by putting a ball court on a 25x40-foot balcony. It's an ingenious and fresh design idea by the firm of Silverman and Cika, blissfully different from the cookie-cutter designs the Parks Department used to turn out by the dozen.

Like pebbles tossed in a pond, vest-pocket parks dropped in the middle of a neighborhood can create wider ripples of reform. Yet for all that a successful small parks program can mean for the city, it is still a compromise—a workable start toward a solution of our ugly urban environment but far from an ideal solution.

Utopia would mean a park or playground—some large, some small—every four or five blocks. For every two communities there ought to be an indoor recreation facility. Our waterfront offers miles of untapped recreation space: parks on unused piers, marinas, even floating swimming pools anchored in the river, as they have in Paris. A nationwide competition could transform post-Fair Flushing Meadow into the 20th century's Prospect Park, still the most beautiful park in the nation and 100 years old this summer.

Safety? Prospect, Central and the other large parks are not as dangerous as most people believe, but they are not exactly snug harbors for nature lovers either. They could be made safer and more useful—well-lit for nighttime tennis players, strollers, bike riders. And if people want to spend a hot summer night sleeping on the grass, why not?

We are, I think, approaching a new awareness of parks and their purpose. It will mean less emphasis on acquiring more acreage and greater effort toward serving more people. Everything cannot be sacrificed for the vest-pocket park program—large projects such as Marine Park (accurately nicknamed "The Dump"), Breezy Point and the Green Belt on Staten Island must be kept open for future generations. But after a generation of neglect of local neighborhood needs, the attempt to catch up must be started. As far as the city's available park land is concerned, it means that to think big we must also think small.

The Shame
of the States

by John F. Kennedy

JUST FIFTY YEARS ago Lincoln Steffens and his fellow muckrakers exposed "the shame of the cities." In city after city, they documented the sorry record of bossism, bribery and graft, the degradation of officials, police and public. Mayors were either the venal bosses of dishonest machines or figureheads for the bosses. The meeting of any Board of Aldermen could be completely cleared, a wag said, by a prankster shouting: "Alderman—your saloon is on fire." It was an age in which Mr. Dooley could observe that city bosses were "fine, strong American citizens—with their hand on the pulse of the people and their free forearm against the windpipe."

Whatever the truth of these charges may have been fifty years ago, they are not true today. Fifty years of reform and reconstruction of municipal government have produced a new breed of able political leaders and civil servants, playing a wholly different and highly competent role in the management of their towns and cities, their states and nation. The old-time machines and bosses, the politically managed police departments, the purchase and control of elections—all of these and other causes for shame have, on the whole, given way to the honest, efficient, democratic kind of municipal administration the voters have rightfully demanded.

Yet our urban areas have only exchanged one set of problems for another. Growth has outrun reform; achievement has been dwarfed by need. State and local governments, for example, have increased their employment twice as fast, in this century, as the rate of growth for the nation's total population and employment. Their expenditures are thirty times the 1900 level, far outstripping the nation's economic growth. In the last ten years alone, the financial demands on local government have doubled. A record proportion of cities are mired in a deficit position. The difficulties of such a position were accentuated last year when tight money policies made borrowing more difficult and more costly; and they are accentuated now by the contraction of investment capital at a time when relief and other needs are multiplying.

Able and devoted city officials are overworked and underpaid. Necessary programs and services are either cut back or defaulted. Far from progressing, most urban communities are hard-pressed just to hold their own.

The shame of our cities today is not political; it is social and economic. Blight and decay in urban government have been replaced by blight and decay in the cities themselves. They suffer from overcrowded and hazardous schools, undermanned with underpaid teachers—halfway education in half-day sessions. They suffer from slum housing, congested traffic, juvenile delinquency, overcrowded health and penal institutions and inadequate parking. They lack parks and recreational facilities, too often crowded out and ignored in the hasty, haphazard growth of the metropolitan areas.

In a blighted city, economic and social malaise go hand in hand. Industries move out, and so do their markets. The city's core tends to become a community of only the very rich and the very poor. Downtown merchants lose their customers and their ability to match the attractiveness of suburban rivals. As the community deteriorates, the tax base shrinks, the tax burden on those who remain grows heavier—and the community deteriorates further.

"The thing generally raised on city land," wrote Charles Dudley Warner, "is taxes."

The efforts of many local governments to eradicate this "shame," to rebuild our cities and restore their health, have been inspiring. But all too often they have had to do the job alone, even though the work affects many living outside the town or city's corporate limits.

The education of our children, the control of air and water pollution, the expansion of airport facilities, provisions for civil defense, the treatment of the mentally ill—these and other problems are not confined within city limits or even to metropolitan areas. They affect us all; they are of concern to us all. Juvenile delinquency bred in city slums seeps steadily outward. The traffic jams of the city become—at least twice a day—the headache of the suburbs.

The burden for coping with these problems rests—logically or illogically, fairly or unfairly—upon our municipal governments primarily. But the harsh facts of the matter are that these local governments receive all too little help and cooperation from Washington and the state legislatures. They are refused adequate Federal and state funds for the programs they need so badly, and for which they have paid so heavily. They contribute the lion's share of Federal and state taxes, but an equitable share is rarely returned to them. They have been pre-empted by the Federal and the state governments from the best sources of tax revenue.

They have been held back and hamstrung by antiquated debt limits, patchwork city charters and prehistoric municipal boundaries which uninterested and distrustful legislatures balk at altering. Often, they have been denied even the right to manage their own affairs.

But a majority of Americans, one hundred million strong, live in the metropolitan areas. They cast the majority of votes, they pay the largest share of taxes. Why do they not exert their power politically to secure their rights and their needs?

This is the root of the problem. For the sad answer is that the urban majority is, politically, a minority and the rural minority dominates the polls. Of all the discriminations against the urban areas, the most fundamental and the most blatant is political: the apportionment of representation in our Legislatures and (to a lesser extent) in Congress has been either deliberately rigged or shamefully ignored so as to deny the cities and their voters that full and proportionate voice in government to which they are entitled. The failure of our governments to respond to the problems of the cities reflects this basic political discrimination.

Rarely, in electing state Legislatures, does an urban vote, in effect, count for as much as a rural vote. At one time, in a then largely rural nation, legislative strength was heavily weighted in favor of rural areas. Though times have changed, many Legislatures have not. They have gerrymandered the shape of legislative and Congressional districts. They have left district lines unchanged (for as long as fifty years) without adjusting representation to population shifts.

In some cases, urban dwellers are "constitutional minorities." The state constitutions are so written that an urban area, no matter how large, cannot win a legislative majority. One method is to give every town or county, regardless of size, one seat in the Legislature. What sounds like equality is in reality rank discrimination.

Whatever the means, the result has been systematically and often deliberately to deny the cities their fair share of political power. Our Legislatures still represent the rural majority of half a century ago, not the urban majority of today.

In one state, 13,000 rural citizens have as many State Senators as four *million* urban dwellers. In another, a city with one-eighth of the state's population has less than one-sixty-eighth of the representatives in its legislative Assembly. There are states where as little as 10 per cent of the people can elect a majority in one house of the Legislature. The citizens of one urban area pay 25 per cent of the state's taxes—but have less than 2 per cent of the legislators who appropriate them. Indeed, in more than half the states, a majority in at least one legislative chamber is elected by less than a third of the voters.

Even in Congress, America's urban majority is not equitably represented. The same malapportioned state legislatures, after all, apportion Congressional seats. When, in 1956, the Senate debated the Mundt-Coudert proposal to apportion electoral votes along the lines of Congressional districts, I learned in startling detail how many of our urban citizens are short-changed in their Congressional representation. In one state, an urban Congressman has 800,000 constituents. A rural Congressman in the same state represents just over 200,000 people. In at least eighteen states, the city-dweller's vote is in effect worth less than his rural neighbor's. In at least seven of the states, a Congressman from a sparsely settled area represents less than half as many people as his colleague from that state's major urban area.

In some states, all urban voters are combined in one out-size district that has no more representatives than a tiny rural area. In others, the metropolitan area is split up by shrewdly but curiously drawn district lines that disperse the city voters into surrounding rural or suburban areas where their minority voice is barely heard. In some states the legislatures have simply failed to redistrict in keeping with urban growth—in others they have redistricted but in a discriminatory pattern.

In a big city in one typical state, the average Congressional district contains 404,000 people. Outside the city, the average district contains 322,000. This is not an uncommon picture of the systematic discrimination that besets the cities. The balance of political power is distorted far over to the rural end of the scale.

None of us, rural or urban, benefits in the long run from this situation. Our politics should not become a battle for power between town and country, between city-dweller and farmer. The principles at stake go much deeper than that. For whenever a large part of the population is denied its full and fair voice in government, the only result can be frustration of progress, bitterness, and a diminution of the democratic ideal. Country and city are interdependent; conflict and discrimination cannot serve the interests of either.

We in the Congress are constantly warned about the centralization of functions in Washington. We are urged to disperse many activities to state governments closer to the people. We are asked to turn back to the states the task of meeting many of the urban problems which Congress—despite its own imbalance of urban representation—has attempted to meet. The present Administration has—first with the Kestenbaum Commission and more recently with a special committee of Governors—explored ways of moving in that direction.

I am not a believer in the omnipotence of Federal bureaucracy; I see no magic attaching to tax money which has flowed to Washington and then back again. But as long as our state legislatures are not fully responsive to the urban areas and their needs, there is no practical way in which Congress can avoid its responsibility for meeting problems that are national in concern.

For all its limitations, Congress stands in shining contrast to many state legislatures in responding to the needs of the city and its people. As a member of Congress, I would not presume to instruct the state legislatures in their responsibilities. But I do insist that Congress cannot yield vital public functions affecting our metropolitan majority to state legislatures dominated by rural minorities. To do so would consign almost two-thirds of a nation to second-class citizenship. As long as democracy is distorted in this fashion, our cities will inevitably turn from unsympathetic state legislatures and seek help from a more responsive source— the Federal Government.

The cities of America cannot afford to become wholly dependent upon unsympathetic and unrepresentative state legislatures for assistance in tackling their problems of urban redevelopment and all the rest. It is apparent now that our growing classroom shortage cannot be met by state aid alone.

It is apparent, too, that we cannot leave it up to the states to fix standards for unemployment insurance payments. Today, when the cushioning effect of this system is most needed, it is woefully inadequate in too many states which have failed to raise their benefit levels since the low-wage days of the depressed Nineteen Thirties. Those on the state level who talk longest and loudest about returning these and other functions to the states ought to take an equally long look at what might well be called in 1958 "the shame of the states"—their unrepresentative state legislatures.

I do not claim that fair and equal representation offers any panacea for the city's ills. Even given sufficient funds and authority, too many of our cities suffer from a lack of trained personnel, from a multiplicity of governing units, and from the political, housing and other personal habits and trends of our population. But whatever their handicaps, our urban officials are more familiar with, responsible for and responsive to our urban needs. The recent example of the strong anti-public-housing Congressman who became a strong pro-public-housing mayor is a vivid illustration of this point.

Housing legislation, school legislation, labor and similar measures of primary concern to our cities have been defeated in the Congress in recent years by narrow margins. Had our urban areas been fully represented, there is every indication that the outcome might have been different. I have no doubt that our cities have experienced similar frustration on roll-calls in our state legislatures —denied their fair share of state funds or the legislation necessary to tackle their problems.

The great difficulty in stating these problems is that there is no apparent solution. Reform of our state legislatures depends upon the unselfishness of our state legislators. They are both the perpetrators and the beneficiaries of the present malapportionment. When they undertake reform—when they restore to our metropolitan areas their full suffrage—many of them do so at their own expense. Even the Congress is reluctant to require fair apportionment as a condition for representation. Appeal to the courts is an unlikely avenue of relief, for the Supreme Court has made clear its belief that such change depends basically upon political, not judicial, processes.

Our greater reliance, therefore, must be on the sheer weight of logic and morality in support of what is right, practical, and necessary. As our cities grow and their problems mount, the pressures for reform will increase. Perhaps an aroused public, a vigorous press, and the force of the democratic tradition will create an irresistible demand for justice to the second-class citizens of the city and its suburbs.

One hundred million citizens—constituting a majority of the nation—will not forever accept this modern day "taxation without representation." If there is a "shame of the cities" today, it is the failure of our urban dwellers and their spokesmen to be aware of these discriminations—and to press more vigorously for their elimination.

To Come to the Aid
of Their Cities

by Joseph S. Clark

IF PRESIDENT KENNEDY'S views prevail, a Department of Urban Affairs and Housing, headed by a Secretary of Cabinet rank, will · be established during the present session of Congress. This does not guarantee the rebirth of our cities, but it does certify to the magnitude of the task, and provide a central focus and guidance which have been so notably absent in the fragmentary, ineffectual efforts of states and cities to stem urban blight.

What are the problems of the cities, and why haven't they been solved at the local level?

Slums are still spreading faster than they are being cleared. There are eleven million sub-standard dwelling units in American cities. These are buildings which, instead of giving shelter, expose their inhabitants to most of the public health and social ills known to modern man.

Blight is eroding commercial and industrial real estate with equally serious repercussions. When deterioration begins, business and industry join the exodus of upper income families, increasing the complexities cities must cope with, and decreasing the resources with which they must do the coping.

From the *New York Times Magazine,* April 30, 1961, copyright © 1961 by The New York Times Company.

Congestion created by the growth in urban populations is intensified by an even greater increase in automobile traffic. Transportation to and from the metropolis, and traffic within, remain unsolved, along with a host of other problems created by overcrowding.

The "free air" of the city is now dangerously polluted. The metropolis that is not already experiencing a water shortage anticipates vast expenditures to meet this growing threat. Police and fire protection, education, welfare and recreation facilities lag far behind the need. Juvenile delinquency, the breakdown of the family, the incidence of emotional illness, and a multiplicity of educational questions continue on the rise.

As the former Mayor of a large American city—and one with a reasonably successful and far-reaching urban renewal program—I believe that unless the Federal Government comes to the rescue our cities, and all they stand for in our civilization, are doomed.

The American city cannot rebuild itself, for several reasons. Despite such individual private-enterprise accomplishments as New York's Rockefeller Center, Chicago's Lakefront, Philadelphia's Penn Center, Pittsburgh's Golden Triangle, immensely larger physical areas have deteriorated and remain untouched—unattractive to the private redeveloper.

On the whole, the early private investments in renewal were made because they were economically sound. The government's help was needed only to assemble and condemn the required land. A little further from the lake, or the river, or the downtown area, the potential value of property for redevelopment purposes drops rapidly. It is, therefore, no longer economic for private enterprise to buy land, clear it, and rebuild.

In addition, much of what has to be done by way of providing new facilities and open areas for the cities falls in the public sector of the economy and has to be supported by government, because there is no immediate profit in the task for the entrepreneur.

Community facilities thus become the responsibility of government, and government has been unpopular during the last eight years. So schools, libraries, recreation centers, sewage disposal plants, off-street garages and so on, which belong to the public sector of the economy, have been starved during most of the Fifties.

Debt limitations and inadequate tax resources, caused by a shrinking economic base, keep cities from doing the job of urban renewal themselves.

Contrary to popular belief, it is not the Federal Government whose financial structure is under the greatest strain—it is our state and local governments. The Federal debt has risen less than 5 per cent in the past fourteen years, while the debt burden, measured in relation to national income, has been cut in half.

State and local debt, meanwhile, has more than quadrupled, far outstripping the rate at which the incomes of these governments and their citizens have risen. City budgets have been balanced only by quadrupling tax levies. Even so, tax resources are not adequate for the expensive job of urban rehabilitation.

For the past twenty years the Federal Government has been helping local communities with $2 of Federal money for each $1 of local funds spent for slum clearance and renewal, and with F. H. A. mortgage insurance for suburban housing.

Only a handful of states have chipped in at all, and those that have contribute white chips rather than blue ones.

As anyone who looks can see, all these efforts combined have barely scratched the surface of urban decay.

Local initiative is frustrated in other directions. City governments' jurisdiction ends at boundaries established long before the current urban sprawl was even envisaged. As a result, the programs that cities plan for recreation, education, garbage collection, sewage disposal and the like, must arbitrarily cease functioning at the city's legal boundaries, even when the contemporary metropolis has spread into an area twice its original size.

Not only is the city prevented from planning effectively, it is also financially strangled by the nature of urban growth. Typically, a sizable percentage of the metropolitan area's inhabitants live in the suburbs and come to the city for jobs, forcing the latter to supply all manner of services to meet their daytime needs. At night they return to the suburbs, taking with them their pocketbooks and the tax money that formerly—before the city's spread—would have helped pay for the police and fire protection, the traffic control, the roads and the bridges that they require by day.

Studies have been made of almost every major metropolitan area in the country, but they have produced little more than a library of frustration. Only Miami and Atlanta have established area-wide governmental units with significant responsibilities.

People seem unready for the drastic changes needed. Government at all levels has failed to concentrate the decision-making processes so that urban problems might be tackled effectively. Most of these matters are being attacked now in piecemeal fashion by private enterprise, voluntary civic effort, local government, sometimes the state, and frequently Federal agencies.

Efforts are too often blocked by insufficient funds, inadequate staff, lack of planning, and little or no coordination of the work of overlapping agencies.

In all candor, those who on philosophical grounds still argue against the Federal Government's playing a greater role in renewing American cities are ignorant either of past facts or of present economics.

Fortunately we have reached a point with the problems of the cities—as I daresay we have with other national problems, such as education and medical care for the aged—where the obvious need for action outweighs any exaggerated, if not imaginary, concern for the foundations of the Republic.

The time has come to mature and sharpen our thinking about the national responsibility for metropolitan affairs in general and urban renewal in particular. We must approach the problems of urban living as a whole, not as a series of separate issues.

This is what the President's program does. The new Department of Urban Affairs and Housing, which it would establish, would have a broad charter to survey the urban scene in its entirety. It would be a point of contact in Washington for harassed local officials. It would have general responsibility for coordinating all Federal activities affecting the city. It would have specific authority to carry out the measures advanced in the President's message.

These measures would provide money and means to build better housing for the elderly and for low- and moderate-income families; give assistance in the development of community facilities and urban transportation; and revitalize our urban areas by reserving open space for future residential development, recreation, and conservation of natural resources.

The Department also would give those Americans who live in urban communities—a large majority of our population—an equal voice with rural Americans in framing national policy, and in directing it where desirable to the improvement of urban life. Finally, it would develop the research and thinking necessary to permit the Congress, the residents of metropolitan areas, and the American people generally, to decide whether saving the city is worth the money and the political reorganization required to do the job.

We are, after all, an urban country—part of an essentially urban civilization. With all due respect to the heritage and traditions of the Democratic party, and many of my own constituents, the family farm is no longer the backbone of the American way of life.

Physically, that way of life has changed radically in the past fifty years. It will obviously continue to change in the years ahead. By 1975 three-fourths of all Americans will live in urban areas. Today more than two-thirds of us are in metropolitan centers. Still, we have not begun to appreciate the changes such rapid urbanization has already made in our culture.

It seems incredible that one of the world's oldest democracies, the world's richest industrial nation and the world's No. 1 power should permit millions of its citizens to live in poverty, disease and misery, but we do. We are a nation of under-developed cities, and there is a new frontier of asphalt lying in wait.

What It's Like to Live in an Experiment

by David Jacobs

ANY TWO-YEAR-OLD is capable of demonstrating the difference between living in a conventional urban apartment building and living
in Habitat, the massive experimental housing complex at Expo 67.
The two-year-old who lives with me, for example, is a chronic
window-watcher. She looks out of a seventh-story New York window (barred for safety) and by pushing my metal file box to the
proper position and standing on it, she is able to assume the regulation posture for window-watching—elbows resting on sill. Most
of the time she watches the windows patterned on the vertical
surface across the street, but if she stretches a little she can see the
street below and keep us informed of the action there. "Car," she
announces, or "bus" or "truck." She must know by now that there
are people down there, too, but she is apparently unimpressed, or
uninvolved, and has not yet found it necessary to report their
presence.

A couple of weeks ago she moved into Habitat for a brief residence, and her first test of its livability was an examination of the
windows. The corner one in the living room was the most attrac-

tive, and because it extended from the ceiling to the floor, the absent file box was not missed. Through one pane she had a magnificent, unobstructed view of the city's busy St. Lawrence River port, and behind the harbor in the hazy dusk the young skyline of old Montreal glowed. The other pane revealed more river, some nearby Expo pavilions, and a new highway that provided the requisite cars, buses and trucks. Through the slenderer room-height window on the other wall, she saw the rest of Expo and the ubiquitous St. Lawrence again, for Habitat is set on a peninsula that juts into the river between Montreal and the islands on which most of Expo is built. And also through that window she saw people—not miniature people far below, but life-sized human beings who waved to her as they strolled right by her window on a real sidewalk 10 stories above the ground. She was delighted.

That, of course, is the most extraordinary thing about living in Habitat: you live in a truly three-dimensional urban environment, in a densely populated and high-rising structure with the vitality of city life distributed up and down as well as along and under. Each unit is an individual, private home with its own garden-terrace and a front door that opens onto an outdoor street. A network of these little streets—more accurately, side streets—leads to nearby elevators and connects with major pedestrian thoroughfares on the second, sixth, and tenth stories. Extending the length of the complex (about 950 feet), each of the major thoroughfares periodically dips down and widens out to form a spacious, good-looking and fully protected playground-park.

Its three-dimensionality alone makes Habitat unique. Of at least equal and probably greater significance is the construction method employed to put it up. As its young Israeli-born, Canadian architect, Moshe Safdie, is first to admit, his concept owes less to Frank Lloyd Wright or Le Corbusier or Walter Gropius than to Henry Ford.

The structure is composed of hundreds of identical precast concrete boxes manufactured in a plant on the site. Inside the plant is an iron mold into which concrete is poured. When the concrete sets, it forms a box 38½ feet long, 17½ feet wide and 10 feet high, which is rolled outside the plant on a gigantic, specially made dolly. Machines move in and sandblast it; wiring and plumbing are installed on the bottom, and floors are laid over the installations; wallboard walls, windows, fixtures are fitted; the kitchen is placed; the remarkable bathroom—two pieces of die-cast Fiberglas forming floor and ceiling, walls, linen closet, bathtub and sink—is dropped in; and the roof, cast separately, is slid into place and secured. Finally a behemoth of a crane—also tailormade—lumbers over, drops its skinny arms and grabs the heavy box, which rises, tilts momentarily, rights itself, and swings into place on top of other boxes, to which workmen quickly fasten it. One, two or three boxes in combination may be used for each house (Moshe Safdie calls each Habitat dwelling unit a house, never an apartment), which may contain from three to seven rooms, in one story or two. The assortment of layouts that the assembling of identical boxes yields is astonishing.

Habitat's physique is, to say the least, imposing: it could be a cluster of pyramided building blocks abandoned by a child giant. From a distance it looks heavy, up close it looks heavier, and from within it looks convincingly as though it were the heaviest anything ever built anywhere. Conceivably this overbearing weightiness might weigh too heavily on the people who have to live with it— one does wish for just a touch of delicacy. Relieving the great bulk, however, are the many sun-letting cavities that are the most splendid visual product of Habitat's staggered structure; they sharpen the colossal angularity of the place and brighten everything. Moreover, for all its weight, the projecting-and-receding building seems in every way preferable to our commonplace urban rows of uprising planks that can bear a man down with their aloof and proper straightness. I also thought it interesting, and funny, that this machine-made architecture, with its scarred gray walls and stacked-block surfaces, should make a 1965 New York skyscraper apartment building of man-laid brick look as though it were untouched by human hands.

This humanistic quality in a product of automation gives Habitat the vaguely familiar character that may explain the surprising, almost uniformly enthusiastic reception it is receiving. After all, with its unprecedented design, engineering and construction system, Habitat makes some genuinely revolutionary implications, and revolutions are supposed to generate controversy. Those of us who have known about the project for some time have, in fact, been anticipating the controversy, rubbing our hands together and waiting for the dragon-fire dialogue to begin. While some Canadian public officials have been opposed to footing the bills and questioning the worth of the experiment, and while a few citizens worried that Habitat is some sort of Communist or Fascist plot, serious architectural criticism has been rare.

One dissenter is the eminent Edgar Kaufmann Jr., of Columbia's architecture school. Writing in *Harper's* magazine on the subject of Canadian architecture, Kaufmann finds Habitat "terrifying . . . repulsive . . . like some giant ancient film set waiting for Frankenstein's monster to shatter its spell." But much as an argument would be welcomed now—by the architect as well as the press—Kaufmann's less subjective criticisms provide no departure points for controversy, because, apparently, he was misinformed about Habitat. He says, for instance, that the "units were too big to be handled by the mightiest machines available and had to be cast in halves. . . ." It is simply not true that the Habitat boxes were cast in halves, and the rest of the statement is misleading: available machinery was never *supposed* to build Habitat. In fact, as important in the experiment as the complex itself was the development of adequate equipment to construct assembly-line architecture in the future.

And by implying that Habitat is valueless as a demonstration of mass-produced housing because of its high cost and production mistakes, Kaufmann has forgotten that the structure is a prototype, that it has done precisely what prototypes are supposed to do: supply actual conditions for extensive—and expensive—trials and errors. There were lots of mistakes—two cranes had to be built because the first was inadequate, to name a costly one—but now they are made and done with and won't be repeated when the next Habitat or a facsimile is built. The machinery exists, the lessons have been learned: the same project that cost close to $15-million to build in Montreal can be rebuilt elsewhere tomorrow for $4-million—with the cost per unit sharply declining as the number of units increases.

I was exposed to that subtly familiar quality of Habitat's—without really being aware of the quality, I'm quite certain—the first time I saw it. That was in the summer of 1966, and only a few of the 158 dwellings were in place. Writing about it, I tried several times to include some reference to the old apartment dwellings of the Pueblo Indians. The relationship, I knew, was awfully superficial: the staggered, piled-up character of both places was the only tie they had, but their essences were entirely unrelated. One was a handcrafted affair, built into the sides of elevations; the other is the machine-made, self-supporting product of a still new technology.

Nevertheless, I finally managed to fit the Pueblos in (just as I have here—by pointing out how little their architecture had in common with Habitat); and since then other writers have also thought of the Pueblos and made similar noncomparisons. A more imaginative writer simply called Habitat a "Mediterranean cluster," which was better inasmuch as it makes no specific reference but lets you know that the structure does have some sort of recognizable character to it; and another forced a comparison to Knossos, the ancient Minoan royal palace and mini-community on Crete—an even farther-out contrast than the Pueblo one. But however weak our allusions, I think they reflect a significant virtue of Habitat: by relating more closely to the architecture of the man-wrought past than to the frigid, precise and increasingly inadequate architecture of the present (from which it is theoretically sprung), it subordinates its revolutionary qualities to its human ones.

I doubt that the significance of this virtue can be overstressed. There are more visionary proposals for urban rehabilitation than Habitat, more sweeping and far-reaching solutions to the problems of urban housing. But while a revolution is essential and immanent if the urban environment of the future is to be made tolerable for a well-balanced population, a man is not likely to subject his wife and children to a violent upheaval. Despite its colossal strength, Habitat is a very gentle revolution. By looking somehow familiar, by providing privacy and activity, the equivalent of a suburban backyard *and* of a sociable city park playground, and the basic facilities that people know and like (their own front door), Habitat has the best chance to succeed at the tricky business of rebellion. Its design and engineering innovations and unprecedented construction method notwithstanding, it is, before it is anything else, a decent place to live.

The small parking areas created by periodic recessions in the layout of Habitat are for visitors; residents' auto spaces are distributed on the ground level (which is invisible from the highway that passes one long side of the complex) under the structure. Next to each parking place is a door, marked with a number corresponding to the resident's house number, and on the other side of the door is a good-sized workroom. I call it workroom, although you might want it to be a storeroom or studio or darkroom: the point is that it is a more than suitable substitute for the basement you would have in the suburbs or the extra room you wouldn't let yourself think about in the city—secluded, safe, away from it all but right there, too.

Not far from the parking place and secret hideout is an elevator; there are three pairs equidistant along the length of Habitat. After rising to your level, you walk along a street—it is never very far— to your home. The streets, incidentally, are half-covered with an arched roof of clear plastic. If it is raining you have a choice and can walk along the uncovered part if you like. If it is snowing you have no choice: the steps that may lead up or down to your house are cored with heat-conducting wires that melt snow and deprive you of the opportunity to trudge.

Our place was an L-shaped, officially "two-and-a-half" bedroom unit on one level, formed with two of the precast boxes. One box contained the living room–dining area, kitchen and enormous closet (the size of a maid's room in some apartments), and the other, the bedrooms and bathroom. Outside, embraced by the two inner walls of the L, was the garden-terrace, which was in fact the roof of a box on the ninth level. Layouts throughout Habitat vary widely, and most three-box duplex houses have two terraces, the lower visible from the upper. Ours was as representative an arrangement as any, however, and one terrace was enough to spoil us for our return to our terraceless apartment in New York.

From an architectural standpoint, the actual Habitat in Montreal, Quebec, is important only as a prototype expression of a new idea in urban architecture. Obviously, the structure itself is of no practical concern to anyone other than the 158 families who will live there. *What is it like to live in Habitat?* means *What is it like to live in a three-dimensional, mass-produced community?*

Without implications for the future of architecture and without applicability to the problems of the present-day city elsewhere, Habitat would be meaningless. The reason I bring this up here is that very soon after our arrival my wife and I deduced that corners had been cut during the construction of the interior in order to keep the ever-rising costs down; that second crane had to be compensated for somehow. The resulting flaws were small annoyances —clumsy door latches, flimsy window tracks, noisy fluorescent lighting and exhaust fan motors, wallboard less than soundproof— and, what's more, they are all without significance. The flaws will not appear when the next Habitat and its offspring are built, and many are still being ironed out of this Habitat. We kept that in mind.

At first the interior seemed to be ordinary enough, the kind of open-spaced, large-windowed arrangement that you see in a lot of new apartments nowadays. The living room–dining area beyond a partitioned-off, compact kitchen, for example, was really one room, the separation defined only because a hanging lamp, suspended about one-fifth of the way along the ceiling, afforded you no choice but to put a dining room table under it. The ceiling itself, just under 10 feet from the floor, looked a little higher than that, probably because the tall, slender windows give the rooms a vertical look. The bathroom, I'm sorry to say, for all its Tomorrowland manufacture looked like a bathroom pure and simple: we had to examine the fixtures closely in order to determine the uniqueness of the construction. The essential difference between it and the conventional bathroom, of course, is that in Habitat the floor, walls, ceiling, bathtub, sinks, and even the linen closet and the casement for a vertically stacked, pullout washing machine and dryer are all parts of a continuous surface—the right angle, for example, at which the sink top meets the wall is here a sharp curve. To the lady who will have to keep the bathroom clean, the continuous surfaces of the room mean fewer seams where dirt collects and only one kind of material to keep clean. Instead of hauling several kinds of cleanser into the bathroom (one for tile floors, one for porcelain sink and tub, one for painted walls), she can make do with one bucket of sudsy detergent.

Except for the bathroom, little in the interior of Habitat could be called avant-garde, but the layout and its features are extremely well thought out. A raised, cast-in rim with a slightly concave top separated the outside of our tub from the floor, functioning as both a drain for escaped shower water and a footrest for drying your legs. The panel separating the kitchen from the dining area was slideable and built over a counter which could be, with the panel aside, a breakfast bar. My wife also promptly noticed that dishes could be stacked on the bar after dinner, the panel then closed, concealing the dirty china from view as the diners retired to the living room proper.

The bedroom-and-a-half turned out to be the second bedroom, an unusually large one with two doors a couple of inches apart. Between the doors on the inside was a room-high, accordion-folded wooden partition which, when extended, made the one room two, each with its own light switches and window. This arrangement, while not unique, reminded me that it ought to be more widespread than it is: it provides a more than generous expanse for a playroom, decorated as one unit, and privacy when two children have different bedtimes and different things to do. It also makes the dwelling—well, not a three-bedroom apartment but more than a two, so two-and-a-half will have to do.

Safdie's custom of calling the dwelling units houses rather than apartments was, I quickly realized, something more than semantic nit-picking. In an apartment, no matter how many exposures you have, the sensation of being in an apartment always exists: you are over someone and under someone; you share an elevator corridor with neighbors; there are often tenants flanking you.

Actually, many of the same conditions exist in Habitat, but you would never know it. There is simply no way of making your downstairs neighbor hear you unless you call on the telephone. Our experiments, consisting of jumping, screaming, pounding and high-fidelitying, were uniformly negative in result. (This is perfectly logical, of course: unlike an apartment building, in which the seventh floor is the ceiling of the sixth story, Habitat consists of separate and independent units. The only shared floor and ceiling is the terrace, but since the concrete is a formidable sound barrier the possibilities for audible harassment are not much greater.)

The most expansive windows are on the walls opening onto the terrace, and through them—and this holds true of most of the houses, not just ours—the view is broad and uncluttered by other Habitat units. The window on the living room wall opposite the terrace faces the street in the air; it is a narrow window, and when the curtains were drawn the privacy we had was uncanny.

Having been raised in suburbs, my wife and I are, naturally, against them. Since we have become parents, however, we concede that suburban life has one, only one, virtue—the patio, or backyard, where a young child can safely play alone and an infant sleep in nice weather. On the other hand, the daily trips to the park, at first regarded as necessary evils in the city, eventually became an event looked forward to as much by my wife as by my daughter—particularly after friendships were formed. The only remaining drawback was that it was something that *had* to be done, and if something that prevented the park trip came up two days in a row, guilt set in.

In Habitat, that one suburban advantage is matched in town, and the urban advantage—the trip to the shared playground-park—remains, made better by being optional. The terrace, enclosed on two sides by the house and on the other two by a high wall, is extraordinary. Floored with wood or brick, large and rustic enough to be crowded with bikes, toys, beach umbrella and what have you without appearing to be cluttered, it even doubles as a garden and triples as a city-type roof-with-a-view. About two and a half feet deep and four feet high, the wall is cast with a U-shaped top. Inside the U is earth in which shrubbery is being planted. Under the earth is a permanent irrigation system that eliminates the need for care:

people who like to garden can, of course, plant anything they wish and trim and pamper to their hearts' content; but those who are not interested can let the leaves fall where they may—against Habitat's rugged exterior it shouldn't matter.

The wall is not solid concrete: if it were the children would have no view. Between the bottom of the planter and the step-high base of the wall is an open area of about 30 inches, made safe by a piece of strong, clear plastic. The top of the plastic fits into a groove under the planter, on the terrace side of the wall; then it curves outward, its bottom edge fitting into a groove near the outside edge of the wall's base. This creates a plastic semi-domed enclosure. When we first entered the house and completed the window-testing ceremony, we tried out the terrace. Our little girl made a bee-line for the wall, climbed onto the base and sat fascinated inside her private enclosure. This became a ritual every time she went outside, which was every time she noticed that outside was right there and accessible—a rarity for a city kid.

We took a walk over to Safdie's, whose house is in the center section (called Red, because of the color of the elevator that services it) of the three major clusters that form Habitat. As the thoroughfare that took us there meandered around combinations of boxes, it was always walled on one side by houses and on the other by a barrier of concrete planks about 60 inches long and 42 inches high. Between each plank a three-inch opening was left, and as soon as the baby noticed one she headed for it and looked through.

When we arrived, Safdie's first two comments were: Did the baby climb into the base of the wall and did she look between the planks? The shape of the plastic—it could have more easily been fastened flat to the outside of the wall—and the openings in the street walls, he explained, were determined solely for the purposes for which my daughter had used them.

Safdie has two kids, and all of Habitat reflects his concern for children. The whole place is, in a way, an enormous play area, suitable for climbing, hiding, seeking, even digging. Remarkably, however, this charming factor is never intrusive, the way it is in many large housing complexes, where the presence of kids hovers over the place long after they've been put to bed. Had I not had my daughter along at Habitat, I doubt that I would have noticed it.

When I evaluated Habitat the first time I suspected that its being restricted to only 158 dwellings was a major drawback to the experiment, and I am more certain of it now. Originally designed to incorporate 1,000 units, it had to be reduced because of the enormous cost. Expo and the three governments (Canadian federal, provincial, and city) that paid the bills cannot be faulted; certainly their willingness to spend so much on a project by an unknown architect is more than commendable.

But if Habitat's size is just one of those things, it is also a very serious flaw. The view, the activity, the townhouse quality of the homes may contradict this, but Habitat as it exists is unfortunately a suburban kind of community. You can't run to the store; you have to drive. The kids can't walk to school; they have to be driven or bused. There is no commerce. At 1,000 units there could have been a small shopping area and some professional offices, perhaps a school and movie theater. For obvious reasons, at Habitat's present size such places couldn't survive.

Officials are hoping that Habitat will act as a catalyst for Montreal's harbor growth, as well it might; and then urban diversification will come. That will be very nice for Montreal, but it will prove nothing about Habitat. (Residential harbor development is the order of the day in many North American cities; the idea has simply caught on, and the nature of the architecture that gets the ball rolling seems to make little difference.)

Habitat's greatest value, it seems to me, is as an urban *renewal* system. I have seen any number of handsome, practical, livable community schemes that would profit any city—provided the city were willing to raze a couple of hundred acres for construction; and no city is willing to do that. Habitat makes no such demand. Flexible, diffusive, it has the unique ability to meander wherever it is needed without plowing under whatever might be worth keeping. Added to its restrictive size, then, the isolated site on which Habitat has been built is experiment drawback No. 2. Regretfully, what is needed now is another experiment.

It takes a lot of money to make something really inexpensive, and lack of money is the reason why Habitat, which Safdie designed to be truly low-cost housing (of which there is at present no such thing), cannot even now be built inexpensively enough. More sophisticated research and development are still needed; computers have to be put to work; gigantic automated machinery for its manufacture has to be made—machinery that will relate to the current Habitat plant the way today's Ford factories relate to the assembly line of the Model T. The basic block must become lighter and stronger and assume a variety of forms. It is conceivable: building Habitat was the biggest step, and that has been taken.

Someday one of the giant industrial corporations that have been giving extensive lip service to the idea of investing vast sums in urban reconstruction will decide to follow through: it will take on the whole upper West Side of New York. Assume that four slum blocks in the 90's between Amsterdam and Columbus Avenues are the starting points. The boxes plunk into place, now joined by precast domes, egg-shapes, disks. East of Columbus, one block down, is another bad street. Up go the units *over* the avenue, which continues uninterrupted on its way; down along the street crawls the Habitat, and because there's a fine old church in the middle of the block, the units stack *around* it and open up a vista in front of it, making it more precious than it was before. Caterpillaring, the architecture makes it all the way down to the Hudson at one point and all the way over to Central Park West at a couple of others.

Then somebody will complain: these houses (which will cost maybe $6,000-$8,000 apiece by this point) are a lot nicer than the place he's paying $500 a month to rent. All right, then, he gets another architect to build him something better.

I don't think Safdie would mind. He claims no monopoly on revolution.

Architecture and
the Architect

by Henry Russell Hitchcock

A TESTAMENT. By Frank Lloyd Wright. Illustrated. 256 pp. New York: Horizon Press. $12.50.

Of the 181 years since 1776—the date of this country's political independence to which Frank Lloyd Wright refers recurrently in *A Testament*—this great American architect has seen approximately half. For seventy of these years Mr. Wright has been designing buildings. It is not too much to say that he is himself a major American monument; nor is current recognition of the significance of his prophet's role in modern architecture limited to his own country. The German magazine Das Kunstwerk has just published its list of the twenty-five most important—or, more accurately, most significant—buildings of the twentieth century. In that list five are by Le Corbusier and four each by Wright and by Miës van der Rohe. In other lists he scores higher than either Le Corbusier or Miës—though he appears not at all, curiously enough, in that of the leading modern Japanese architect, Kenzo Tange.

Mr. Wright has little use for critics, and it is unfortunate that it must, for the most part, be critics who will review his book. But if he has written that "architectural criticism of the modern is oftentimes bitter, sometimes sweet, seldom even wide-awake [and] wholly lacks inspiration because it lacks the appreciation that is love," he has also admitted that "some of our own critics could be appreciated—Lewis Mumford, early Russell Hitchcock, Montgomery Schuyler and a few others." Perhaps the later Russell Hitchcock may be forgiven for reviewing the latest Wright, since the only architect who might be considered of equal stature—Le Corbusier—would be anathema to him.

Recurrently throughout this book Mr. Wright stresses that architecture is more important than the architect. In his case there are many admirers who do not agree with him; but I think one may properly say of *A Testament* that its greatest value lies in the 210 well-chosen and well-reproduced illustrations. These add notably to the visual documentation of the executed work and projects of the architect, ranging all the way from a house elevation (probably of 1890, but dated by the author 1888) to several major designs of the present year.

Ten or more of the early designs have never been published before, and the fifteen dating from the post-war years have been available for the most part only in magazines. The book will be almost as necessary for any shelf of books on twentieth-century architecture as the great monograph on Wright's early work, published in Berlin in 1910, which is so rarely obtainable today.

Those who study the latest projects presented here (such as the Mile High Skyscraper scheme of 1956) or, if in New York, look at the Guggenheim Museum now rising on Fifth Avenue will realize that Mr. Wright has, at eighty-eight, lost none of his creative vitality as an architect. They may, however, have some difficulty in understanding the sharp distinction he makes repeatedly between "exuberance" and "excess." Certainly the projects for Philadelphia's Beth Sholem Synagogue of 1954 and above all that for the Arizona Capitol of the present year are more exuberant than anything he has built in the last thirty years. They are balanced, however, by other current designs, such as that for the Christian

Science Church of Bolinas, Calif., and the Music Building of Florida Southern College in Lakeland, which well illustrate the serenity that he insists must go hand-in-hand with exuberance.

Mr. Wright is a writer of notable verve as well as an architect of genius. His *Autobiography* of 1932 is properly rated as a major American literary document, and the last decades have seen the reprinting of most of his other more ephemeral writing. Not for nothing is he a Celt and proud of it; while the heterodoxy of his distinguished uncle, the Rev. Jenkin Lloyd Jones, lives on in this artist who is himself a Baptist minister's son. The greater part of this book is more of a sermon than a testament. Mr. Wright lives in an eternal present (this must, indeed, be one of the secrets of his eternal youth), and the enemies of his early, his middle and his later days tend, as has always been the case with him, to merge in his polemics.

It is pointless to complain of inaccuracies in his references to others—no one would look in such a text for precise historical fact but only for psychological atmosphere—yet he is at least as inaccurate, or vague, in his references to his own life. In the vital matter of his exposure to the "gifts" of the Frederick Froebel kindergarten system, the earliest formative influence upon him, one might get the impression that he was three at the time his mother brought them home; he was actually nine.

The motivation of his departure from the room just before Miës van der Rohe spoke at the banquet in honor of that great foreign architect upon his arrival in Chicago remains mysterious. The unkind might suspect that the clue lay in the parenthetic "Accent on the *I*" that he injects in the text after quoting his introduction: ". . . I give you Miës van der Rohe." Yet anyone interested in Mr. Wright's extraordinary career can only regret that he has not included more such episodes from his later years as he himself sees them.

Sermons are supposed to do you good and so will Mr. Wright's if you don't take them all in one dose as a reviewer must. These latest are somewhat clearer in their meaning than some of his earlier ones have been, and the vocabulary less private. They make the most sense—as interpretation of Wright's purpose, at least, if not as detailed guides for architectural conduct—if one can suspend one's sense of chronology and thus sense that they represent not his reaction to the immediate present of the Nineteen Fifties but to the entire seventy years during which he has been building. Studded with aphoristic sentences, they have something of the sensuous verbal appeal of the poems of Dylan Thomas or the speeches of James M. Curley. For example, he writes that the "static checker-board of the old city is pattern already in agony . . . not living, but rather hanging by its eyebrows from its nervous system."

The short section of the book entitled "The New Architecture" is less (or perhaps I should say more) time-bound. It offers rather clear evidence of what Mr. Wright sees as the possibilities of architecture today. The short paragraphs, The Earth Line, The Modular of the Kindergarten Table, Character Is a National, are familiar doctrine and apply to his work at the opening of the century as much as to his work of today. But Tenuity Plus Continuity and Space are forward-looking. The quality of the architect's imagination as applied to the basic means of architecture has certainly not deteriorated.

Whether one likes this or that among the successive periods of Wright's work is as irrelevant as whether one prefers this or that period of Picasso. The protean character of Wright's contribution is underlined by *A Testament*, both in its text and in its illustrations. No one interested in this eminent American architect can do without his writings, of which we may happily hope *A Testament*, despite its title, will not be the lest.

How Civilized Can Urban Man Be?

by Allan Temko

THE CITY IN HISTORY: Its Origins, Its Transformations and Its Prospects. By Lewis Mumford. Illustrated. 657 pp. New York: Harcourt, Brace & World. $11.50.

Among the splendid generation of American humanists born at the close of the last century—the generation which completed the native cultural revolution launched by Emerson—Lewis Mumford has always occupied a special place, possibly because he very early established himself as the finest environmental writer of his time. *The Story of Utopias*—an appropriate first title—appeared in 1922. *Sticks and Stones*, which in some ways remains the best book on American architecture, followed two years later; and although the young author could not then have known how far his interest in environment would lead him, Edmund Wilson had the perspicacity to note, in 1926, that Mr. Mumford promised to become "someone important." In 1934 *Technics and Civilization* brilliantly verified that prediction. Four years later another major volume, *The Culture of Cities*, came from the press as an incontestable masterpiece.

Indeed, the book was a landmark in urban literature. Mr. Mum-

From the *New York Times Book Review*, April 16, 1961, copyright © 1961 by The New York Times Company.

ford brought to his study of the city not only penetrating insight but a passionate affirmation of human values, which he saw everywhere being weakened or destroyed by the spread of megalopolitan chaos. He regarded the city not as the helpless victim of inchoate forces, but as a stricken living organism which itself can be a formative factor in culture. Indeed, in the "symbolic" organization of the medieval town, it was a dynamically creative factor. In the insensate cities of modern times, however, negative forces were uncontrolled, and as Mr. Mumford inspected the cancerous growth of large cities, he diagnosed still deeper social maladies.

Urban civilization was headed for catastrophe, he reasoned, unless our cities were decongested and decentralized; he proposed the establishment of a regional "bio-technic" order which would renew mankind's association with the natural world. In 1938 he knew that time was short, and humane regional undertakings such as T. V. A. all too rare; with harrowing accuracy he foretold an eruption of hell on earth: the psychotic totalitarianism, mass exterminations, barbarous tortures, and widespread urban devastation of World War II.

Twenty-three years have passed since Mr. Mumford delivered this prophecy, yet the world seems little the wiser. Except for a few intelligently governed cities such as Stockholm, the rise of Megalopolis is in sight in every part of the globe, not least in the United States. Millions of acres of open land are senselessly devoured each year. Planners such as Robert Moses, eager to shuttle still more thousands of motor cars at ever decreasing speeds over longer and longer highways, are still powerful. In the urban core, the violent slums spread malignantly, and the skyscrapers go up, and up, often on the most inappropriate sites; for example next to Grand Central Station. Congestion increases.

That Mr. Mumford has chosen this moment to speak out once more—in a magnificent sequel to *The Culture of Cities* which may well stand as the crowning achievement of his life's work—is a measure not only of his unique stature in modern letters and his indomitable intellectual vigor, but also of the now almost incredible gravity of the environmental problem.

Time may again be running out, Mr. Mumford warns in this

massive book, which at every point is more profound in its findings, more searching in observation, more comprehensive in scholarship, and more despairing in tone, than was the earlier volume. We have reached the point, as the author abundantly demonstrates, where the absolute extinction of the city is conceivable on a global basis. After Megalopolis the final Spenglerian stages of cultural disintegration are Tyrannopolis, the city of parasitic Caesarism, and Necropolis, the city of death.

Even if urban civilization is not wiped out in a nuclear and bacteriological apocalypse, there remains the clear possibility that the whole world will become "a vast urban hive," which of course would be another form of death for the city. "The fact that the same signs of overgrowth and overconcentration exist in 'communist' Soviet Russia as in 'capitalist' United States," he declares, "shows that these forces are universal ones, operating almost without respect to the prevailing ideologies or ideal goals." Thus we may be faced with the prospect of a dehumanized world, ruled by the "cybernetic deity" and its secretive priests, manipulated by "professional illusionists," and populated mainly by unthinking automatons who are doomed to "mandatory consumption" administered by a "tentacular bureaucracy."

If he holds this to be a probability rather than a possibility, Mr. Mumford nevertheless has marshaled evidence from more than five thousand years of urban history to support his conclusion that only a final choice exists between reorganizing the city on a "positive" basis or witnessing its extinction by "negative" forces. Though scoffing critics, who forget the precision of his earlier forecasts, may dismiss his fervent exclamations as a messianic jeremiad (and it is worth noting that certain academic circles consider his works merely "uplifting generalities") this great book—praise I accord with due caution—should last as long as books last.

For *The City in History* plumbs both the life-giving and death-dealing aspects of urban civilization through depths of time and expanses of space which no other writer has explored in quite this particular way, analyzing both the spiritual and physical remains of cities. As such, the book is more than urban history: it is moral philosophy of a high order and tragic poetry. Mr. Mumford has gone far beyond *The Culture of Cities*, of which he retained only so much as he was "not skillfull enough to improve or resourceful enough to expand"; and although in the earlier book he was content to halt at the Middle Ages, he now goes backward to the dawn of history.

From this and other prehistoric shrines, where men first deliberately transformed physical surroundings into symbolic representations of the cosmos, Mr. Mumford carries the story forward, on a prodigious scale, through the neolithic village, the early cities of Mesopotamia and Egypt, the Greek *polis*, and its meretricious successor, Imperial Rome, and finally—returning to the ground of *The Culture of the Cities*—the medieval Renaissance and baroque cities, and the industrial metropolis.

A long, beautifully sustained biological metaphor unites this epic. The city is depicted poetically—and possibly, although it is hard to endorse Mr. Mumford here, with intuitive scientific exactness—virtually as a living creature. To Mr. Mumford, venturing here and elsewhere on terrain which many archaeologists hesitate to enter, the village is the "embryonic" city where every significant urban institution with the single, but all-important exception of war, is discernible; house, shrine, cistern, public way, *agora*; and even rudiments of systematic morality, government, law, and justice, as represented by the Council of Elders.

Yet when the young city enters the light of history, as precociously developed as a new god, it seems almost instinctively to have developed evil ways, for its first acts, like those of a spoiled child on the sand, were to construct walls and a citadel, and to crush its neighbors. This brings Mr. Mumford to his major interpretative dilemma, and it is to his credit that he faces it squarely. Does the very institution of the city, he asks, carry in itself inherent seeds of destruction which repeatedly have impelled urban civilizations to ruin and death? Mr. Mumford's verdict is, yes.

Freudian psycho-pathology, after all, has long confirmed the formidable strength of suicidal compulsions and both Freud and Jung have attempted to apply the principle of collective unconscious behavior to whole societies. Mr. Mumford accepts this as the only explanation of the "schizoid" or "ambivalent" character which cities have displayed from the beginning: a "bifurcation" of symbiotic and predatory impulses. The first "urban implosion"— the dynamic concentration, and almost sudden miraculous increase, of human and material resources within the walled precinct of the king—resulted in undeniable valuable benefits, but nevertheless the city from the start "has also served, throughout most of its history, as a container of organized violence and a transmitter of war."

Thus the apparently sound young organism was plagued by a "paranoid psychal structure" which resulted in "purposeless materialism"; and no matter how strong, how beautiful, the city grew, lovely Venice for example, the "infantile trauma remained to warp the development of all subsequent societies." And after Mr. Mumford has recorded the cruel follies, the wholesale slaughter, the inhuman degradations that have marred every phase of urban civilization but reached peaks of unspeakable horror in the death houses such as Rome, who can say that this "lethal" psycho-genetic factor, built into the arrogant walls, the locked granary, the impenetrable chamber of the priest, the awesome throne room of the landlord-king, should not be held responsible?

It is precisely this irrational agent that Mr. Mumford fears will overthrow modern civilization, whose atrocities in the last forty years make Rome's seem negligible by comparison. He likens our society to a car without driver, steering wheel, or brakes, but crammed with demoralized passengers, hurtling toward destruction.

Happily, however, the picture is not completely grim. Borrowing a figure from Arnold Toynbee, the author points out that brute materialism may be "etherealized" by a predominantly healthy society. Walls can vanish, moats become lakes, fortresses make way for libraries and hospitals. And the glory of this book is the humane warmth that Mr. Mumford brings to his exposition. He finds invincible positive forces flowering, often as a tender bud among ruins, but also occasionally blossoming among great fountains and arbors in the garden of civilization: the green quadrangles of medieval Oxford; Swiss and Dutch cities, even commercial Amsterdam which shows how much can be done when mercantile acquisitiveness is subordinated to over-all civic interest.

These healthy elements are also found in aristocratic Bath; the romantic nineteenth-century park and its companion, the romantic suburb, now a museum piece where it is not degraded and over-run. It was out of this romantic suburb that Ebenezer Howard's great concept of the garden city grew.

To Mr. Mumford, understandably enough, perhaps the most meaningful triumph of the human spirit was Greece at its finest. This was not complacent and bellicose Athens, which, as he observes in a superb critique of the Acropolis, made the fatal error of finally worshiping the *polis* as a god. Rather, it was Olympia the shrine of the healthy body and rational art; Delphi, where the Greeks achieved what we ourselves so desperately need, a sane association of the "measure and clarity of Apollo" and the "darkness and ecstasy" of Dionysus; and Cos, the home of healing medicine and pure waters.

The principles of civilized life, then, have long been apparent to wise men. If we embrace a program of positive action, if we repeat throughout the world innovations such as the new towns and green belts which have been established around London and Stockholm, if we rebuild our urban cores on the human scale of post-war Rotterdam, if we will only "slow down" as Mr. Mumford insists we must, and stop hoping to fly to the moon when we must first recover our "human selves," and above all if "the sterile dreams and sadistic nightmares that obsess the ruling élite are banished, there will be such a release of human vitality as will make the Renaissance seem almost a stillbirth." We shall not have achieved Christianopolis perhaps, still less Utopia, yet we shall have averted Necropolis, and built the City of Man.

Suggested Reading

BECAUSE THIS is a compact list, I have made some arbitrary rules. No author is represented by more than one title, although some of these writers produced several outstanding and pertinent works. Also, I have favored books that focus on the historical problems of permanence and change, and I have sought a variety of approaches to these problems.

Lewis Atherton, *Main Street on the Middle Border,* Bloomington, Indiana University Press, 1961 (Quadrangle paperback).

Edward D. Baltzell, *Philadelphia Gentlemen,* New York, Macmillan, 1958 (Free Press paperback).

Claude Brown, *Manchild in the Promised Land,* New York, New American Library, 1966 (Signet paperback).

Theodore Dreiser, *Sister Carrie,* New York, Doubleday, 1900 (many paperback editions).

Ray Ginger, *Altgeld's America,* New York, Funk & Wagnalls, 1958 (Quadrangle paperback).

Charles N. Glaab and A. Theodore Brown, *History of Urban America,* New York, Macmillan, 1967 (Macmillan paperback).

Sidney Glazer, *Detroit: A Study in Urban Development,* New York, Twayne, 1965.

Michael Harrington, *The Other America,* New York, Macmillan, 1962 (Penguin paperback).

Geoffrey Hellman, *Bankers, Bones and Beetles: The First Century of the American Museum of Natural History*, New York, Natural History Press, 1968.

John Hersey, *The Algiers Motel Incident,* New York, Knopf, 1968 (Bantam paperback).

Jane Jacobs, *The Death and Life of Great American Cities,* New York, Random House, 1961 (Vintage paperback).

Robert S. and Helen M. Lynd, *Middletown,* New York, Harcourt, Brace, 1924 (Harvest paperback).

Blake McKelvey, *Urbanization of America, 1860–1915,* New Brunswick, N.J., Rutgers University Press, 1962.

Malcolm X, *Autobiography,* New York, Grove, 1965 (Dell paperback).

Seymour Mandelbaum, *Boss Tweed's New York,* New York, Wiley, 1965 (Wiley paperback).

Lewis Mumford, *The Highway and the City,* New York, New American Library, 1964 (Mentor paperback).

Lincoln Steffens, *Autobiography,* New York, Harcourt, Brace, 1931 (Harvest paperback).

Bayrd Still, *Milwaukee,* New York, Society Press, 1965.

Frederick B. Tolles, *Meeting House and Counting House,* New York, Norton, 1963 (Norton paperback).

Richard C. Wade, *Slavery in the Cities,* New York, Oxford University Press, 1964 (Galaxy Books paperback).

Sam B. Warner, Jr., *Streetcar Suburbs,* Cambridge, Mass., Harvard University Press, 1962 (Atheneum paperback as *The Process of Growth in Boston, 1870–1900*).

Edith Wharton, *The House of Mirth,* New York, Scribner, 1905 (several paperback editions).

Frank Lloyd Wright, *The Living City,* New York, Horizon, 1958 (Mentor paperback).

Index

A Note on the Editor

RAY GINGER was born in Memphis, Tennessee, and studied at the University of Michigan and Western Reserve University. He is the author of *Six Days or Forever?: Tennessee versus John Thomas Scopes; The Bending Cross: A Biography of Eugene Victor Debs; Altgeld's America: The Lincoln Ideal versus Changing Realities;* and *Age of Excess: The U.S. from 1877 to 1914.* He is now Professor of History at the University of Calgary.

New York Times Books
published by Quadrangle Books

American Foreign Policy Since 1945
edited by Robert A. Divine

American Politics Since 1945
edited by Richard M. Dalfiume

American Society Since 1945
edited by William L. O'Neill

Cities in Trouble
edited by Nathan Glazer

The Meaning of the American Revolution
edited by Lawrence H. Leder

Modern American Cities
edited by Ray Ginger

Nazis and Fascists in Europe, 1918-1945
edited by John Weiss

Available in Paperback and Cloth Editions
Current Catalog On Request